Building PowerPoint® Templates

Step by step with the experts

Echo Swinford and Julie Terberg

800 East 96th Street,
Indianapolis, Indiana 46240 USA

BUILDING POWERPOINT TEMPLATES

COPYRIGHT © 2013 BY QUE PUBLISHING

ISBN-13: 978-0-7897-4955-0

ISBN-10: 0-7897-4955-6

Library of Congress Cataloging-in-Publication data is on file.

First printing September 2012

TRADEMARKS

WARNING AND DISCLAIMER

BULK SALES

Que Publishing offers excellent discounts on this book when ordered in quantity for bulk purchases or special sales. For more information, please contact

U.S. Corporate and Government Sales
1-800-382-3419
corpsales@pearsontechgroup.com

For sales outside of the U.S., please contact

International Sales
international@pearson.com

EDITOR-IN-CHIEF
Greg Wiegand

EXECUTIVE EDITOR
Loretta Yates

DEVELOPMENT EDITOR
Charlotte Kughen

MANAGING EDITOR
Sandra Schroeder

PROJECT EDITOR
Seth Kerney

COPY EDITOR
Paula Lowell

INDEXER
Tim Wright

PROOFREADER
Jovana San Nicolas-Shirley

TECHNICAL EDITOR
Ric Bretschneider

EDITORIAL ASSISTANT
Cindy Teeters

BOOK DESIGNER
Julie Terberg

COVER DESIGNER
Julie Terberg

COMPOSITOR
Bumpy Design

CONTENTS AT A GLANCE

TABLE OF CONTENTS

THREE FOR THE PRICE OF ONE

Hi, I'm Ric. You don't know me, but I really like you. Why? Because you're obviously a PowerPoint user and I've spent much of my professional life trying to understand you and make your life better. I have always cared about your success and tried to help you. You're just going to have to trust me on that.

I think that's the main reason why Echo and Julie asked me to write this foreword. Sure I helped with some of the editing, which was easy enough given my background. But it's also why it was hard to settle on one proper introduction. There's so much for you to understand here. And I wanted you to understand. One introduction wouldn't really do it. So I wrote the following three. I hope you understand why by the end. But then again, nobody reads this part, anyway.

CONGRATULATIONS, YOU'RE WORKING IN MULTIPLES NOW

Right away, I can tell that you're courageous, curious, and not satisfied with the way things are in your use of PowerPoint. I'm basing this upon the fact that you're reading the introduction to a book with an incredibly focused and singular subject: making great PowerPoint templates.

The average presentation hacker who is just trying to knock out another "slideument" because their boss required it isn't interested in making better templates. They just grab another default template, or they reuse somebody else's presentation. But not you. You understand the importance of good templates. You are close to the secret.

Templates manifest the power of multiples.

Multiples are powerful things. You do a good job once, taking your time to do it right and true, and it ripples through all the jobs that come afterwards making them similarly good. It ripples through all the people who use that template to construct a well-formed presentation. And it ripples through the audiences who sit through all those presentations, enhancing their ability to get the presenter's message.

Multiples.

It doesn't matter if you're doing this for yourself, your client, a small organization or a huge conglomerate. What matters is the fact that if you do a bad job, that bad job multiplies, proliferating a lack of attention to detail, clumsy operation, or simple confusion and failure. It's fundamentally essential to be good when your work is the basis for other's work.

Let me tell you a little insider story from the PowerPoint team. One that repeated itself many times.

When we were reviewing a problem or design glitch in a new version of PowerPoint, some-one would inevitably ask what percentage of people would encounter it, and by that how important was it to fix? There was always the question of whether we could let it slide, not fix it. The common answer was that even if it affected as little as one percent of PowerPoint users, that one percent could easily fill a professional football stadium. That put real perspec-tive on the problem, thinking about the users in that way, as if they were in that stadium watching us build the product they'd eventually use. And they were all hoping we'd do well, and not fumble *their* ball.

Understand that you can make a similar difference, and that it can start right here.

I'M NOT THIS CRAZY

I suppose you could blame some of PowerPoint's problems on me, and that's why I was asked to write this forward. Just the forward, I'm not crazy enough to take on a whole book. You see I spent close to 17 years working at Microsoft, and all of that time on the PowerPoint program. There's a lot I'm proud of from that time. But don't worry; I won't bore you with the list. There are also many things I really wish we'd done a better job on, things that really could make a difference in how people communicate. And helping users create good tem-plates is high on that list.

The current incarnation of PowerPoint templates resulted from the intersection of work that became PowerPoint in Office 2007. In that release the team took on an insanely large update to the application, changing the core of what made the program work. We built a new text engine that would make text in graphics work the same as standard text. We created a new graphics engine with insanely cool effects and new ways to communicate your points out-side of bulleted lists. And we created a new file format for PowerPoint, based on XML that was eventually recognized as a world-wide standard. We basically rebuilt PowerPoint for the 21st century.

Any one of those areas could have kept the team busy for few years working towards a single release. To take on all three at the same time was obviously crazy, but absolutely necessary to keep PowerPoint the great communications tool users expected it to be.

And the team nearly killed itself doing it.

But they did it.

Of course there were a few warts, things that could have been done better if there'd been time. Make no mistake, PowerPoint is a great application, and it ships with a great set of tem-plates painstaking created by talented folks.

But it's not as easy to make your own templates as it should be. It's actually quite difficult, not obvious how to get it all done right.

And that's why we're all here with Echo and Julie.

WHO ARE ECHO AND JULIE?

Echo Swinford and Julie Terberg are many things. Both are talented designers with tons of knowledge about PowerPoint. Both are outspoken and highly critical commentators on PowerPoint function and operation. And both are *PowerPoint MVPs*.

The MVP program is one of the most brilliant innovations at Microsoft. The Microsoft MVP organization identifies and "anoints" individuals outside of the company as Most Valuable Professionals for applications such as Word, Excel, PowerPoint, Windows, and even less glamorous areas like programming tools and server products. These MVPs are given access to the relative Microsoft product team to provide feedback on the application, and help other regular users who are having trouble. Part of my responsibilities on the PowerPoint team was to serve as a point of contact for the *PowerPoint MVPs*.

Over the years Julie and Echo asked hundreds of questions on how PowerPoint and, more to the point, how templates worked. I guess that would be better said how they were *supposed* to work, or how they could be made to work better. Faced with these issues I typically had to run off to ask other engineers about relatively obscure bits of information. And I do mean obscure. It was not unusual for us to sit down in front of a computer and review the program code to determine what was going on in a given situation. And all too often we found that things weren't working quite correctly, that there were bugs or other design flaws, and those were not pleasant things to have to report back. Not pleasant at all.

It was all well and good that these questions got answered, because the answers typically helped another user out of an immediate jam. And it identified areas we needed to fix in upcoming versions of PowerPoint. But what wasn't obvious to many was that Echo and Julie were amassing a level of specific and precious information that most folks within Microsoft wouldn't themselves have been able to lay their hands on. What went into Echo and Julie's notes rarely got lost.

So who are Echo and Julie, the authors of this book? They're uncompromising, detail oriented, aggressive, occasionally sarcastic, and often rude. OK, maybe Echo more than Julie on that last bit. In other words they're the best advocates for teaching you how PowerPoint works you could possibly find. They know PowerPoint so well that each has actually been brought in to teach Microsoft employees how to use PowerPoint more effectively. They're the teachers you want, the ones you need.

You're in good hands. Go learn how to change your PowerPoint world.

Ric Bretschneider
July 31, 2012
http:/www.ricbret.com

ABOUT THE AUTHORS

Echo Swinford began her career in the industry by convincing the boss to keep the presentation development work in house. This forced Echo to learn PowerPoint in a hurry!

Fast forward 15 years and Echo has completed her master's degree in New Media at the Indiana University-Purdue University at Indianapolis School of Informatics. She is the co-author of *The PowerPoint 2007 Complete Makeover Kit*, author of *Fixing PowerPoint Annoyances*, and the expert voice and instructor behind *PowerPoint 2010 LiveLessons (Video Training)*. She's tech edited a slew of other books and is constantly learning more about PowerPoint. Based in Indianapolis, she travels frequently, supporting clients worldwide with presentation and template consulting, development, and training.

A Microsoft PowerPoint MVP since 2000, Echo has been a featured speaker for the Presentation Summit (formerly PowerPoint Live) user conference since its inception. In her spare time she fights with the Theme Builder, fosters cats for the Humane Society of Indianapolis, and trades sanity checks with Julie Terberg at least three times a day.

Julie Terberg has worked in the computer graphics industry since the time of CRT monitors, 8-inch floppy discs, and film recorders. Her background includes a BFA in Industrial Design, years of experience behind the scenes in business theater, and more than a million slides served (with backup files to prove it).

Julie is the principal of Terberg Design, based in Michigan, where she lives with her husband and two teenage kids. She loves helping her clients by developing visual concepts that better communicate with an audience.

Julie has been a Microsoft PowerPoint MVP since 2005. She is the co-author of *Perfect Medical Presentations* and she was the tech editor for *The PowerPoint 2007 Complete Makeover Kit*. As a contributing author to *Presentations Magazine*, Julie won editorial awards for her Creative Techniques columns. She enjoys speaking at the Presentation Summit user conference, where she met and instantly bonded with Echo Swinford.

DEDICATION

We dedicate this book to all the PowerPoint warriors out there. We hope this book makes it easier for you to create templates that won't come back to haunt you.

ACKNOWLEDGMENTS

We could never have written this book without each other. It took a collaboration of minds, the result of a deep friendship that extends well beyond the common bond of working with presentations. We're grateful for each other's talents, experiences, and neverending support.

Sincere gratitude to our editor Loretta Yates and the team at Que who produced this book: Paula Lowell, Charlotte Kughen, and Seth Kerney.

A huge thank you goes to Ric Bretschneider for his technical expertise and insight.

We would also like to thank all the PowerPoint MVPs past and present (and a couple of honorary ones) for their support, guidance, helpful tips, useful custom tools, and especially their friendship. We couldn't ask for better colleagues. A special shout out to Steve Rindsberg, Stephanie Krieger, and Beth Melton for their unique subject matter expertise.

Thanks to Rick Altman for hosting the Presentation Summit, a unique community-building conference where we can help users face to face. And a special thank you to Dave Paradi for bugging us to do this book for so long.

From Julie: A very special thank you to Bob, Jacob, and Megan for your patience and support. Many thanks to Echo for talking me into this project and for talking me off the ledge now and then!

From Echo: Thank you, Julie, for agreeing to work with me on this project and for making room on your ledge for me!

WE WANT TO HEAR FROM YOU!

As the reader of this book, *you* are our most important critic and commentator. We value your opinion and want to know what we're doing right, what we could do better, what areas you'd like to see us publish in, and any other words of wisdom you're willing to pass our way.

We welcome your comments. You can email or write to let us know what you did or didn't like about this book—as well as what we can do to make our books better.

Please note that we cannot help you with technical problems related to the topic of this book.

When you write, please be sure to include this book's title and author as well as your name and email address. We will carefully review your comments and share them with the author and editors who worked on the book.

Email: feedback@quepublishing.com

Mail: Que Publishing
             ATTN: Reader Feedback
             800 East 96th Street
             Indianapolis, IN 46240 USA

READER SERVICES

Visit our website and register this book at quepublishing.com/register for convenient access to any updates, downloads, or errata that might be available for this book.

SETTING THE STAGE

We work with PowerPoint templates every day, often collaborating on the same projects. Sometimes a client provides an existing template to use when creating a new presentation. Other times, we're asked to troubleshoot issues that our clients are having with their templates. Let's just say that a *lot* of presentation templates cross our desks, and they all have problems!

On the plus side, many companies trust us to design and build their templates and to ensure that the new templates will work correctly for hundreds, or thousands, of users.

Before Microsoft PowerPoint 2007, a template could easily consist of a slide master and title slide master. That scenario changed dramatically with the addition of themes, a new slide master/slide layout relationship, custom layouts, the introduction of Office Open XML file formats, and so on. Building a PowerPoint template suddenly meant many more steps to follow, along with additional elements to understand and address. Not much information is available on working with templates, and what is out there oversimplifies the process, or it's technically deep and not written for the average user.

Creating a well-built PowerPoint template can provide a huge return on investment (ROI) for your company. Think about it: A poorly constructed template forces users to make many manual adjustments to their slides. If these adjustments cost each user an extra 10 minutes of work per day, that's 40 hours a year *per user*. A whole week's worth of work gone, just like that. Unfortunately, this scenario is quite common. We often hear from users who are forced to waste time trying to create presentations using a broken template.

After years of dealing with problematic templates and building new ones from the ground up, we've learned what works and what doesn't. We want to share our best practices and hopefully save you a lot of time and headache.

Follow along as we take you through the process step by step. The people who use your new templates will thank you.

WHAT THIS BOOK IS ABOUT

This book explains all the parts and pieces that make up a PowerPoint template and includes details for building a template that will work well beyond your desktop.

We show you what to look out for and specific things to consider when making decisions for your template. By reading this book, you'll learn how to build a template that actually helps those who will use it for presentations.

The information applies to Microsoft PowerPoint 2007 and 2010 (for Windows). Chapter 15, "Creating Themes and Templates on a Mac," features supplemental information on Microsoft PowerPoint for Mac 2008 and 2011.

HOW TEMPLATES HAVE CHANGED

A PowerPoint template contains preformatted elements (backgrounds, colors, placeholders, and so on) that serve to establish a basic level of consistency for a series of slides or presentations. Although their functionality has dramatically changed over the years, the concept of a template has been around in some manner since PowerPoint was first published in 1987. Subsequent versions of PowerPoint also featured design templates, which you might recognize as having a POT extension. Figure 1.1 shows the PowerPoint 2003 interface, with design templates accessible from the Slide Design task pane.

Design Templates

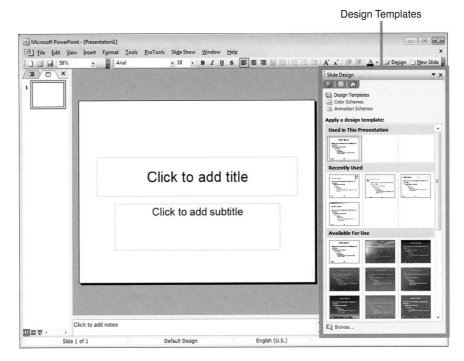

FIGURE 1.1

Design templates were accessible from the Slide Design task pane, as shown here in the PowerPoint 2003 interface.

In these early iterations, a typical PowerPoint presentation template consisted of a slide master and title slide master. When building new slides, users could select from a series of predefined slide layouts for different types of content. Figure 1.2 includes all the slide layouts available in PowerPoint 2003. These slide layouts were automatically generated by PowerPoint, based on the slide master formatting. Although helpful, they were also sometimes limiting: You could not add placeholders to these layouts or make custom layouts to better suit your presentation content.

PowerPoint 2007 was the game changer, including some of the biggest modifications and improvements in the application's history. The updated program now featured customizable slide layouts along with advanced graphic capabilities and an expanded color palette. One of the most obvious differences was the program interface, shown in Figure 1.3, featuring the Ribbon and contextual tools. PowerPoint 2010 (and 2008/2011 for Mac) follow this same structure.

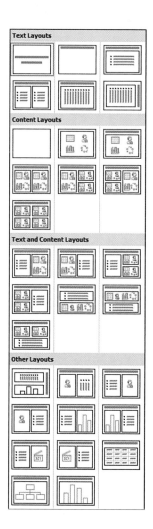

FIGURE 1.2

Slide layouts in PowerPoint 2003, and prior versions, offered a range of placeholder configurations to accommodate different types of content.

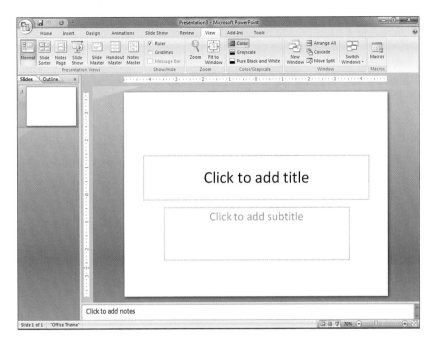

FIGURE 1.3

The most visible difference in PowerPoint 2007 was the program interface, comprised of the Ribbon and contextual menus.

Microsoft Office 2007 introduced new file formats, written in what was to become the Office Open XML format. To reflect this change, PowerPoint file extensions were updated to include an "X" (for XML) or an "M" (for macro-enabled XML) at the end of the extension. These include PPTX for presentation files, POTX for PowerPoint template files, and PPSX for presentations set to open full screen.

Along with new file formats, Office 2007 introduced themes. Chapter 2, "Parts and Pieces," covers themes in more detail, but for now the most important thing to understand is that a theme is a set of colors, fonts, and effects that can be applied to (and included with) Word, Excel, and PowerPoint files.

NOTE

Although Microsoft Word and Excel are mentioned, their use is not a topic for this book and is only included here as orienting background. Certain theme elements and functions differ between Office applications. This book focuses on PowerPoint-specific features.

PROBLEMS WITH POWERPOINT TEMPLATES

Here are some issues we frequently see in troublesome templates. Do any of these look familiar to you?

- Chart text is the same color as the background.

- Charts are filled with unexpected colors.

- Two-line titles don't fit in the title placeholder, often disappearing off the top of the slide or overlapping the body text.

- Titles and body text appear to shift position on subsequent slides.

- The fonts on your slides do not look like the headings and body font specified in the template.

- The first level of text in a placeholder is formatted without bullet points. When typing text on a slide, you're unable to use the Tab key (or Shift+Tab keys) to apply a bullet character when moving text to another level.

- Footers show up in large sizes and in odd positions.

- Newly created tables do not match the table included on the sample slides.

- The fonts and colors on handouts or notes pages do not match the rest of the template.

- There are so many slide layouts that you must scroll the layouts gallery to see them all.

- The template file size is too large for an email attachment.

- Sample slides include shapes filled with colors that do not match the theme colors.

You're not alone. You can avoid all these problems; we show you how.

In addition to the listed issues, a problem we see all the time is folks attempting to upgrade their PowerPoint 97 or 2003–format templates (PPT, POT) by opening them in PowerPoint 2007 or 2010 and simply saving them in the new XML-based file format (PPTX, POTX). Although you might think this is a logical way to "upgrade," it actually fails horribly. A template upgraded in this manner has huge issues with colors—they don't map properly. Other weirdness can also occur, such as chart text matching the slide background (for example, white chart text on a white slide background). These things are a dead giveaway that the template was the product of a botched update.

In fact, we've witnessed so many strange issues that occur when updating old templates for use in PowerPoint 2010 or 2007 that we refuse to do it. We always start over and rebuild from scratch. Our advice is that you do the same. There—you have been warned.

On the flipside, you shouldn't create a template in the newer versions of PowerPoint for people who are still working with older versions. We see this problem all the time, too. People build a template in PowerPoint 2010 or 2007 and save it as a PowerPoint 97–2003 format for users who are still working in those versions. The assumption is that because it uses a PPT extension, it must be compatible with PowerPoint 2003 or earlier. That's just wrong.

Sure, PowerPoint 2003 users can, of course, open the old PPT file format, but it doesn't mean the template works properly for them. These down-saved templates are still PowerPoint 2007 and 2010 XML-based files under the hood; in PowerPoint 2003 they are, at best, difficult to use and PowerPoint gets the blame for the difficulty, of course. Although many reasons exist for why this approach is problematic, the major issues involve differences between color schemes, slide masters, and slide layouts.

So let us reiterate: Create XML-based templates (PPTX or POTX) in PowerPoint 2007 or 2010 (or 2008 or 2011 on the Mac). Create 97–2003 format templates (PPT, POT) in PowerPoint 2003 or prior (2004 or prior on the Mac). If you do build cross-platform (on Mac for PC use or vice versa), be sure to test the template on the other platform before rolling it out.

There—you have been warned. Again.

WHO SHOULD USE THIS BOOK?

This book is designed for intermediate or advanced PowerPoint users who already build templates and want to improve their work or for those who want to add template development to their skill set. If your company has recently upgraded from PowerPoint 2003, you'll find the information you need to build templates for newer versions of the program in this book.

Assuming that you have more than a basic understanding of PowerPoint features and commands, our instructions are brief and include information specific to this process. We try not to bore you with obvious commands such as, "Click the Close button to shut the dialog box."

HOW TO USE THIS BOOK

Chapters 2–9 include detailed information about themes, parts of a template, and the steps you need to follow when building a template. We suggest you read through this material and follow along with the tutorials to become familiar with the process and techniques. Building a template can be a very circular process. Don't get discouraged.

When you're ready to build a template of your own, gather all template assets (colors, backgrounds, logos, and so on) and follow the steps in order. Because the process is so recursive at times, we've included a summary of key steps in the Appendix, "Key Steps to Building a Template."

If you're starting over and developing a completely new look for your template, Chapter 10, "Designing a Template," features best practices.

When presenting a series of charts, maintaining some consistency for common elements is important. A well-formed template and chart templates can help. See Chapter 11, "Understanding Charts and Chart Templates," for details.

You can build themes and templates with PowerPoint alone, but sometimes your design requires more customization than the application offers. In that case, you need to use the Microsoft Theme Builder or manually edit the XML code. Chapters 12, "Using the Theme Builder Utility to Customize Your Theme," and 13, "Editing PowerPoint and Theme File XML," help you get started. Before distributing a new template to everyone at your company, be sure to read Chapter 14, "Deploying Your Template or Theme."

Creating themes and templates in PowerPoint for Mac is quite similar to the process for PC versions of PowerPoint, but a few differences exist between the platforms. Read Chapter 15 for more information.

We've compiled all of the key steps to building a template into a quick reference list, available in the Appendix. See the book website at http://www.quepublishing.com/title/0789749556 for all the files necessary to complete the chapter tutorials, links to sites and add-ins, bonus files, and other information.

IN THIS CHAPTER

- Understanding the differences between themes and templates
- Learning which elements make up a theme
- Learning which elements make up a template

2

INTRODUCING TEMPLATES AND THEMES

In talking to our clients, we have discovered that a lot of confusion surrounds themes and templates. That's completely understandable because themes and templates are similar, and they contain many of the same elements. You can use PowerPoint to create both themes and templates, which further contributes to the confusion. If we refer to them by their proper names—Office themes and PowerPoint templates—you might have a head start on understanding the differences and a good pneumonic to help keep them straight!

This chapter covers the differences between themes and templates. We also describe the various parts that comprise them.

CREATING CUSTOM THEMES

Although you can go a long way in creating a theme within PowerPoint, sometimes you need a level of customization that PowerPoint can't provide. For this purpose, you can use a separate tool (Microsoft Theme Builder) or edit the XML code (Office Open XML). Throughout this book, we call out specific theme elements that you can customize with the Theme Builder or with XML editing. Chapter 12, "Using the Theme Builder Utility to Customize Your Theme," features detailed information on using the Theme Builder tool, and Chapter 13, "Editing PowerPoint and Theme File XML," includes instructions for customizing themes by editing the XML code.

THEMES VERSUS TEMPLATES

Themes were first introduced with Microsoft Office 2007. A theme file (.THMX) is Office-wide, which means that PowerPoint, Word, and Excel can share a set of common colors, fonts, and effects. Themes are a big help when you need to create a report or document that pulls together pieces from these three applications. When you apply Office themes, your Word, Excel, and PowerPoint files actually look like they go together!

For PowerPoint specifically, a theme also includes formatting information for slide masters and slide layouts. Themes do not contain content, so things such as sample slides and pre-populated footers are not included.

An Office template (.DOTX, .POTX, .XLTX) is a "starter" file, made specifically for Word, PowerPoint, or Excel. Templates are pre-formatted files that save time and help to create consistent-looking documents. As Figure 2.1 shows, every template is based on a theme. The colors, fonts, and effects that make up a theme are embedded, if you will, into the template.

A PowerPoint template (.POTX) goes a step further than a theme (.THMX), as it *does* include any sample slides or pre-populated footers saved with the template. If you have no need for the sample content a template can include, then you could base your files directly on the theme.

The theme is the underlying chassis of all templates. If templates are based on the same theme file, the same colors, fonts, and effects are available when the user begins typing or chooses objects from the galleries (SmartArt, Shape Styles, and so on); this is true no matter if it's a Word, Excel, or PowerPoint template.

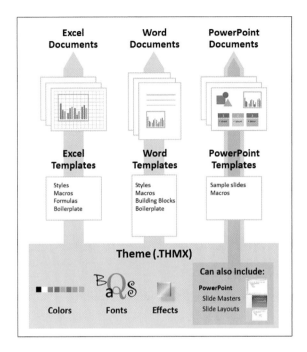

FIGURE 2.1

Office documents are based on templates, which are based on theme elements.

If a theme is Office-wide, then why should you bother with separate Word templates, Excel templates, and PowerPoint templates? Theoretically, you could just distribute one .THMX file, but you must consider a couple of issues when doing so:

- As mentioned earlier, .THMX files do not contain content, which means they have no sample slides, no pre-populated footers, no Word macros, no autotext, and none of the other things that are often included in Word, PowerPoint, or Excel templates. Templates can include this content.

- Users don't understand what a .THMX is; they expect to receive a template.

To make a theme in PowerPoint, simply create your template: Select colors, fonts, and effects from the Design tab and then set up your slide master and layouts. When the template is complete, save the file as a .POTX and then immediately save it again as a .THMX file. Voilà! There's your theme. It's just like the template, but any sample slides (and other content) are removed from the theme.

The Themes gallery is on the Design tab in PowerPoint (see Figure 2.2). When you save a theme, it displays as a thumbnail in this gallery. You can quickly change the style of your presentation by selecting a different theme.

More button

FIGURE 2.2

The Themes gallery is located on the Design tab of the Ribbon. Click the More button to the lower right to expand the gallery.

PARTS OF A THEME

A theme consists of three main parts: colors, fonts, and effects. The choices you make for these settings affect how graphics and text appear in your template and on slides created with the template.

THEME COLORS

There are 12 colors in a theme, including two light and two dark colors, six accents, and separate colors for a hyperlink and followed hyperlink. A list of theme color sets is accessible from the Design tab (see Figure 2.3). Click the Colors button to expand the list, and then select Create New Theme Colors at the bottom to open the dialog (see Figure 2.4) where you can create new theme color sets.

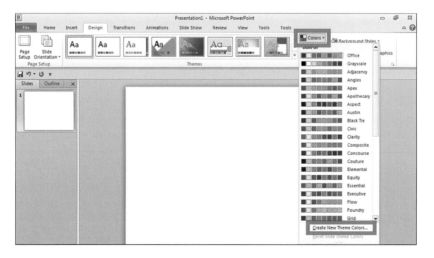

FIGURE 2.3

From the Design tab, click the Colors button to access a list of available theme color sets.

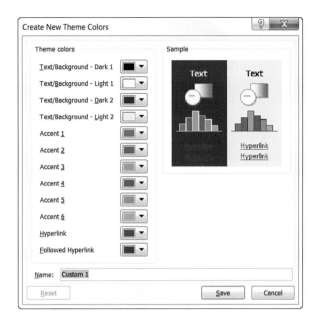

FIGURE 2.4

The Create New Theme Colors dialog shows the current color set when you open it. In this case, you see the theme colors for the default blank PowerPoint template.

Figure 2.4 shows the Create New Theme Colors dialog box, where you can see the theme colors, including those for hyperlink and followed hyperlink. The first four colors include two light and two dark values. These four colors populate the Background Styles gallery, which is shown in Figure 2.5. You can access the Background Styles gallery from the Design tab.

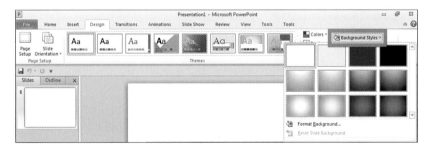

FIGURE 2.5

The background styles in this gallery are based on combinations of the two light and two dark values from the color theme along with subtle, moderate, and intense background fill styles.

The relationship between the light and dark theme colors is crucial because these defaults help ensure that your text is visible regardless of the color of your background. (See Chapter 3, "Getting Started: Set Up a Theme," for details on defining theme colors.)

The six accent colors populate various galleries within the PowerPoint interface. They appear in all Theme Colors galleries as well as the Chart Styles, Table Styles, Shape Styles, SmartArt Styles, and Picture Recolor galleries. Charts automatically populate with accent colors, in order from Accent 1 through Accent 6. (Read more about charts in Chapter 11, "Understanding Charts and Chart Templates.")

Theme Colors galleries display when you click any fill, outline, or font color option throughout the PowerPoint interface. The top row of the Theme Colors gallery shows theme colors: Light 1, Dark 1, Light 2, Dark 2, Accent 1, Accent 2, Accent 3, Accent 4, Accent 5, and Accent 6. (see Figure 2.6). The palette of colors below includes tints and shades of the theme colors.

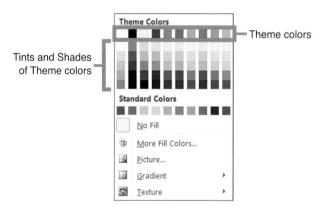

FIGURE 2.6

A Theme Colors gallery.

The Shape Styles gallery is located on the Drawing Tools Format tab and on the Home tab of the Ribbon. To expand the Shape Styles gallery, which you see in Figure 2.7, click the More button on the lower-right side of the Shape Styles group.

The Chart Styles gallery is located on the Chart Tools tab, which appears when you select a chart on a slide. As with other quick-style galleries, click the More button to expand this gallery, as shown in Figure 2.8. The first column in the Chart Styles gallery is based on variations of Dark 1. The multi-colored chart styles in the second column are based on the accent colors in order, and columns 3 through 8 are monochromatic variations based on Accents 1 through 6.

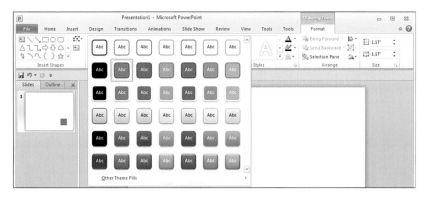

FIGURE 2.7

The Shape Styles gallery is populated with theme colors Dark 1 and Accents 1 through 6.

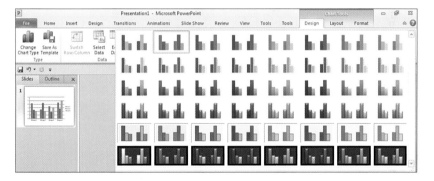

FIGURE 2.8

Options in the Chart Styles gallery are mostly based on Accent colors 1 through 6 combined with various effects styles.

Table styles are also based on theme colors, with various combinations of Dark 1, Light 1, and the six accent colors coming into play. Most of the styles in the section of the Table Styles gallery labeled Best Match for Document also use the theme's effect styles, as you can see at the top of Figure 2.9.

Default SmartArt diagrams are based on Accent 1. Other color options are available, as you can see in Figure 2.10. From the SmartArt Tools Design tab, click the Change Colors button to open the gallery. Text in SmartArt diagrams is always based on Light 1 and Dark 1 colors. The SmartArt shape fill colors are based on Accents 1 through 6.

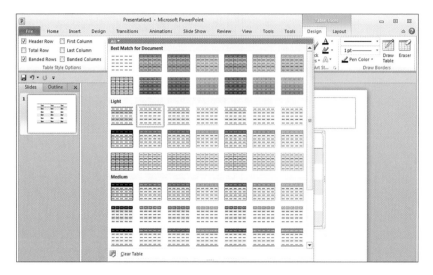

FIGURE 2.9
The Table Styles gallery.

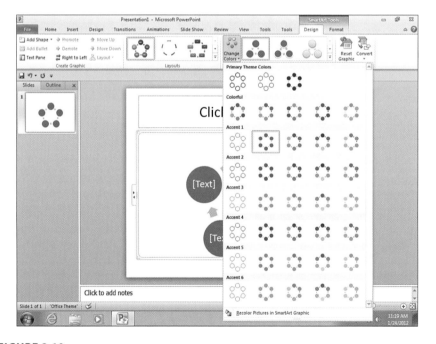

FIGURE 2.10
SmartArt's Change Colors gallery offers various options based on theme accent colors.

To access the Picture Color gallery, shown in Figure 2.11, select a picture on your current slide. From the Picture Tools Format tab, click the Color button. Picture recolor styles include options based on Dark 2 and Light 2 theme colors as well as dark and light versions of Accents 1 through 6.

The Hyperlink and Followed Hyperlink colors do not appear in Theme Colors or any of the other galleries. The Hyperlink color applies only to text with a defined hyperlink. The Followed Hyperlink color appears *only* in Slide Show mode, after a hyperlink has been clicked.

FIGURE 2.11

Picture color styles include washouts and sepia tones and variations based on Accents 1 through 6.

THEME FONTS

Every theme includes two font settings: one for the Headings font and another for the Body font. You can select the same font for both (as do many of the default themes). The Headings font automatically applies to the Title placeholders on the slide master and lay-outs. The Body font applies to everything else. If you're consistent in choosing the Headings or Body font when you create or update content, you'll find it very easy to replace a font presentation-wide if you need to. (See Chapter 3 for more information on understanding and choosing fonts.)

You can access theme font sets from the Design tab. Click the Fonts button to expand the list. The list displays all available theme font sets with a thumbnail preview of the Headings and Body fonts for each theme. Theme fonts are labeled (Headings and Body) in the font gallery on the Home tab and the Mini toolbar that appears when you select text (see Figure 2.12).

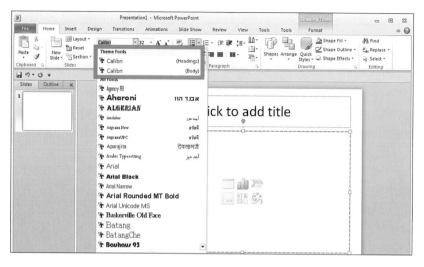

FIGURE 2.12

Theme fonts are labeled in the Font gallery.

THEME EFFECTS

Theme effects govern the appearance for graphic objects. These effects can include settings for shape fills, outlines, bevels, shadows, and more. Three levels of graphic effects are defined in a theme: subtle, moderate, and intense. These include varying degrees of lines, fills, and effects that range from simple fills and outlines to three-dimensional shading. Users can select from these theme effects in the Shape Styles, Chart Styles, Table Styles, and SmartArt Styles galleries. Chapter 3 covers theme effects in more detail.

Unlike theme colors and theme fonts, which you can define within PowerPoint, you must use the Microsoft Theme Builder or manually edit the XML code to create custom theme effects. (For details on using the Theme Builder to create custom theme effects, see Chapter 12.)

PARTS OF A POWERPOINT TEMPLATE

As mentioned at the beginning of the chapter, a template (.POTX) includes a theme as its foundation. Even if you begin with a blank PowerPoint template, your colors, fonts, and effects reflect the default settings of the Office Theme. When you make a change to theme colors, fonts, or effects, the new settings are applied throughout the template. Consequently, if you choose an entirely new theme, a complete set of new colors, fonts, and effects is applied to the whole template.

A PowerPoint template also includes a slide master and slide layouts (with placeholders for content), a handout master, and a notes master. (A template can have multiple slide masters; refer to Chapter 4, "Formatting the Slide Master," for more information.)

SLIDE MASTER

If you've used legacy versions of PowerPoint, you're familiar with the basic concepts of slide masters and understand their influence on slides within a presentation. With the introduction of new file formats and themes in PowerPoint 2007, slide masters have changed significantly.

The slide master directs the formatting for all the slide layouts within a template. (For the programmers among you, it's a classic parent-child relationship.) The child layout inherits its settings from the slide master (see Figure 2.13). These settings include the Background style as well as placeholder formatting, size, and position. When you apply formatting to the placeholders on the slide master, those settings trickle down to the corresponding place-holders on the slide layouts below. You can read more about slide masters, placeholders, and slide layouts in Chapters 4, 5, and 6.

TIP

Start by editing the slide master first. Make all formatting and position adjustments, and then move on to any slide layout adjustments. Why? If you make any changes to a placeholder on a slide layout, that placeholder is disassociated from the slide master. From that point on, when you tweak the slide master, you must make the same change manually on that slide layout.

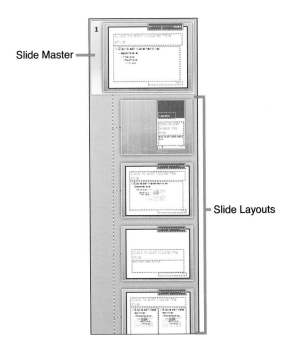

FIGURE 2.13

The large thumbnail is the slide master; the smaller thumbnails are the slide layouts.

SLIDE LAYOUTS

By default, each slide master has 11 associated slide layouts: Title Slide, Title and Content, Section Header, Two Content, Comparison, Title Only, Blank, Content with Caption, Picture with Caption, and two Vertical layouts. These are pictured in Figure 2.14.

Generally, only nine of these layouts show up in the New Slide or Layouts gallery. The two Vertical slide layouts are included for right-to-left language formats. Only users who have enabled right-to-left languages (such as Chinese or Japanese) see the two Vertical layouts in the galleries.

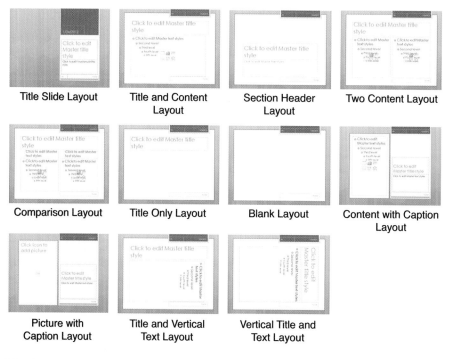

Title Slide Layout	Title and Content Layout	Section Header Layout	Two Content Layout
Comparison Layout	Title Only Layout	Blank Layout	Content with Caption Layout
Picture with Caption Layout	Title and Vertical Text Layout	Vertical Title and Text Layout	

FIGURE 2.14

There are 11 slide layouts in a default PowerPoint template.

PLACEHOLDERS

Placeholders are pre-formatted containers for content (such as text, pictures, charts, and so on) that make creating consistently formatted slides easy. The placeholders included on the slide master and slide layouts (see Figure 2.15) have a direct relationship to the placeholders you see on a slide in Normal view. Placeholder types include the following:

- Content

- Text

- Picture

- Chart

- Table

- SmartArt

- Media

- ClipArt

A Content placeholder is unique in that it accepts any of the other seven types of content (for example, you can put a picture or a chart in a Content placeholder). All the slide layouts have different placeholder configurations, offering a variety of arrangements and content types. When creating new slides, you can select the layout that best suits your slide content.

Three Footer placeholders are also included on the slide master and slide layouts. These placeholders include the Date, Slide Number, and Footer information for the presentation. You can find more detailed information on formatting footers in Chapter 4.

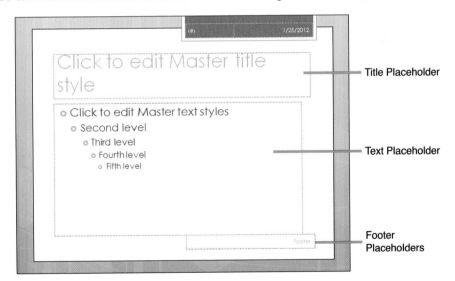

FIGURE 2.15

Placeholders are included on slide masters and slide layouts.

HANDOUT MASTER

You use the handout master to define how handout pages print. You can choose from the available options for Handout Orientation, Slide Orientation, and number of Slides per Page. Note that you *cannot* customize or resize the slide placeholders on the handout master; you must choose from the options available on the ribbon. Header and Footer placeholders are fully editable; you can move, resize, or reformat them as needed.

NOTES MASTER

The notes master defines how Notes pages are formatted for printing. You can make adjustments to any or all the placeholders on the notes master. You can move and resize the Slide placeholder or add an outline or Shape Effects. You can custom format the text placeholder, too. Add bullets, adjust indents and line spacing, and resize or reposition as you like. You can also reformat the Header, Date, Footer, and Page Number placeholders. Chapter 7, "Formatting Notes and Handout Masters," covers formatting and customizing Handout and Notes Masters.

IN THIS CHAPTER

- Creating a color theme
- Choosing theme fonts
- Selecting theme effects

3

GETTING STARTED: SET UP A THEME

Now that you're familiar with the pieces that comprise a template, it's time to learn how to put them together.

The next few chapters take you through building a template step by step. Follow along in PowerPoint, building a sample file as you become comfortable with the process. (The tutorial files are available at http://www.quepublishing.com/title/0789749556.)

Numerous decisions go into a template design. From color and font selections, to background styles and layout arrangements, many choices affect how the template looks and how it will work for users. In reality, the design process begins long before you open PowerPoint because you must make decisions about these things before you start working.

After you've gone through the steps to build a practice template and are ready to create a template for yourself or your company, we suggest that you read Chapter 10, "Designing a Template."

This chapter covers the steps to defining your theme elements: the colors, fonts, and effects that form the foundation of a template.

UNDERSTANDING THEME COLORS

The color scheme is one of the most important parts of a template. Setting up the colors correctly is imperative because your choices affect the appearance of everything moving forward. Not only do the colors influence background styles and placeholder text, theme colors populate all the style galleries as well.

If you're working with a specific existing color scheme, such as a corporate identity, you might already have a set of RGB values in hand and think you're ready to plug them into a new color theme. Or perhaps you're working with an existing template and wondering why certain things don't look right on your slides. Sound familiar? You're not alone because this template issue is a common one. Read this section to learn how theme colors work and how extremely important the order in which you position them is.

As mentioned in Chapter 2, "Introducing Templates and Themes," there are 12 colors in a theme. These include two light, two dark, six accents, hyperlink, and followed hyperlink colors (see Figure 3.1).

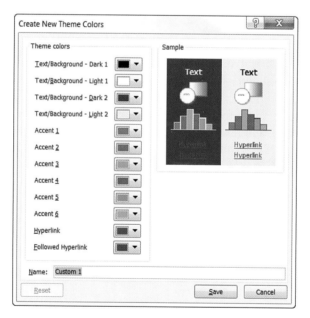

FIGURE 3.1

The Theme Colors dialog box includes settings for 12 colors.

TEXT/BACKGROUND COLORS

The first four color chips are designated as Text/Background - Dark 1, Light 1, Dark 2, and Light 2. These colors work together to ensure that your text is visible, no matter if your background is light or dark.

CAUTION

Even though Dark 2 and Light 2 color chips are designated as text colors (as shown in Figure 3.1), they are never automatically applied to text when you change background styles.

Background styles are based on the four light and dark colors (see Figure 3.2). When setting up a new template, you choose one of these styles as the background. (Read more on background styles in Chapter 4, "Formatting the Slide Master.")

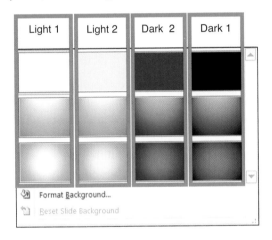

FIGURE 3.2

Choose one of the Background Styles when you set up a new template.

Text always defaults to either Dark 1 or Light 1, whichever is the opposite value from the value you chose for the background style. For instance, if you select a dark background style, the default text color is Light 1. Choose a light background style, and the default text color is Dark 1. You can see the various background and text color combinations in Figure 3.3.

FIGURE 3.3

Text colors default to Dark 1 or Light 1 theme colors, whichever is opposite in value from the current background style.

WHY ARE BACKGROUND STYLES IMPORTANT?

Presentations are delivered in a wide range of venues: ballrooms, boardrooms, classrooms, and so on, each with a different type of projector and a different amount of ambient light in the room. To accommodate these different venues and lighting situations, presenters often need to change their slides from light to dark backgrounds and vice versa. For instance, in darker rooms, white or light backgrounds appear to glow because there's so much bright light projecting onto the screen. This can make reading text and looking at the screen for a long period of time difficult for an audience. For situations like this, a presenter might want to change all the content to a dark background with light text.

Background styles are also important in another common scenario: When pasting slides from one presentation into another, you have to make sure all the text is visible on the new background. If you properly built both templates, with light and dark theme colors assigned to placeholders and backgrounds, your text automatically converts to the proper value.

Considering that text defaults to either Light 1 or Dark 1, you must choose colors that contrast well against the background colors. You want all text to be legible for the audience, right? Quite often in the default color themes, you see white and black chosen for Light 1 and Dark 1. These colors make sense because they offer the highest contrast you can achieve.

If you select a color other than Light 1 or Dark 1 for a text placeholder—such as Accent 1, for instance—it does not automatically switch from light to dark when you change the background style.

How do you determine what colors to assign to Light 2 and Dark 2? Generally, you can define them as the lightest and darkest background colors other than black and white. For instance, let's say you decide on forest green backgrounds with white text for the primary template design. For the alternative lighter version, you decide on celery green backgrounds with black text. Assign celery green to Light 2 and forest green to Dark 2. Easy decision.

What happens if you've changed Dark 1 to charcoal so all your text (including charts, tables, and SmartArt) is gray? In this situation, it might be helpful to include black in the color palette so you can assign it to Dark 2 (see Figure 3.4).

Background color: Light 1 (White)	Background color: Light 2 (Tan)	Background color: Dark 2 (Black)	Background color: Dark 1 (Charcoal)
Text color: Dark 1 (Charcoal)	Text color: Dark 1 (Charcoal)	Text color: Light 1 (White)	Text color: Light 1 (White)

FIGURE 3.4

If you change Dark 1 to a color other than black, it helps users if you assign the color black to Dark 2.

CAUTION   *Chart text, table text, and SmartArt text always pick up either the Dark 1 or Light 1 color. For consistency, select Dark 1 or Light 1 when formatting all text placeholders.*

ACCENT COLORS

The six accent colors form the basic palette for your presentation graphics. As demonstrated in Chapter 2, all the style galleries are filled with the accent colors. It's important that all accent colors stand apart from the background colors and that they look harmonious as a group.

The order of the accent colors is significant. Charts populate with the accent colors in numerical order, from Accent 1 through Accent 6 (see Figure 3.5). When determining the order of accent colors, consider how they will look next to one another in a column or bar chart.

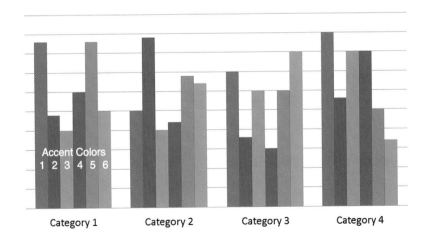

FIGURE 3.5

Charts automatically fill different series with accent colors, in order from Accent 1 through Accent 6.

SmartArt graphics also pull from accent colors, although "colorful" SmartArt begins with Accent 2 in most SmartArt diagrams (see Figure 3.6).

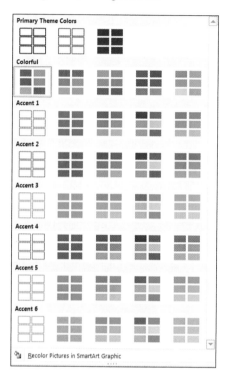

FIGURE 3.6

The SmartArt gallery is populated with all six accent colors, along with tints and shades of these colors. Note that the Colorful style options begin with the Accent 2 Theme Color.

COLOR IS SUBJECTIVE

Some people have strong opinions about colors they like or don't like. Certain colors, such as red or black, can have negative connotations. Pink can be perceived as feminine, unprofessional, or weak. Some executives hate purple. Colors also have various connotations in different cultures.

In the early stages of the template design process, develop a few sample slides that show theme colors in action. Project these sample slides and review the colors with key decision makers. Tweaking the color theme before distributing a template is better than finding out later that certain colors just aren't working. Consider that highly saturated colors might become brighter and overpower other colors when projected. Subdued hues might become dimmer or washed out. Dark colors can also be tricky; you might discover some appear even darker, almost black, when projected. Take a look at Chapter 10 for more information on designing a template.

For most corporate templates, accent colors are derived from a branding color palette. Make sure you have the RGB values for all corporate colors because you need them to set up the theme colors in PowerPoint. (If you're starting from scratch and need ideas for choosing accent colors that work well together, see Chapter 10.)

We can't stress enough that colors appear vastly different when projected versus printed on paper. Before finalizing a template, projecting sample slides to review colors, contrast, and legibility is best. Tweak the color values as needed and project again to test. These preliminary steps might seem like a lot of extra work, but the time involved early in the process can save you hours of rework later.

You need to consider some things as you set up your proposed accent colors for early testing. The goal is to achieve contrast (foreground and background colors are distinguishable from each other) and harmony (they look pleasant as a set) for all six colors. Considering how these colors will apply to content in future presentations is helpful. Keep in mind that a column chart might use all six accents. When one color is lighter or brighter than the rest, that data series tends to stand out or appear highlighted. For this reason, it's best to choose accent colors that are of relatively similar intensity.

Figure 3.7 shows the Office Theme accent colors in relation to all four background colors. This format works well for preliminary color exploration; you can quickly check for contrast and harmony.

You can also create slides on light and dark background colors, using filled textboxes for each of the proposed accent colors. Create a slide for each light and dark background color. Draw six textboxes on each and fill them with the proposed accent colors (see Figure 3.8). You can quickly see whether there's enough contrast with the backgrounds, how the accent colors work together, and how text contrasts with each accent color.

The best advice regarding accent colors is to test them thoroughly with various types of content (charts, SmartArt, tables, and so on), on light and dark background styles, and in different presentation environments (for example, on a boardroom projector or web-conference platform).

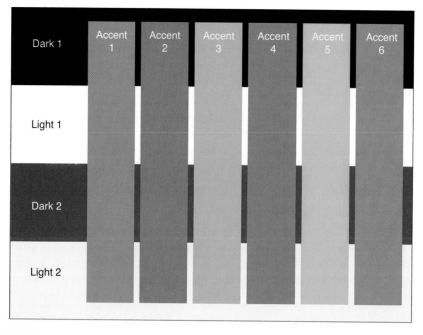

FIGURE 3.7

This graphic demonstrates the Office Theme colors. All six accent colors overlap the four background colors.

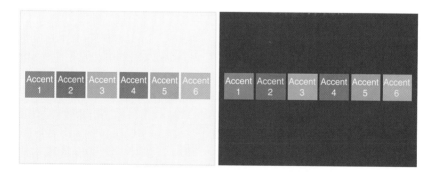

FIGURE 3.8

Create example slides to see how the accent colors look together and to determine whether they have enough contrast with the backgrounds.

TIP

While you're developing your color theme, you might want to use the Shape Fill tool on the Home tab of the Ribbon to manually format test colors. This is easier than repeatedly editing the color theme while you're in this development phase.

HYPERLINK AND FOLLOWED HYPERLINK COLORS

The Hyperlink and Followed Hyperlink colors do not appear in Theme Colors or any of the other galleries. The Hyperlink color applies only to text with a defined hyperlink. The Followed Hyperlink color displays only in Slide Show mode after a hyperlink has been clicked. We recommend repeating one of the accent colors for the Hyperlink color. It should differ from the body text color so it stands out a little, calling attention to linked text. A Followed Hyperlink is usually more subdued in value because it signifies a link has already been clicked. (There's no need for attention at this point.) A medium gray works well in most cases for the Followed Hyperlink color. See Figure 3.9 for examples of Hyperlink and Followed Hyperlink colors.

Alterum expetendae sit et paulo

- Lorem ipsum dolor sit amet
- Etiam dapibus vulputate ipsum id auctor neque dignissim in laoreet
  - Mauris id libero ut ligula condimentum eleifend
    hyperlink color
  - massa consectetuer adipiscing elit portittor
    followed hyperlink color

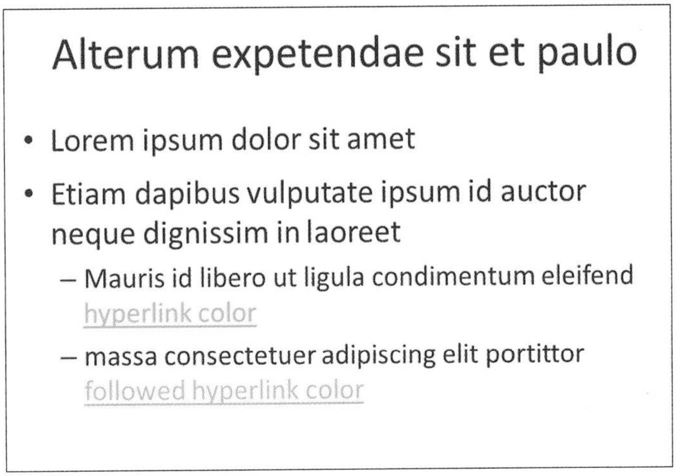

FIGURE 3.9

The Hyperlink color should stand out from body text. The Followed Hyperlink color should be more subdued, signaling that the link has already been clicked.

PRESERVING LEGACY COLORS

Our clients often ask us why colors change on objects when they paste old slides created in PowerPoint 2003 (or earlier) into PowerPoint 2007 or 2010. The change is actually related to the theme colors and the way PowerPoint maps color scheme slots between older versions and newer ones. It's kind of confusing, but read on for an explanation.

As you might know, older versions of PowerPoint have only four accent colors. See the sample 2003 accent colors pictured on the top row of Figure 3.10. Being the diligent template creator you are, you create a color theme in PowerPoint 2010 that uses the same colors for the first four accents (shown on the middle row of Figure 3.9). This should help users because everything uses the same colors, right?

Unfortunately, when your users paste their old slides into PowerPoint 2007 or 2010, anything that used Accent 3 and Hyperlink or Accent 4 and Followed Hyperlink in the older version picks up the Hyperlink and Followed Hyperlink colors in the current version of PowerPoint. They don't pick up Accent 3 and Accent 4 colors as you would expect. (Don't shoot the messenger!) And because the Hyperlink and Followed Hyperlink colors don't display in any of the Theme Color galleries, users have no way to understand what's happening—they just think that PowerPoint has randomly changed all the colors.

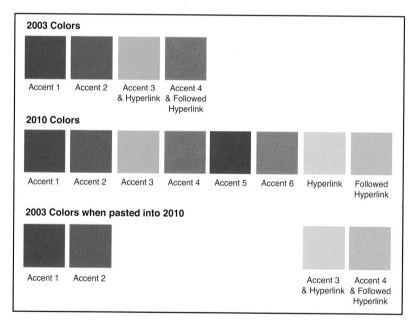

FIGURE 3.10

Unfortunately, when you paste slides from older versions of PowerPoint into newer versions, objects mapped to Accent 3 and Hyperlink or Accent 4 and Followed Hyperlink get mapped to Hyperlink and Followed Hyperlink colors.

If you're struggling with this, here's what to do:

1. Format your Hyperlink and Followed Hyperlink colors in PowerPoint 2010 to match Accents 3 and 4 from the PowerPoint 2003 color scheme.

2. Then use these colors again for Accents 3 and 4 in PowerPoint 2010.

This is pictured in Figure 3.11. It's not a perfect solution, but trust us—the users will thank you for it.

FIGURE 3.11

If you match the Accent 3 color to Hyperlink and Accent 4 to Followed Hyperlink, your users won't know the difference and objects seem to pick up the correct color when legacy slides are pasted into PowerPoint 2007 or 2010.

APPLYING BUILT-IN THEME COLORS

Each of the built-in themes includes a color scheme. One of them might work well for your template design or at least be a good starting point. When selecting from the available themes, you want to be able to see the colors in action. The best way to do this is to start with a colorful sample slide that includes a chart or a SmartArt diagram.

To apply one of the built-in color themes, follow these steps:

1. On the Design tab, select the Colors gallery to view the built-in theme colors (see Figure 3.12).

2. Scroll through the list and hover on different color schemes. Your current slide colors change, showing you a preview of the new theme colors.

3. Click on a set of theme colors to apply it to your current PowerPoint file.

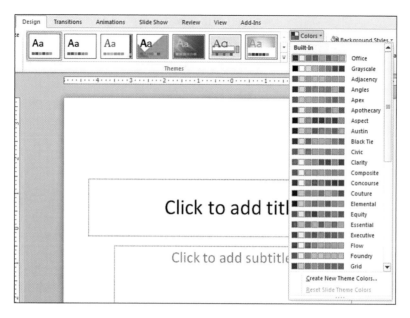

FIGURE 3.12

As you hover through the list of built-in theme colors, your current slide colors will dynamically change, showing you a preview of the new colors.

DEFINING CUSTOM THEME COLORS

If the stock color themes don't quite work for your template or if you have a set of RGB values you need to use, then you must create a custom color theme. To do so, follow these steps:

TUTORIAL

1. On the Design tab, click the Colors button to open the gallery.

2. At the bottom of the Colors gallery, select Create New Theme Colors.

3. To edit each theme color, click the color swatch to open the Theme Colors gallery and then click More Colors. The Standard tab in the Colors dialog box displays a honeycomb of basic colors (see Figure 3.13).

4. Switch to the Custom tab to have access to 16 million colors. At the bottom of the Custom window, you can type in values for Red, Green and Blue (see Figure 3.14).

5. Input the RGB values shown in Figure 3.15 to build the tutorial template theme colors.

6. Give this color scheme a name, such as Tutorial, and click Save. The new theme colors are applied to your current PowerPoint file.

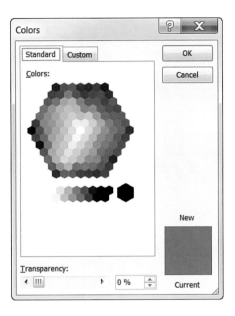

FIGURE 3.13

Use the standard color tab to select from a basic palette.

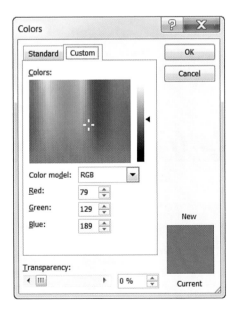

FIGURE 3.14

Use the Custom tab to input RGB color values.

FIGURE 3.15

Type in these RGB values to create your tutorial color theme.

When you save a new theme colors file on your system, the name appears in your Colors gallery. This will not be the case for other users' systems. Although theme colors are coded into and travel along with a template or theme file, users do not see the custom theme colors name listed in their Colors gallery.

If you find later that you need to change any of the values in the color theme you created, you can right-click the theme color's name and choose Edit. Make your changes and save, retaining the original color theme name.

SUPER-FAST, CUSTOM THEME COLORS

Typing in RGB values for 12 colors is tedious and time consuming. Fortunately, two add-ins are available to help you speed up the task. The OfficeOne ProTools Color Picker is $19.95 (USD) for a single user license, and there are substantial discounts for multiple licenses. The Color Swatch Add-In for PowerPoint 2007 and 2010 is a free add-in.

OfficeOne ProTools Color Picker makes picking up and applying any color simple. With the ProTools Color Picker, you can choose colors for fills, outlines, fonts, shadows, glows, and more. It displays a magnified view of pixels surrounding your cursor and also shows you the RGB values in hexadecimal and decimal formats. You can write down the decimal RGB values and use them to create new theme colors *or* use the Color Picker in combination with another brilliant add-in for the fastest color themes ever.

When developing a new color theme, start with a blank slide and create 12 filled rectangles to represent all the colors in a theme (see Figure 3.16). Use the ProTools Color Picker to pick up and fill these rectangles with colors from branding documents, websites, or with colors from graphics and images that you plan to use in the new template.

The next step involves a wonderful tool called the Color Swatch Add-In for PowerPoint 2007 and 2010. This free add-in is available at http://skp.mvps.org/swatch.htm.

FIGURE 3.16

Create a slide that includes shapes filled with the 12 colors you want to use for theme colors.

Click the Create Swatch Slide button and a new slide is added to the front of the presentation. You see 12 swatches, as shown in Figure 3.17, that represent the current color theme, along with 12 empty swatches that you can define as custom colors for your theme.

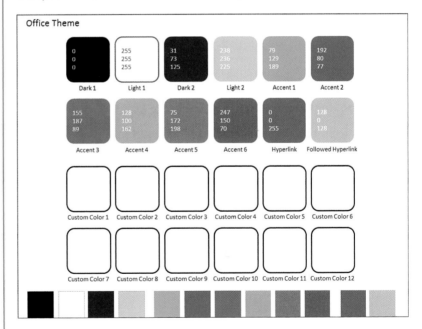

FIGURE 3.17

Copy your original 12 filled rectangles to the new Color Swatch slide. Use the OfficeOne ProTools Color Picker to pick up and apply each color to the corresponding swatch.

Copy the 12 filled rectangles from your original slide (refer to Figure 3.16) to the new Swatch slide (see Figure 3.17). Move the shapes to the bottom or off the slide area so they don't cover the swatches. One at a time, select each shape on the Swatch Slide and use the Color Picker to fill with the corresponding new color.

When you're finished filling the Swatch Slide with new colors, click the Apply Swatch to Color Theme button. Type in a name for your color theme and you're done.

There are links to both the Color Swatch Add-In and the ProTools Color Picker Add-In at http://www.quepublishing.com/title/0789749556. Thank you to Shyam Pillai and Chirag Dalal for developing these helpful tools!

DEFINING THEME FONTS

Theme fonts include two settings, one for headings and another for body. The Heading font applies to all Title placeholders and the Body font applies to all other text, including all other placeholders and default text in charts, tables, SmartArt, and individual textboxes. This helps establish a consistent look for text throughout a presentation. You can choose from the built-in theme font sets or create a custom font set.

SELECTING FROM BUILT-IN THEME FONTS

When you're setting up a template or theme and deciding what fonts to use, the built-in font sets are a good place to start. To choose one of them, follow these steps:

1. Open a blank presentation or continue with the presentation from the previous exercise in which you defined custom theme colors.

2. From the Design tab, select Fonts. In this gallery, you can choose from any of the built-in font sets, as shown in Figure 3.18.

3. Scroll down the list and hover over different theme names; your slide text will dynamically change to show you a live preview of the theme fonts.

4. Click on a theme font set to apply it to the current file.

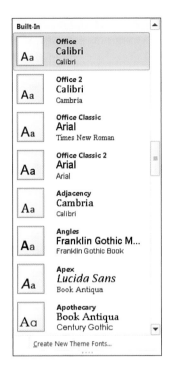

FIGURE 3.18

The Built-In Theme Fonts gallery offers many choices for sets of theme fonts. As you scroll through the list, hover on a theme name to see a preview of the fonts on your current slide.

WHY FONT CHOICES ARE LIMITED FOR TEMPLATES

Before you select just *any* font for your template, realize that your choices are extremely limited. This is one of the most confusing, and often frustrating, issues for PowerPoint users. You have hundreds of fonts available on your computer, so why can't you choose any one of them for a template?

The reason is that the fonts you select might not be available for everyone else who uses the template. Theme fonts *must* be present on a user's system or else they are automatically replaced by another font. This can create problems because when a font is replaced, text might resize, callouts might not align with other elements, text can extend beyond the edge of the slide, and line breaks might become inconsistent.

Fonts are installed on a computer system during the installation of various programs, starting with the operating system. Let's say you have Windows 7, Office 2010, and Adobe Creative Suite 5.1. All these programs come with a collection of fonts, but the options you selected during installation determine which fonts are actually loaded.

Think about the limitless combinations possible with various operating systems and software programs. What about Mac users? Windows XP? Perhaps you work for a worldwide corporation, with thousands of users and various language configurations. Only a slim chance exists that everyone at your company has the exact same list of fonts.

The logical solution would be to embed the fonts into the template. Unfortunately, this is not practical for a few reasons: most fonts cannot be embedded into a template, embedding does not work with theme files, PowerPoint won't warn you if the font is not embeddable, and PowerPoint on the Mac will ignore embedded fonts. If you're considering using licensed or free fonts for a template, read the "Purchased Fonts and Embedding" section later in the chapter.

CREATING CUSTOM THEME FONTS

To create a custom theme font set, do the following:

1.   From the Design tab, select Fonts, then Create New Theme Fonts.

2.   Select a Heading font.

3.   Select a Body font.

4.   Type in a name for your theme font set.

5.   Click Save.

You can select the same font for both Heading and Body. Many of the built-in font themes are set up this way.

TUTORIAL

To continue with the tutorial template, do the following:

1.   From the Design tab, select Fonts, then Create New Theme Fonts.

2.   Select Cambria for the Heading font and Calibri for the body font.

3.   Type in the name **Tutorial** and click Save (see Figure 3.19).

The new fonts set is saved to your system and is applied to your current PowerPoint file.

When you save new theme fonts to your system, *you* see the new name listed in the Custom section of the Fonts gallery as pictured in Figure 3.20. This will not be the case for other users. Although the settings for theme fonts do travel with a template or theme file, other users cannot see the theme font set listed in their Fonts galleries.

FIGURE 3.19
Select a Heading font and a Body font, and then type in a new name for your theme fonts.

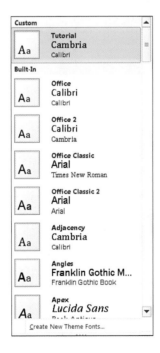

FIGURE 3.20
The new Tutorial theme in the Custom section of the Fonts gallery.

Sometimes you need to change the Heading or Body font, or both. Instead of creating a new set of theme fonts each time you make a change, you can edit the existing file. In the Fonts gallery, right-click the current theme font set's name and choose Edit. Make your changes and save the file, retaining the original name.

CAUTION   *When you create your own theme fonts, certain language settings are not included in the underlying XML code. These language settings are included in the built-in theme fonts. If you're creating a template for multinational use, selecting from built-in font sets and then changing the fonts later in the Theme Builder or directly in the XML might be a good idea. For details, see Chapter 12, "Using the Theme Builder Utility to Customize Your Theme," and Chapter 13, "Editing PowerPoint and Theme File XML."*

CHOOSING THE RIGHT FONTS

Just like the decisions you make for theme colors, the choices you make for fonts will have a lot of impact down the line. Theme fonts will populate all placeholders and default text and appear in (just about) every future slide created with the template.

One thing to consider when choosing fonts is that the characters in each font have personality and style. Some fonts look more contemporary whereas others can appear dated or retro. The fonts with the most personality are referred to as *ornamental* or *display* fonts. They have more distinctive letterforms and are not well-suited for body fonts (Chiller, Juice ITC, or Mistral are examples).

Legibility is the most important visual characteristic for a presentation font. You should choose fonts that are simple in design and form so that the letterforms are distinguishable at smaller sizes (consider chart labels or table data, for instance). This is why most presentation professionals suggest using *sans serif* fonts. *Serifs* refer to the small features at the end of letter strokes, as in the classic typefaces Times New Roman or Palatino Linotype. *Sans* means "without," so *sans serif* describes letterforms that do not have these extensions. See Figure 3.21 for some examples of sans serif fonts.

Some serif fonts work well for larger text sizes and are completely appropriate choices for Heading fonts. (Figure 3.22 shows some examples of serif fonts.) So, why not use them for body text? Serif characters are generally formed with thick and thin strokes. At small sizes, the thin strokes can break up or disappear, which makes reading text difficult. Think about chart labels as a baseline for smaller font sizes. You want to ensure that even the smallest text is clearly legible.

As stated earlier in the chapter, when selecting fonts you must consider *everyone* who will be using that template to create, edit, or display presentations based on that template. The theme fonts must be present on a user's system for the template to work properly. If the template (and subsequent presentations) will be shared among many users, you must stick with fonts that are common to all.

Consider the following scenarios to help you determine which fonts to choose for your theme.

Arial

Arial Black

Calibri

Candara

Century Gothic

Corbel

Euphemia

Franklin Gothic Medium

Tahoma

Verdana

FIGURE 3.21

Sans serif fonts are the best choices for body fonts. This list includes just a few examples.

Book Antiqua

Bookman Old Style

Cambria

Century

Constantia

Courier New

Garamond

Georgia

Nyala

Palatino Linotype

Plantagenet Cherokee

Times New Roman

FIGURE 3.22

This list features a few serif fonts, which look best at larger text sizes.

SCENARIO 1: CREATING A SINGLE-USE TEMPLATE

In this situation, you're designing and building a template on the computer that will display all presentations created with that template. Perhaps the presentations will only be printed, converted to PDF, or output to video from this system. (If there is *any* chance the presentation will be shared elsewhere, see Scenario 3.)

In this case, the sky's (almost) the limit. You can select any font from your Fonts gallery within PowerPoint, including fonts that your company has purchased licenses for. (Hello, branding fonts!)

Many fonts are installed with Microsoft Windows and Microsoft Office. Figure 3.23 includes a sample list of fonts that might be installed with specific versions of these programs.

The fonts shown in Figure 3.23 are not a definitive list of fonts available for PowerPoint templates. The list is subject to differences depending on installation options for each system. For more information on fonts, visit http://www.microsoft.com/typography/fonts/.

Arial (Bold, *Bold Italic*, *Italic*)	**Eras Bold ITC** (Demi, Eras Light, Eras Medium)	*Mistral*
Arial Black	Euphemia	Modern No. 20
Agency FB (**Bold**)	FELIX TITLING	*Monotype Corsiva*
Arial Narrow (Bold, **Bold Italic**, *Italic*)	Footlight MT Light	*Niagara Engraved*
Arial Rounded MT Bold	*Forte*	*Niagara Solid*
Baskerville Old Face	Franklin Gothic (Book, *Book Italic*, **Demi**, **Demi Cond**,	Nyala
Bauhaus 93	**Heavy**, ***Heavy Italic***, Medium Cond)	Old English Text MT
Bell MT (**Bold**, *Italic*)	Franklin Gothic Medium (**Italic**)	*Onyx*
Berlin Sans FB (**Bold**, **Demi Bold**)	Freestyle Script (Bold, *Bold Italic*, *Italic*)	*Palace Script MT*
Bernard MT Condensed	*Freestyle Script*	Palatino Linotype (**Bold**, ***Bold Italic***, *Italic*)
Bodoni MT (**Black**, ***Black Italic***, Bold, *Bold Italic*, *Italic*)	*French Script MT*	Papyrus
Bodoni MT Condensed (**Bold**, ***Bold Italic***, *Italic*)	Gabriola	*Parchment*
Bodoni MT Poster Compressed	Garamond (**Bold**, *Italic*)	Perpetua (**Bold**, ***Bold Italic***, *Italic*)
Book Antiqua (**Bold**, *Bold Italic*, *Italic*)	Georgia (**Bold**, ***Bold Italic***, *Italic*)	PERPETUA TITLING MT (**BOLD**)
Bookman Old Style (**Bold**, ***Bold Italic***, *Italic*)	*Gigi*	Plantagenet Cherokee
Bradley Hand ITC	Gill Sans MT (**Bold**, ***Bold Italic***, *Italic*, Condensed, Ext Condensed Bold,	*Playbill*
Britannic Bold	**Ultra Bold**, **Ultra Bold Condensed**)	Poor Richard
Broadway	Gloucester MT Extra Condensed	*Pristina*
Brush Script MT	Goudy Old Style (**Bold**, *Italic*)	Raavi (**Bold**)
Calibri (**Bold**, *Bold Italic*, *Italic*)	**GOUDY STOUT**	**Ravie**
Californian FB (**Bold**, *Italic*)	*Kunstlerschreibschrift*	Rockwell (**Bold**, ***Bold Italic***, *Italic*)
Calisto MT (**Bold**, ***Bold Italic***, *Italic*)	*Harlow Solid Italic*	Rockwell Condensed (**Bold**)
Cambria (**Bold**, *Bold Italic*, *Italic*)	Harrington	**Rockwell Extra Bold**
Candara (**Bold**, *Bold Italic*, *Italic*)	High Tower Text (*Italic*)	*Script MT Bold*
CASTELLAR	**Impact**	*Segoe Print* (**Bold**)
Centaur	Imprint MT Shadow	*Segoe Script* (**Bold**)
Century	*Informal Roman*	Segoe UI (**Bold**, ***Bold Italic***, *Italic*, Light, Semibold)
Century Gothic (**Bold**, ***Bold Italic***, *Italic*)	*Jokerman*	**SHOWCARD GOTHIC**
Century Schoolbook (**Bold**, *Bold Italic*, *Italic*)	*Juice ITC*	**Snap ITC**
Chiller	Kristen ITC	**STENCIL**
Colonna MT	*Kunstler Script*	Sylfaen
Comic Sans MS (**Bold**)	Lucida Bright (*Italic*, **Demibold**, ***Demibold Italic***)	Tahoma (**Bold**)
Consolas (**Bold**, *Bold Italic*, *Italic*)	*Lucida Calligraphy*	Tempus Sans ITC
Constantia (**Bold**, *Bold Italic*, *Italic*)	Lucida Console	Times New Roman (**Bold**, ***Bold Italic***, *Italic*)
Cooper Black	Lucida Fax (*Italic*, **Demibold**, ***Demibold Italic***)	Trebuchet MS (**Bold**, ***Bold Italic***, *Italic*)
COPPERPLATE GOTHIC BOLD	*Lucida Handwriting*	TW Cen MT (**Bold**, ***Bold Italic***, *Italic*)
COPPERPLATE GOTHIC LIGHT	Lucida Sans (**Demibold Roman**, ***Demibold Italic***)	TW Cen MT Condensed (**Bold**, **Extra Bold**)
Corbel (**Bold**, *Bold Italic*, *Italic*)	Lucida Sans Typewriter (**Bold**)	Verdana (**Bold**, ***Bold Italic***, *Italic*)
Courier New (**Bold**, ***Bold Italic***, *Italic*)	*Magneto*	*Viner Hand ITC*
Curlz MT	Malandra GD	*Vivaldi*
Edwardian Script ITC	*Matura MT Script Capitals*	*Vladimir Script*
Elephant (*Italic*)	Microsoft Sans Serif	**Wide Latin**

FIGURE 3.23

A sample list of fonts installed with Microsoft Windows Vista and Windows 7, Microsoft Office 2007 (Small Business, Professional, Ultimate, Professional Plus, Enterprise versions) and Microsoft Office 2010 (Standard, Professional, Professional Plus versions).

SCENARIO 2: CREATING A TEMPLATE FOR USE IN A SMALL GROUP

Let's say you work for a small company. You know for a fact that everyone in the company has the same computer setup: the same operating system and same version of Microsoft Office. When creating templates for an ideal (and surprisingly uncommon!) situation like this, you might choose from any of the fonts that appear in your PowerPoint font list.

Remember though: If presentations are shared beyond this small group of users, you run the risk of font substitution for those who have a different computer setup from the original group. Don't forget, this includes your clients, your vendors, and anyone else to whom you might send the presentation.

In this scenario, planning ahead for the inevitable shared presentation is best. Make sure any fonts that you're using can be embedded with the presentation. You must test this thoroughly! PowerPoint won't always warn you when a font cannot be embedded. Also be aware that, because most embedded fonts will not travel with a template, everyone at your company must know how to embed fonts when saving a presentation *and* remember to do so!

CAUTION

To embed a font in a presentation, do the following:

1. Choose File, Save As.

2. Click the Tools button, and then click Save Options.

3. Check the Embed Fonts in the File box.

4. Choose Embed All Characters and click OK.

Remember, though, most fonts will not embed in a template. And be careful when embedding a font into a presentation because PowerPoint might not warn you if the font has not actually been embedded.

Also, if any chance exists that a presentation will be viewed on a Mac system, forget embedding altogether and see Scenario 3. Mac versions of PowerPoint cannot embed fonts, and they cannot use fonts that have been embedded. (Read on for more information about purchased fonts and embedding.)

SCENARIO 3: CREATING A TEMPLATE FOR A LARGE GROUP OF USERS

In this most-common situation, it's better to be safe (and boring) than sorry. With little information about end users' systems, sticking with fonts from the list shown in Figure 3.24 is the best option. These fonts are common to most users.

Arial (**Bold**, ***Bold Italic***, *Italic*)	**Impact**
Arial Black	Juice ITC
Book Antiqua (**Bold**, *Bold Italic*, *Italic*)	Kristen ITC
Bookman Old Style (**Bold**, ***Bold Italic***, *Italic*)	Lucida Console
Bradley Hand ITC	*Lucida Handwriting*
Calibri (**Bold**, **Bold Italic**, *Italic*)	Microsoft Sans Serif
Cambria (**Bold**, ***Bold Italic***, *Italic*)	*Mistral*
Candara (**Bold**, **Bold Italic**, *Italic*)	*Monotype Corsiva*
Century	Nyala
Century Gothic (**Bold**, ***Bold Italic***, *Italic*)	Palatino Linotype (**Bold**, ***Bold Italic***, *Italic*)
Comic Sans MS (**Bold**)	Papyrus
Consolas (**Bold**, ***Bold Italic***, *Italic*)	Plantagenet Cherokee
Constantia (**Bold**, ***Bold Italic***, *Italic*)	*Pristina*
Corbel (**Bold**, **Bold Italic**, *Italic*)	Raavi (**Bold**)
Courier New (**Bold**, ***Bold Italic***, *Italic*)	Segoe Print (**Bold**)
Euphemia	*Segoe Script (**Bold**)*
Franklin Gothic Medium (*Italic*)	Sylfaen
Freestyle Script	Tahoma (**Bold**)
French Script MT	Tempus Sans ITC
Gabriola	Times New Roman (**Bold**, ***Bold Italic***, *Italic*)
Garamond (**Bold**, *Italic*)	Trebuchet MS (**Bold**, ***Bold Italic***, *Italic*)
Georgia (**Bold**, ***Bold Italic***, *Italic*)	Verdana (**Bold**, ***Bold Italic***, *Italic*)

FIGURE 3.24

When creating a template for a large group of users, choosing from this list of fonts that are common to most users is best.

To make your font decisions easier (or for you designers, utterly frustrating), the choices from this list of 45 common fonts are further limited by character legibility and font style. As discussed in the first part of this section, sans serif fonts are preferable for presentations. You can eliminate many of the display fonts such as Freestyle Script, French Script MT, Juice ITC, Mistral, Papyrus, and so on because they're impractical choices for templates. The characters do not scale well, which makes reading text at smaller sizes difficult. There's always an exception to the rule, so you could make a case for choosing one of the display fonts as the Heading font.

PURCHASED FONTS AND EMBEDDING

Although we would all love to use unique fonts for presentation templates, the reality is that this proposition is risky in regard to PowerPoint. Here are a few things to consider regarding embedding purchased or free fonts:

- As mentioned earlier, most fonts cannot be embedded in a template and theme files do not support embedding. Theme fonts must be installed in order for anyone to use these files.

- Your company might have purchased the rights to use certain fonts for all company documents and presentations. The fonts work just fine on employees' systems. But typical font licensing does not extend beyond internal company usage (distributing the fonts to anyone outside your company is illegal). This means that anyone outside the company (such as ad agencies, marketing firms, event companies, and so on) must purchase a licensed copy of the fonts. If theme fonts cannot be embedded or distributed, PowerPoint makes substitutions for them, often with disastrous results.

- Many sites offer free fonts; most of which are display or decorative fonts and unsuitable for body text. Be aware that many of these fonts have incomplete character sets, which means you might not have all the symbols you need. Also, some free fonts can overwrite legitimate fonts on your system if the filenames are the same.

- Many fonts cannot be embedded at all, and those that can might have license restrictions that limit embedding to print and preview purposes only. Most type foundries do not allow editable embedding of their fonts, and do not offer licenses for fonts that will embed with a template. Adobe OpenType fonts are not embeddable in any Office program (these fonts have an .OTF extension). Only TrueType fonts (.TTF extension) *can* be embedded, but even then, not all TrueType fonts are embeddable. You must test the font embedding capabilities to be sure.

- PowerPoint might not warn you that a font is not embeddable. When you save a presentation, it might look like fonts are embedding. You must test the file by opening it on a system that does not have the fonts installed. You might discover the fonts have been replaced instead of embedded.

- Even if the fonts are embeddable (and tested), can you be sure that all employees will know how to embed fonts and *remember to do so*?

- Embedded fonts increase the presentation file size.

- Mac versions of PowerPoint cannot use fonts that have been embedded. Because the newest versions of PowerPoint for Mac and PC are very similar, you should consider that your presentations might be viewed on a Mac system.

- If your company has a large budget, you could purchase custom-built, open-licensed fonts to embed in your templates. This is an expensive proposition and requires thorough testing to ensure the embedded fonts work on other systems. Remember though, Mac versions of PowerPoint cannot use embedded fonts at all.

NOTE *Feel free to copy this section and pass it along to key decision makers for your corporate templates.*

Think carefully and test thoroughly before choosing uncommon or licensed fonts for corporate templates. The purpose of a template is to establish basic design parameters that help to maintain some consistency among a group of users creating presentations. Not enough control exists over font embedding and font substitution to outweigh the risks when distributing a template to a large number of people.

For more details about embedding fonts with PowerPoint, visit the PPTFAQ at http://www.pptfaq.com/FAQ00076_Embedding_fonts.htm.

UNDERSTANDING THEME EFFECTS

If you've used a newer version of PowerPoint, you've most likely seen theme effects in action. When you open the Shape Styles, Chart Styles, SmartArt Styles, and Table Styles galleries, you can see how the current theme effects influence graphic fills, lines, bevels, and shadows. More importantly, you can change the theme effects to better suit your template design.

PowerPoint's built-in theme effects include pre-programmed settings that specify degrees of intensity for fills, lines, and special effects such as shadows and bevels. Effects are grouped into three style levels: subtle, moderate, and intense. Subtle effects typically consist of flat color fills without shadows. Moderate effects take things up a notch by including gradients or shadows, perhaps. Intense styles usually have the most effects, including bevels and texture fills. See Figure 3.25 for examples of the three levels of effects. These levels are combined to create the styles you see in the various galleries throughout PowerPoint.

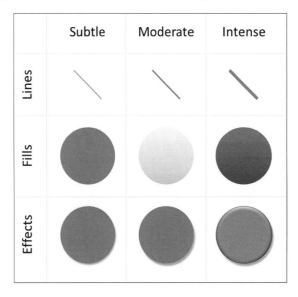

FIGURE 3.25

The settings for theme effects are grouped into three style levels: subtle, moderate, and intense.

PowerPoint includes 40 built-in sets of theme effects. Every theme has a different set of effects, each with its own unique characteristics. For example, some themes have a metallic look; others look frosted. The Equity theme (see Figure 3.26) has a vertical line pattern fill. The Paper theme (see Figure 3.27) includes a texture fill.

FIGURE 3.26

The Equity theme effect features vertical line fills.

FIGURE 3.27

A texture fill is included in the Paper theme effect.

You cannot edit the built-in theme effects using PowerPoint, nor can you build custom theme effects with PowerPoint. If you're interested in building custom theme effects, see Chapter 12.

You can often make do by selecting one of the built-in effects schemes. Just choose one that works well with the look and feel of your template design.

When you're developing a new template, you have to consider what style of effects best suits the template design. Think about how shapes, charts, tables, and SmartArt will look when different levels of effects are applied to them. Ultimately, the people creating slide content will be able to apply any style available in the galleries. You can determine which styles will populate these galleries by selecting an effects scheme that complements the template.

To see the differences between the built-in theme effects, try creating a sample slide with various types of content (see Figure 3.28). Include shapes, a chart, a SmartArt graphic, and a table with different levels of effects applied to this content. When completed, you can roll over the theme names in the Effects gallery to see how different themes look with this content.

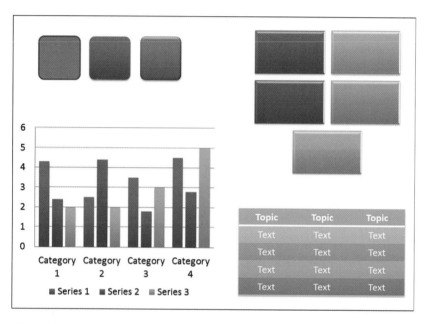

FIGURE 3.28

A sample slide with various types of content and fill styles can help you determine which built-in effect theme works best with your template design.

To build a sample slide like the one shown in Figure 3.28, follow these steps:

1. Add a new slide using the Blank slide layout.

2. Draw a rectangle, select the Format tab, and open the Shape Styles gallery. Apply one of the styles from the second row (demonstrating subtle fill effects).

3. Copy the rectangle you drew in step 2 and apply a style from the fifth row (moderate effects).

4. Copy the rectangle you created in step 3 and apply a style from the last row (intense effects). Move the rectangles (if necessary) to make room for the rest of the sample content.

5. Insert a chart, using the default data. Resize the chart and move it to a corner of the slide.

6. From the Chart Tools Design tab, open the Chart Styles gallery and apply a style from the third row. This style features moderate effects.

7. Insert a SmartArt graphic. The Basic Block List works well for this purpose.

8. From the SmartArt Design tab, open the SmartArt Styles gallery and select the first style in the 3-D category (Polished), which includes intense effects. To get a better look at the effects applied to various accent colors, select Change Colors and apply the first style from the Colorful section. Resize and move the SmartArt graphic as needed.

9. Insert a table. The example slide includes a 3 × 5 table. Including sample text in your table can help you check legibility when effects are applied.

10. From the Table Tools Design tab, open the Table Styles gallery and apply a style from the Best Match for Document section. Resize and move the table, if necessary, to complete the sample slide.

11. On the Design tab, click Effects to open the gallery (see Figure 3.29). Roll over each of the thumbnails to preview the effects on your current slide. You must click on an Effects scheme to apply it to the current file.

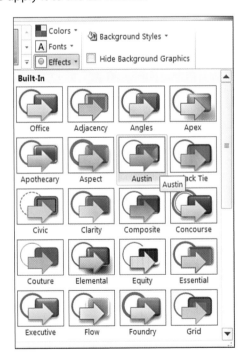

FIGURE 3.29

Roll over the thumbnails in the Effects gallery to see how each theme changes the settings on your sample slide.

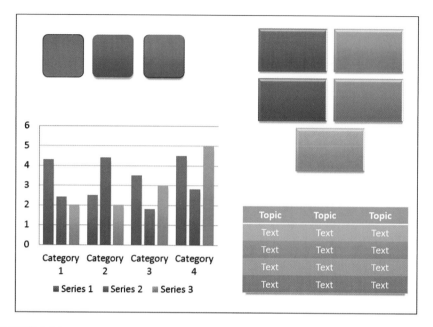

FIGURE 3.30

The Pushpin theme effects feature a more subdued design style.

Some of the theme effects include bevels, and others have glows or reflections. A few have texture fills. If your template is more suited to a subtle graphic style, consider choosing a simpler theme, such as Foundry or Pushpin (see Figure 3.30). Be cautious when choosing a more intense theme (for example, Equity, Flow, or Metro). Some intense effects make fills lighter, which can make text harder to read. Also, when all the graphics in a presentation include extreme special effects (glows, bevels, shadows, textures, and so on), the results can be visually overwhelming and distracting from the content, as shown with the Opulent theme in Figure 3.31. When in doubt, test the theme effects on a wide range of slides with different types of content.

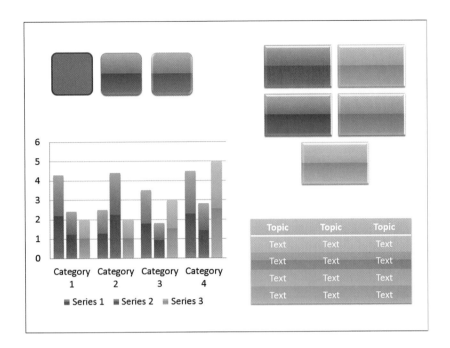

FIGURE 3.31

The Opulent theme features a high gloss gradient fill for moderate and intense effect styles.

IN THIS CHAPTER

- Defining the page setup
- Applying theme colors, fonts, and effects
- Choosing a background style
- Setting up guides
- Formatting placeholders

FORMATTING THE SLIDE MASTER

The slide master holds primary formatting information for a template. Slide layouts inherit their settings from the master, and slides inherit their settings from the layouts (see Figure 4.1). These settings include theme fonts, colors, effects, background styles, and placeholder settings. Also, any graphics, pictures, or logos placed on the slide master appear on all the slide layouts.

When you edit the slide master, the changes trickle down to all the layouts. This doesn't work in reverse. Changes made to slide layouts won't affect the slide master.

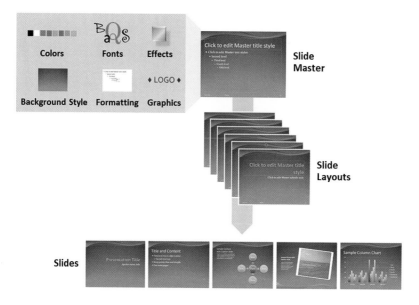

FIGURE 4.1

Slide master formatting is automatically applied to all slide layouts.

You must format the slide master first and then move on to the slide layouts. Why is the order important? Because when you make formatting changes to a placeholder on a slide layout, that placeholder becomes disconnected from the slide master. From this point on, that layout must be edited manually. If you later go back to the slide master and make further changes to that placeholder, those settings no longer apply to the orphaned layout.

This chapter takes you through the steps to set up a slide master. These steps include defining the page size; selecting theme colors, fonts, and effects; applying a background style; and formatting the title, body, and footer placeholders.

BEGIN WITH A NEW, BLANK PRESENTATION

If you were following along with the steps in Chapter 3, "Getting Started: Set Up a Theme," you might have a file open in PowerPoint that you used to set up theme colors, fonts, and effects. Close that file and open a new, blank presentation. Whenever you're building a template, starting with a clean slate is always best.

NOTE   *We're often asked to fix templates that aren't working properly, and our answer is always the same—we insist on rebuilding rather than risking a faulty repair. Starting over from scratch is safer than trying to fix a broken template.*

DEFINE THE PAGE SETUP

The default page setup for a PowerPoint presentation is sized for an on-screen show with an aspect ratio of 4:3. (This ratio describes the proportional relationship between the slide width and height.) If you're creating a template the same size as the PowerPoint default, you can skip this step and move on to "Choose a Background Style."

If you're developing a widescreen template, or any other size besides the default, you have to change the dimensions in the Page Setup dialog. You can access the Page Setup dialog from two places: on the Design tab and the Slide Master tab. Either way works the same; changes made to Page Setup apply to the entire template.

NOTE   *You cannot mix slide dimensions within the same presentation.*

As you can see in Figure 4.2, the Page Setup dialog includes multiple options for sizing your template. The default template is sized for an On-screen Show (4:3), the most common size for presentations. Slide width is 10", and slide height is 7.5". For a standard-sized template, keep the default settings as they are.

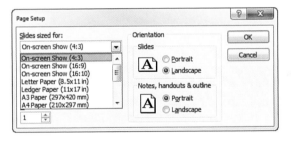

FIGURE 4.2
The Page Setup dialog includes many different size options.

The next choice in the size drop-down menu is On-screen Show (16:9). In recent years, 16:9 has become the most common aspect ratio for computer displays and widescreen projectors, driven by the 1080p standard for high-definition television.

Another option for widescreen page size is 16:10. Some laptops, monitors, and projectors display this ratio. If you're creating a template for presentations that will be shown on a widescreen display or projector, you should match the aspect ratio for that particular output. When in doubt, checking this setting early in the template development process is best.

Although PowerPoint provides both of these widescreen options in the page setup dialog, we don't recommend using the dimensions provided. Why? If you choose Slides Sized for

On-screen Show (16:9), you'll see that the width changes to 10", and slide height changes to 5.63". If anyone copies default-sized 10" × 7.5" slides into a widescreen presentation sized 10" × 5.63", all the font sizes, placeholder settings, and shapes will be greatly distorted. In addition, the content will be larger than the slide and will have to be resized.

A better method to set up a 16:9 widescreen template is shown in Figure 4.3. In the Page Setup dialog, change the slide width to 13.33" (keep the slide height at 7.5"). Click OK. That's all you have to do. By keeping the height the same as a standard-sized slide, you can more easily work with content from existing 4:3 presentations. Shapes are still distorted, but at least the font sizes remain the same.

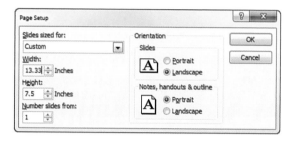

FIGURE 4.3

Format a 16:9 widescreen template using 13.33" for the width and 7.5" for the height.

To format the page size for a 16:10 template, change the slide width to 12". Again, keep the slide height at 7.5", which makes working with content from standard-sized presentations easier.

RESIZING SLIDES FROM STANDARD TO WIDESCREEN (OR VICE VERSA)

Shapes and pictures get distorted when you convert slides from standard to widescreen formats. Fortunately, a couple of PowerPoint add-ins are available that make properly resizing slide content between various presentation sizes easier. PPTools Resize is available at http://www.pptools.com/resize/index.html, and Aspect is available at http://www.pptalchemy.co.uk/Aspects.html.

TUTORIAL To continue building the Tutorial template, use the Page Setup default setting: On-Screen Show (4:3).

SELECT THEME COLORS, FONTS, AND EFFECTS

The next step in setting up your template includes applying theme colors, fonts, and effects. Chapter 3 explains how to create new theme colors, how to select and save theme fonts, and how to choose from available theme effects. If you followed along with the tutorial instructions, you have both theme color and font sets named *Tutorial* saved on your system. If not, you can go back to Chapter 3 for instructions.

On the Slide Master tab of the ribbon, click the Colors button to open the Theme Colors gallery. The top of this gallery displays all the custom color sets that you have saved on your system. The gallery also includes all the built-in theme colors.

TUTORIAL For the Tutorial template, choose the color set named Tutorial, as shown in Figure 4.4.

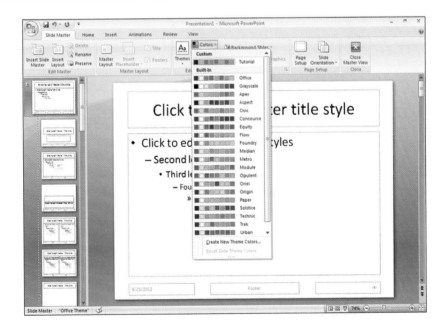

FIGURE 4.4
Click on a theme color set to apply it to the template.

In the same location on the Ribbon, click the Fonts button to open the Theme Fonts gallery. This gallery includes any custom theme font sets that you've saved on your system, as well as the built-in sets.

Choose the font set named Tutorial to continue setting up the Tutorial template, as shown in Figure 4.5.

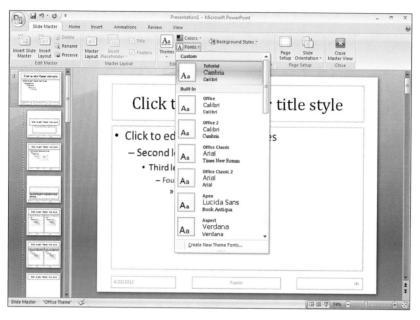

FIGURE 4.5

Click on a theme font set to apply it to the template.

Chapters 2 and 3 explain how theme effects influence the appearance of graphic elements. These effects include settings for shape fills, outlines, bevels, shadows, and more. You cannot edit or create theme effects using PowerPoint; you must do this type of customization using the Theme Builder or by manually editing the file's XML code (see Chapters 12 and 13).

On the Slide Master tab, open the Theme Effects gallery. When building a new template, you should choose a set of effects that complements your design. See Chapter 3 for instructions on how to set up a slide with various types of content to help you see differences between the built-in theme effects.

For the Tutorial template, click the effects set called Module (as shown in Figure 4.6).

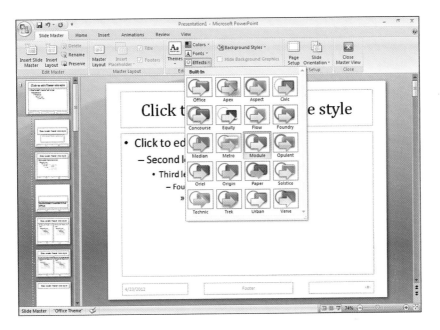

FIGURE 4.6

Click on one of the built-in theme effects sets to apply it to the template.

APPLY A BACKGROUND STYLE

After you've defined the theme colors, fonts, and effects for your template, the next step is to apply a background style. Background styles are often misunderstood and frequently forgotten. You should recognize that applying a background style is a critical step in the template build because it helps to ensure that text is visible and contrasts with the background.

Background styles and text colors work in tandem. Choose a dark background style and your text is automatically light. Choose a light style and text is dark. When you apply the background style first, your text color automatically picks up the opposite value and therefore should always be visible.

What text is affected by this setting? When you apply a background style, the slide master title and body placeholders automatically pick up the Light 1 or Dark 1 theme color. See Figure 4.7 for an example of both light and dark colors applied to the slide master.

CAUTION

Changing placeholders to any color you like is possible. There's a catch though: Chart text, SmartArt text, and table text always default to Light 1 or Dark 1 colors! To maintain consistency, stick with the default Light 1 or Dark 1 color on the body placeholder.

FIGURE 4.7

Text and background colors are formatted to work together to ensure that text is visible against the background.

On the Slide Master tab, click the Background Styles button to open the gallery (see Figure 4.8). Hover on any of the thumbnails to see a live preview of the background style on the current slide master.

FIGURE 4.8

Click on a background style to apply it to the template.

As shown in Figure 4.9, the Background Styles gallery includes three rows of fills based on the four light and dark theme colors. The default styles include solid fills, offset radial gradient fills, and centered radial gradient fills.

NOTE

Many of the built-in themes have custom background styles. To see these custom styles, open a new, Blank presentation (separate from your Tutorial template in progress). On the Design tab, click one of the Built-In Themes, such as Pushpin, Module, or Paper, to apply it to your current file. Click the Background Styles button to see the types of fills that are built into that particular theme. This level of customization cannot be done in PowerPoint. You must use the Theme Builder or manually edit the file's XML code to create custom background styles. See Chapters 12 and 13 for more information on using the Theme Builder and editing a file's XML code manually.

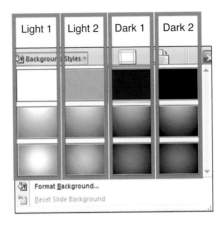

FIGURE 4.9

Background styles are based on the four light and dark theme colors, and they include three fill types.

CREATE A CUSTOM, GRADIENT FILL BACKGROUND

What if you want to use a gradient other than the ones included in the Background Styles gallery? Start by selecting a solid fill color style from the top row. Choose a color that is closest in value to your new gradient. If the new gradient is predominantly dark, select Background Style 3 or 4. If the new gradient is very light, choose Style 1 or 2. (When you hover on the thumbnails, the tooltip identifies the Style number.) Click on a background style to apply it to the template. From the Ribbon, click the Background Styles button again, and then click Format Background. Format the gradient fill with your new settings and choose Apply to All (see Figure 4.10).

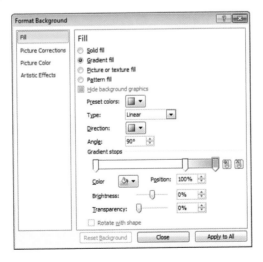

FIGURE 4.10

Create a custom gradient fill in the Format Background dialog.

When choosing colors for a new background gradient, we suggest using tints and shades from the same column below one of the theme colors. For instance, if your gradient transitions from medium to dark gray, you could select tints and shades from the Dark 2 column. Figure 4.11 shows a gradient formatted with the Dark 2 theme color and two shades of the same theme color. The benefit to choosing colors this way becomes apparent if you change theme colors down the road. The background gradient keeps similar values, but picks up the new hue. You have less control over the results if your gradients are formatted using multiple theme colors.

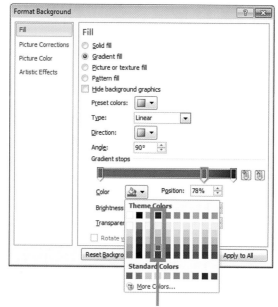

Theme colors column of tints and shades

FIGURE 4.11

When creating a custom gradient fill for a background, select tints and shades from the same theme color column.

FORMAT A PICTURE FILL BACKGROUND

If your template design features a picture fill background, you must begin by choosing a solid Background style that is close in value to the picture. This forces text to pick up the contrasting light or dark color. If you have a predominantly light picture, choose a light background style. If you have a dark picture, choose a dark background style. You will add the picture fill next.

RESIZE AND FORMAT A PICTURE FOR YOUR BACKGROUND

To size a picture for a template background, you need two pieces of information: page size and display resolution. *Page size* is your template width and height in inches. *Display resolution* is the width and height, in pixels, of the projector or monitor that will be used to show presentations based on the template. Image quality will only be as good as the display used when presenting the show.

For a standard-sized presentation, the page size is 10" × 7.5". Historically, the most popular desktop monitor and projector resolution has been 1024 × 768 pixels. These pixel dimensions are equal to a 10" × 7.5" slide background. If the projectors at your company use this resolution, then you can size the template background picture at 1024 × 768 pixels.

Display resolution is continuously changing and improving. Your projector(s) might be capable of a higher resolution, perhaps 1280 × 1024 pixels or greater. Newer laptops and monitors are capable of much higher display resolutions. The point here is you need to determine the most common display resolution that will be used to present slide shows based on the template you're building. Size your background picture for that resolution.

If you work with Photoshop or other image editing applications, you might be used to working in inches versus pixels. When you set up the dimensions for your Photoshop document at 10" × 7.5" and the DPI (dots per inch) at 102.4, your image is exactly 1024 × 768 pixels. This size should be fine for textural backgrounds and other pictures that do not include fine details. Highly detailed pictures look better at a higher resolution because they include more pixels. The result is larger file sizes, though. You need to strike a balance between picture quality and file size, which might require saving and projecting a couple of test files.

Although DPI is a term that pertains to print quality, you can consider this figure equal to pixels per inch (PPI) when sizing pictures in Photoshop (or another image editing program). When you increase the DPI setting, the pixel dimensions get larger—more PPI are included in the picture. A page size of 10" × 7.5" at 120 DPI translates to 1200 × 900 pixels. Remember, file size increases when you include more pixels. An image at this size could be around 2MB, which might be okay if you use the same background throughout your template However, if your template includes more than one background picture, the file size increases accordingly.

Understand that increasing the DPI or pixel dimensions does *not* improve the quality of a smaller-sized picture. Begin with an image that is at least the same size or larger than your target size. You can resize a picture to be smaller, but you can't scale up without compromising quality.

Widescreen monitors and projectors are more prevalent these days. If you are developing a template for widescreen presentations, size the picture background to match your template page size as well as the widescreen projector (or monitor) resolution. Many configurations exist for widescreen projectors. Ask for this information or find it in the projector manual before you begin building the template.

When you're finished editing the picture, save it as a .PNG file. If prompted for Interlace options upon saving, choose None. We recommend using the .PNG format versus .JPG format for pictures in PowerPoint. .PNG files maintain their quality when compressed, whereas .JPG files lose detail and degrade in quality with compression. Unfortunately, picture compression is automatically turned on in PowerPoint. This is a default setting. You must deactivate image compression for every PowerPoint file or edit the system registry to turn it off completely. Learn more about image compression in PowerPoint at http://www.pptfaq.com/FAQ00862_PowerPoint_2007_and_2010_make_pictures_blurry-_loses_GIF_animation.htm.

NOTE

You can insert a picture directly onto the slide master instead of using the picture fill method. Editing an inserted picture is easier than making changes to a background picture fill, especially when the original artwork has not been provided. The biggest difference between the two methods is that the inserted picture will appear in grayscale and black-and-white modes (for printing), whereas a background picture fill will not show.

USE DIFFERENT BACKGROUND STYLES IN A TEMPLATE

You can change the background style or fill on any individual slide layout. Choose the background style most common throughout your template design and apply it to the slide master. Individual slide layouts can be then customized with other backgrounds as needed. See Chapter 5, "Formatting the Default Slide Layouts," for more instructions on changing the background on a slide layout.

FORMAT THE BACKGROUND IN THE TUTORIAL TEMPLATE

TUTORIAL

The Tutorial template includes a picture background, as shown in Figure 4.12. We've scaled the picture for a standard-sized presentation. To format the background in your Tutorial template, follow these steps:

1. Download the file called gray_texture.png from http://www.quepublishing.com/title/0789749556.

2. On the Slide Master tab in the Ribbon, click the Background Styles button to open the gallery.

3. Click on Style 3 (solid gray) to apply it to the template.

4. Click the Background Styles button again, and then click Format Background.

5. In the Format Background dialog, choose Picture or Texture Fill, then Insert from: File. Locate the picture gray_texture.png, click Insert, and then Apply to All. Close the dialog box.

FIGURE 4.12
The Tutorial template is formatted with this picture background.

SET UP GUIDES

Before you format and reposition placeholders on the slide master, set up the guides. Guides help you establish an underlying structure for the template. Use them to maintain consistent size and position for placeholders as you format the slide master and slide layouts.

Guides are turned off by default. To make them visible, right-click the slide layout and choose Grid and Guides. You can also press the keyboard shortcut, Alt+F9. You see two dashed lines that intersect in the center of the slide. When you drag a guide across the slide area, you see a small number that tells you the horizontal or vertical position for that guide.

Turn on the ruler to make positioning guides easier. On the View tab of the Ribbon, select the check box next to Ruler.

The slide area is divided into quadrants, with 0,0 at the center point. Keep the center guides in place as visual reference for the middle of a slide.

Hold the Ctrl key and drag a guide to make a duplicate. Drag the duplicate to a new position on the slide.

We recommend adding guides around the perimeter of the slide master, approximately .5" to .75" from each edge (see Figure 4.13).This is known as a *safe margin*. You want to keep text and other important visual information safely away from the slide edges (and instruct users to do the same when adding slide content). Objects that are close to these edges might be cut off when projected if the projector is not aligned properly. From a design perspective, planning for space around the most important elements on the slides is important. Titles and text that appear too close to the edges can make a presentation look crowded and poorly planned. Plan your slide master with some breathing room around all the placeholders.

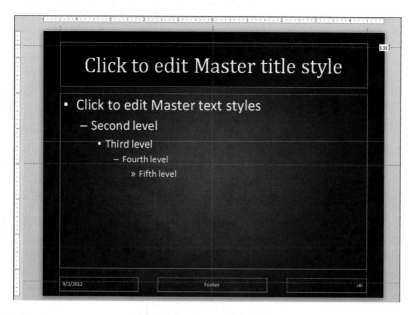

FIGURE 4.13

Add guides to define margins around the perimeter of the slide.

Guides are helpful for positioning and sizing placeholders on the slide master and slide layouts. We suggest adding horizontal guides to indicate the top, bottom, and sides of the title and body placeholders. Figure 4.14 shows all the guides in place on the tutorial slide master.

TUTORIAL Set up guides on the slide master for your Tutorial template.

1. Using your now visible ruler to position them, duplicate and reposition two vertical guides at 0.5" from the left and right edges of the slide area. The number displayed on each guide shows 4.50.

2. Duplicate and reposition two horizontal guides approximately 0.5" from the top and bottom edges of the slide. The number shown on the guides should be 3.33.

3. Duplicate a horizontal guide in the top half of the slide and reposition at 2.25". Use this guide to align the bottom of the title placeholder.

4. Duplicate another horizontal guide in the top half of the slide and reposition at 1.75". This guide anchors the top of the body placeholder.

5. Duplicate a final horizontal guide in the lower half of the slide and reposition at 3.00". This guide establishes the bottom of the body placeholder.

FIGURE 4.14

The guide setup on the tutorial slide master includes three vertical and five horizontal guides. Set up guides before resizing and repositioning placeholders.

SMART GUIDES IN POWERPOINT 2010

Smart guides are a new alignment feature in PowerPoint 2010. When two or more objects are aligned with each other, a smart guide automatically appears as a dashed line extending slightly beyond the aligned objects. These smart guides come in very handy during slide layout and development, but they're not substitutes for drawing guides set at specific positions on the slide.

ADD SHAPES, LOGOS, OR PICTURES

This step is optional and depends on your particular template design. If your design calls for accent shapes, lines, or pictures, you can add them to the slide master before or after formatting the placeholders. Remember that any graphics you add to the slide master appear on all the slide layouts. Add elements that are common to most of the slide layouts. You can hide these elements on layouts that call for a different design.

The Tutorial template design includes a gradient-filled rectangle, positioned behind the title placeholder. To add this rectangle, do the following:

1. Draw a rectangle on the slide master at the top of the slide.

2. Extend the rectangle to span the width of the slide.

3. The bottom of the rectangle should extend just below the second horizontal guide. Figure 4.15 shows the rectangle in place. (Rectangle dimensions are 10" × 1.58".)

4. Format the rectangle with a linear gradient fill. The angle should be 0°. Include two gradient stops with black for both colors.

5. Position the first gradient stop at 0%, and the second stop at 100%. Change the second stop to 100% Transparency.

6. Change the Shape Outline to No Outline.

7. On the Home tab, click Arrange, then Send to Back.

FIGURE 4.15

The tutorial slide master features a gradient-filled rectangle behind the title placeholder.

TUTORIAL

For corporate templates, including a company logo on the slide master is common. For example purposes, we have added a logo to the slide master of the Tutorial template. Figure 4.16 shows the logo in place on the tutorial slide master. Use the following steps to add this logo to your tutorial slide master:

1. Download the logo MT_logo_white.png from http://www.quepublishing.com/title/0789749556.

2. On the Insert tab, click the Picture button, select the logo and click Open.

3. With the logo selected, on the Picture Tools Format tab, change the width to 1.75". The height scales proportionately.

4. Drag the logo to the lower-right corner of the slide master. Using the arrow keys, nudge it into position so the logo characters are resting on the bottom and right guides. You can move the page number placeholder out of the way.

5. With the logo selected, on the Home tab, click Arrange and then Send to Back.

FIGURE 4.16

The sample tutorial logo is positioned against the bottom and right guides.

NOTE

We don't recommend including a logo on every slide. Content should be the focus of a presentation. A small, detailed logo can be distracting, and it takes up valuable space. Plus, the more you add to your slides, the more cluttered they become. A logo on the title slide and closing slide should suffice. Still, many companies might request that templates for their company include a logo on each slide because of requirements from their marketing or legal departments.

WHICH FILE FORMAT SHOULD YOU USE FOR LOGOS?

Although you can insert many different picture file types into PowerPoint—.JPG, .PNG, .EMF, .BMP, .EPS, and so on—only a few of them are suitable formats for logos.

.EMF and .WMF files work well for most logo designs. These vector file formats are made up of scalable shapes that you can resize without any loss in quality. Another advantage to using these file types is that you can ungroup them in PowerPoint, converting the artwork to Microsoft drawing objects. After the conversion you can easily recolor the logo shapes, changing dark colors to light or vice versa.

.EPS files are another vector format type. We don't recommend using this format in PowerPoint because the image quality is not as good as .EMF or .WMF files. Curved and angled shapes in .EPS files can appear very jagged in PowerPoint. Plus, when you ungroup an .EPS file to convert it to Microsoft drawing objects, an outline is automatically applied to any filled shapes. This makes the logo appear thicker than intended. If you receive an .EPS logo for use in a template design, open the file in an image editing program (Photoshop or other) and resave the logo as a .PNG.

.JPG and .PNG are the two most common raster file formats. Raster files consist of a finite number of colored pixels, and they do not retain quality when scaled larger in size. The .PNG file format works great for logos. .PNG files do not lose quality when compressed and details hold up at smaller sizes. You can also save a .PNG file with a transparent background, enabling you to insert the logo over a colored PowerPoint background. Although the .JPG format might be common, we do not recommend it for logos. .JPG files lose quality upon compression. PowerPoint automatically compresses pictures upon file saves (unless you disable this feature). This compression can be disastrous for a detailed logo. Refer to the earlier section, "Format a Picture Fill Background," for more information about .JPG compression.

FORMAT THE TITLE PLACEHOLDER

Quite a few formatting issues exist with the default title placeholder that you should address when building your templates.

The default title placeholder is formatted at 44-point font size, which seems quite large in relation to the body text size. This difference is more pronounced on slides with charts and chart labels. Smaller title sizes such as 28, 32, or 36 point work best for most templates.

The title placeholder is center aligned—a poor choice for slide titles. It feels formal, like a report title or book cover, and titles never begin in the same place on subsequent slides.

Left-aligned titles work best for a template because the text always begins in the same position from slide to slide.

Another issue with the default title placeholder is the vertical alignment set to Middle. This means that text always begins in the middle of the placeholder. This might look fine if all slides in a presentation have one-line titles, but that is rarely the case. The problem with middle alignment becomes apparent in a series of slides that include both one-line and two-line titles, as shown in Figure 4.17. A two-line title splits in the middle of the placeholder, moving the first word to a higher position than a one-line title. The amount of space between title and content also changes in this scenario. These inconsistencies can be visually distracting.

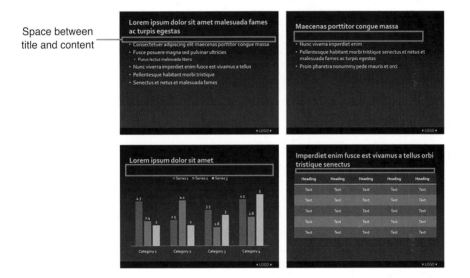

FIGURE 4.17

Middle-aligned titles begin in different positions for one and two lines of text and have inconsistent space above content.

Plan better for titles of various lengths by using the Bottom vertical alignment for title placeholders. Text will always appear in the same position on the lower line, maintaining consistent space above the content. Two-line titles wrap upward in the placeholder. Figure 4.18 shows the Align text button and dialog on the Home tab.

The height of the default title placeholder also poses a problem for two-line titles. The placeholder is too short to accommodate two lines of text at 44 pt size. Autofit is set to shrink text on overflow, which forces two-line titles to shrink to 40 point. Titles are inconsistently sized throughout a presentation, and sometimes the line spacing decreases. Planning a title placeholder that comfortably fits a two-line title without resizing is best.

FIGURE 4.18

Change the title placeholder alignment to Bottom for better visual consistency among titles of different lengths.

We recommend that you set the Autofit option to Do Not Autofit. Right-click the title placeholder and choose Format Shape. On the Text Box tab in the Format Shape dialog, select Do Not Autofit.

Line spacing on the title placeholder is set for Single spacing. This setting creates a large gap between multiple lines of text, especially at larger sizes. If you change Line Spacing to Multiple at 0.9, that gap decreases to 90% of a single line space. Certain fonts and very large font sizes can accommodate smaller spacing, such as 0.8 or so. Test any line spacing changes by typing two lines of text and looking for any overlap (see Figure 4.19 for an example). Make sure that characters with ascenders (h, k, l) or descenders (q, y, p, g, j) don't obscure or touch each other.

FIGURE 4.19

Test line spacing adjustments to avoid overlapping characters like these.

When formatting the title placeholder, confirm that the font color is assigned to the correct theme color. You can select a different color, but we suggest you choose from the Theme Colors gallery. If the theme colors ever change in the future, your font color will update automatically. Be aware that if you choose any color outside of the theme, that color does not automatically update when you apply a new theme. Choosing such a color could be an intentional decision on your part, should you always want that color to remain the same.

You can reposition the title placeholder on the slide master. Place it wherever it suits your template design. You can also change the height and width of the placeholder as needed. Just don't delete the title placeholder on the slide master. Later, you can omit it from specific, custom slide layouts.

A couple of other things to check when formatting the title placeholder include the following:

1. Verify that the title placeholder is assigned to the correct theme font. On the Home tab, in the Font group, you see the word (Heading) after the font name (see Figure 4.20).

FIGURE 4.20
Confirm that the title placeholder is assigned to the Heading theme font.

2. Right-click and select Format Shape. In the dialog box, select the Text Box tab. Under Autofit, select Do Not Autofit. This prevents the title font size from shrinking and helps to maintain consistency.

3. In the same dialog box, confirm that Wrap Text in Shape is selected.

TUTORIAL

To continue formatting the slide master for the tutorial, make the following changes to the title placeholder, as shown in Figure 4.21:

1. Change the font size to 32 point.

2. Change the paragraph alignment to Left.

3. Change the vertical alignment to Bottom.

4. Change the line spacing to Multiple: 0.9.

5. In the Format Shape dialog select the Text Box tab. Under Autofit, select Do Not Autofit.

6. Adjust the height of the placeholder to fit within the top two guides. (The placeholder height will be 1.08".)

FIGURE 4.21

The title placeholder on the tutorial slide master is formatted with the new settings, alignment, and positioning.

FORMAT THE BODY PLACEHOLDER

The body placeholder includes more levels and settings, so it requires more custom formatting than the title placeholder.

The default text size for the first level is 32 point. This size works well for a template *if* you're certain that users will limit the amount of text on their slides. Our clients typically request a smaller size. To resize all levels at once, select the body placeholder (do not click the placeholder text), and on the Home tab, click the Decrease Font Size button (see Figure 4.22). This method decreases all the levels proportionately.

Although you can specify any size you like in a placeholder, we recommend that you stick with the sizes listed in the Font Size gallery. When a user selects increase or decrease font size, PowerPoint changes the text to the nearest size listed in the gallery. It does not scale text sizes proportionately. For example, let's say you choose 22 point for first-level text and 20 point for the second level on the body placeholder. When you click the Increase Font Size button, the first level and the second level become 24 point. The sizing hierarchy is gone.

The bullet characters in the default body placeholder are simple, and that's good. Decorative bullet points are distracting. The function of a bullet point is simply to indicate a new list item. Consider using basic shapes such as circles and squares instead of diamonds, arrows, or 3D shapes.

Decrease Font Size button

FIGURE 4.22

Use the Decrease Font Size button on the Home tab to reduce all text level sizes at once.

Although picture bullets are an available option, they can be problematic. Unlike symbol characters, picture bullets will not change from a light to dark color or vice versa to contrast with a new background style. Also, picture bullets from a Windows PowerPoint file do not work properly on a Mac; the bitmap will be lost, and an unpredictable character will be inserted.

The second-level bullet character in the default body placeholder is an en dash (not a hyphen, but a special character). Some people like to use this character for lower-level bullets. Others think it looks like a minus sign, especially when the line of text next to it begins with a number. You can always keep the design very simple by using the same character for all levels. To change all the bullet characters for all levels in the body placeholder at the same time, use the following steps:

1. Select the edge of the body placeholder (do not click the text in the placeholder).

2. On the Home tab, click the arrow next to the Bullets button to open the gallery, and then select Bullets and Numbering.

3. Choose one of the styles from this gallery (see Figure 4.23), such as the Filled Round bullets or the Filled Square bullets, or click the Customize button to select a different character. The Customize button opens the Symbol gallery, as shown in Figure 4.24. Check that the first option is set to Font: (Normal Text). Be careful selecting characters from other fonts; they might not be available for everyone using the template.

4. Change the size if you like; 80% or 90% often works well for a square or round bullet.

5. Select a theme color for the bullets. If you leave Automatic selected, the bullet character is the same color as the body text.

6. Click OK.

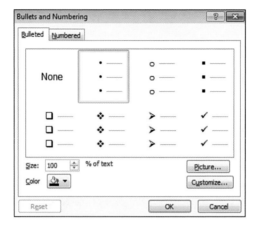

FIGURE 4.23

Choose a simple shape from the Bullets gallery.

FIGURE 4.24

The Symbol gallery includes all the characters available for your font. Select a simple shape when choosing a custom symbol for bullets.

WHAT IF YOUR TEMPLATE DESIGN CALLS FOR NO BULLET CHARACTERS?

A popular convention for slide design is to format text without any bullet characters. Text is visually separated with line spacing, and bullet characters aren't really necessary. Sometimes this includes only first-level text; subsequent levels are still bulleted.

The easiest way to achieve this look is to select the bulleted text on a completed slide and click the Bullets button to turn them off. Bullet symbols disappear and multiple level sizing and indents remain intact. Notice that we specified "completed slide" and not slide master. Turning off bullets on the slide master causes problems in slide editing mode. When you enter text on a slide and press Tab to demote your text to the next level, it doesn't pick up the new level formatting. You must use the Decrease List Level and Increase List Level buttons on the Home tab to get the correct formatting. Getting used to reaching for the Ribbon can be a challenge when you're used to the Tab and Shift+Tab shortcuts.

A workaround is available for no-bullet formatting on the slide master or slide layouts. Instead of a standard bullet character, you can select the "space" bullet character. In the Bullets and Numbering dialog, click Customize to open the Symbol gallery. Choose the first character in the gallery, what looks like a blank box. Figure 4.25 shows the space character highlighted in blue. The default bullet size is 100%; if you keep this setting, there will appear to be a big gap on the left side of your text. Change the bullet size to 25% (the smallest allowed) and edit the indentation settings to move the text over to the left. (For first-level text, try 0.1" for indentation before text and 0.1" for hanging indentation.)

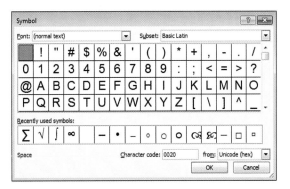

FIGURE 4.25

Select the space character instead of a traditional bullet symbol when formatting the body placeholder with a non-bulleted level.

Using this method for "no-bullet" formatting makes using the Tab and Shift+Tab shortcuts that we're all used to easy. One caveat: If users try to turn bullets points on, they won't see any symbols; you have to inform them of the no-bullet style.

The default body placeholder is formatted with single-line spacing. This presents the same problem as the title placeholder: Lines of text are too spread out. Tighter line spacing looks better and helps to improve readability. To change line spacing for all levels, follow these steps:

1.   Select the edge of the body placeholder (do not click the placeholder text).

2.   On the Home tab, click the Line Spacing button, and then click Line Spacing Options. Change the option for Line Spacing to Multiple at 0.9 (see Figure 4.27).

3.   Click OK to accept the changes.

CAUTION

An option is available to set Line Spacing Exactly at "XX" point size. You determine exactly how many points the space will be. We advise against using this setting because the line spacing doesn't adapt to changes with the body font size. When text sizes decrease, line spacing remains at exactly the specified point size. This can create tremendous gaps between lines of text.

The next issue involves *paragraph spacing*, the amount of space between each level of text in the body placeholder. The default paragraph spacing is set at fractional increments, and in most cases, the spacing is too small to distinguish breaks between paragraphs. Consider each bulleted item on a slide as a paragraph. You want the points to be visually separated for easier reading. See Figure 4.26 for an example of bulleted text set at the default paragraph spacing versus increased spacing before each level.

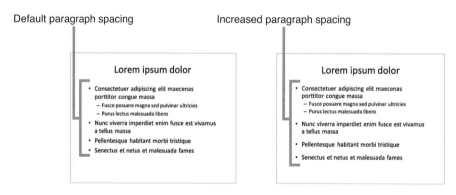

FIGURE 4.26

Increased paragraph spacing helps to visually separate bulleted text for easier reading. You have the option to set spacing before and after a paragraph. Adding space to both settings is not necessary; one will suffice.

Rather than editing each level individually, it's faster to make a global change to all levels first. You can then go back and increase the spacing for the first few levels. To change the spacing before paragraphs in the body placeholder, use the following steps:

1. Select the edge of the body placeholder (do not click the placeholder text).

2. On the Home tab, click the Line Spacing button, and then click Line Spacing Options.

3. In the Paragraph dialog, use the increase and decrease arrows in the Spacing Before field to change the size in 6-point increments. (For any other number, type the size in the box.) Change this setting to 6 points (as shown in Figure 4.27). This size works well for the majority of the smaller levels of text.

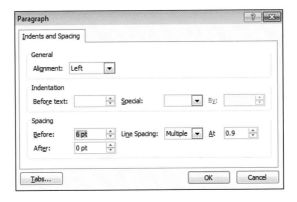

FIGURE 4.27
Select the body placeholder and globally change the Line Spacing to Multiple at 0.9 and Spacing Before to 6 points.

Now you can increase the paragraph spacing on the first few levels of text to allow for more space between the larger text sizes. To change the spacing before each level, do the following:

1. Click inside the placeholder on the level of text that you want to change (the cursor changes to a blinking line between characters).

2. On the Home tab, click the Line Spacing button and then click Line Spacing Options.

3. In the Paragraph dialog, use the increase and decrease arrows in the Spacing Before field to change the size in 6-point increments. (For any other number, type the size in the box.)

4. For first-level text, increase the spacing to 12 points or so. Experiment on a sample slide to determine the spacing that works best for your template design.

5. Repeat these steps for the second and possibly the third level in the placeholder. You can try 10 points and 8 points for these levels. Again, experimenting on a sample slide helps to find the spacing that works best for your template. The remaining levels have already been changed to 6 points.

Indentation settings are another concern with the default placeholder. The default settings might work just fine for some templates, especially if you're not too concerned about multiple levels of text. The problem is that the indents for various levels are not set up proportionately to one another. You can see this on the default slide master in Figure 4.28. Notice where the second-level bullet point is positioned in relation to text on the first level. The bullet is farther away on the third, fourth, and fifth levels.

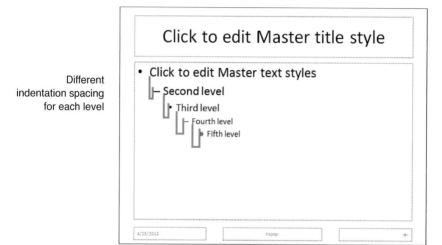

FIGURE 4.28

On the default body placeholder, indentation settings are not proportionately equal for all text levels.

Select the first level of text in the placeholder and open the Line Spacing Options dialog. You see that the indentation before text is 0.38", and the hanging indent is also 0.38". Try resetting both indents at 0.25". The default settings for second-level indentation are 0.81" and 0.31". If you change these to 0.5" and 0.25", the second-level bullet point aligns with the left edge of the first-level text (see Figure 4.29). Continue editing both indentation settings for all remaining levels.

Different bullet symbols, fonts, and font sizes demand different indent settings. Setting up a sample bulleted slide can help determine what indentation settings work for your particular template design.

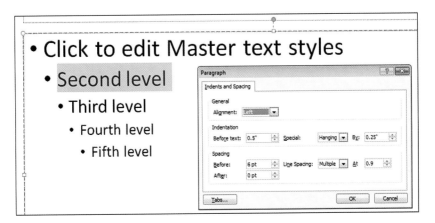

FIGURE 4.29

Change both indentation settings to ensure that bullet spacing is proportionate from level to level.

HOW MANY TEXT LEVELS SHOULD YOU FORMAT?

On the default slide master, you see five levels of text. Not many people know that PowerPoint enables you to format and use up to nine levels! Whether you format all nine levels on the slide master is really up to you and your clients. A pretty safe bet is that most users do not need any of the levels beyond the third or fourth ones. (Keeping these levels visible on the slide master and formatting them is best anyway.) The best presentation slides include very little text without multiple levels at all.

That said, there are always exceptions to the rule. Somewhere, somehow, someone is using PowerPoint to format documents or simply likes the ability to indent up to nine levels. You can format levels six through nine by adding them to the slide master. Press Enter and Tab after the fifth level to add the sixth, and so on. Add these levels prior to any formatting on the body placeholder.

The default body placeholder is set for left paragraph alignment. There's no reason to change this. We read from left to right; our eyes are accustomed to reading chunks of text that begin on the left side. Center- and right-aligned text is more difficult to follow because new sections or paragraphs do not begin in the same place every time. Justified text belongs in a newspaper column (and maybe not even there).

Reposition and resize the body placeholder to suit your template design. Just don't delete the placeholder from the slide master altogether or you'll end up with a template that doesn't work properly. Later, you can opt to leave it off certain custom slide layouts (refer to Chapter 5).

There are a couple of final settings to check on the body placeholder. Make sure the font is assigned to the correct theme font (Body). The font color should be assigned to the Light 1 or Dark 1 theme color. In the Format Shape dialog, ensure that Wrap Text to Shape is selected and Autofit is set to Shrink Text on Overflow.

TUTORIAL

To format the body placeholder for the Tutorial template, use the following steps. (See Figure 4.30 for visual reference of the following changes.)

1. With the body placeholder selected, from the Home tab, click the Decrease Font Size button to reduce the size for all levels.

2. Change the bullet character to Filled Round Bullets, color Accent 3.

3. Change the line spacing to Multiple 0.9.

4. Change all Before line spacing to 6 points. On the first level of text, change the Before line spacing to 12 points.

5. Select the first-level text, change the indentation before text to .3" and the hanging indent to 0.3".

6. Make the following changes to the other levels:

   • Second level: .6" and .25"

   • Third level: .85" and .2"

   • Fourth level: 1.05" and .2"

   • Fifth level: 1.25" and .2"

7. Adjust the top edge of the placeholder to align with the horizontal guide at 1.75" and adjust the bottom edge to align with the guide above the footers at 3.00".

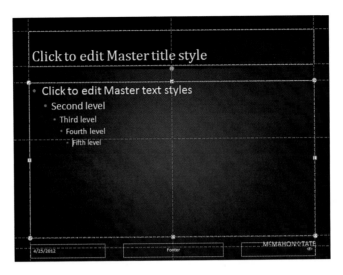

FIGURE 4.30

Many formatting changes are made to the default body placeholder on the Tutorial template slide master.

FORMAT THE FOOTER PLACEHOLDERS

You should include and format the footer placeholders on the slide master. Don't delete them or you'll lose all functionality for those who want to include them in their presentations. You can always turn off the footers when formatting slide layouts (refer to Chapter 5).

You can change the font size, color, alignment, and position of footer placeholders. Your template design influences these settings. The default size for footers is 12 point. They can be smaller—8 point or 10 point, for instance. Layout choices are up to you; you can reposition footers wherever it best suits your design.

TUTORIAL On the Tutorial template slide master, format the footer placeholders as follows (for an example of the formatted footers, see Figure 4.31):

1. Select all three footer placeholders and change the font size to 10 point and paragraph alignment to Left.

2. Change the font color to white, Text 1, Darker 25%.

3. Change the height for all three placeholders to 0.25".

4. Use the up arrow key to nudge all the placeholders until they rest on top of the bottom guide. (Zoom in for greater accuracy.)

5. Select the page number placeholder and edit the width to 0.5". Align this placeholder with the left edge of the body placeholder (the left vertical guide).

6. Select the footer placeholder and change the width to 4". Move this placeholder a bit to the right of the page number placeholder.

7. Select the date placeholder and change the width to 1". Move this placeholder a bit to the right of the footer placeholder.

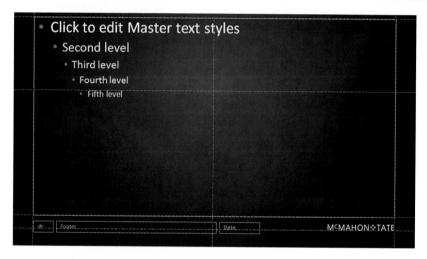

FIGURE 4.31

The footers are resized and repositioned on the Tutorial template slide master.

RENAME AND PRESERVE THE SLIDE MASTER

Before you move on to formatting the slide layouts, you should rename and preserve the slide master. In the slide thumbnails pane, right-click the slide master (the topmost, large thumbnail) and click Rename Master. Right-click the slide master thumbnail again and click Preserve Master. This setting prevents a slide master from being deleted from a presentation with multiple masters, even when the master is not currently applied to any slides.

TUTORIAL

To make these changes in the Tutorial template:

1. Right-click the slide master thumbnail on the top left and select Rename Master from the menu.

2. Change the layout name to Tutorial and click Rename.

3. Right-click the slide master thumbnail again and click Preserve Master (as shown in Figure 4.32).

FIGURE 4.32

Rename and preserve the slide master to prevent it from being deleted.

WORKING WITH MULTIPLE SLIDE MASTERS

With the ability to change individual slide layouts and add unique, custom layouts to a template, you might never need more than one slide master. Cases exist where multiple slide masters can be helpful, though.

Some templates include a light and dark version of every slide layout. Figure 4.33 demonstrates the use of two slide masters in the Tutorial template, as they appear in the layout gallery. The best way to accomplish this is to format one version of the slide master and all associated slide layouts, then duplicate that slide master and change the background style (light to dark or vice versa). You can tweak individual elements and placeholder settings on slide layouts, as needed.

Another case for multiple slide masters is a template that includes unique colors, logos, or other elements that are specific to different divisions, products, or groups. This situation could apply to a specific event with many presenters. The template would include multiple slide masters and layouts unique to each presenter.

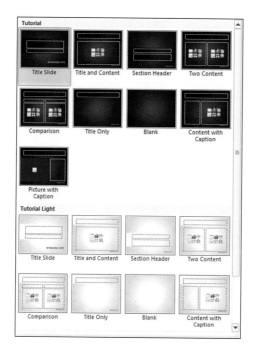

FIGURE 4.33

Multiple slide masters are helpful when you want to include distinctly different versions of all slide layouts.

IN THIS CHAPTER

- Overview of slide layouts
- Uses for each slide layout
- Formatting slide layouts

FORMATTING THE DEFAULT SLIDE LAYOUTS

Chapter 4, "Formatting the Slide Master," explains the importance of formatting the slide master before making any changes to the layouts. Slide master formatting influences all the layouts; this does not work in reverse. Any changes made to the layouts do not affect the slide master.

Slide layouts provide a variety of placeholder configurations. These preformatted layouts make developing a cohesive-looking presentation that includes different types of content easy.

Eleven slide layouts are included with the templates and themes shipped with PowerPoint, including the Blank template (Office Theme). These default layouts (shown in Figure 5.1) are called Title Slide, Title and Content, Section Header, Two Content, Comparison, Title Only, Blank, Content with Caption, Picture with Caption, and two Vertical layouts.

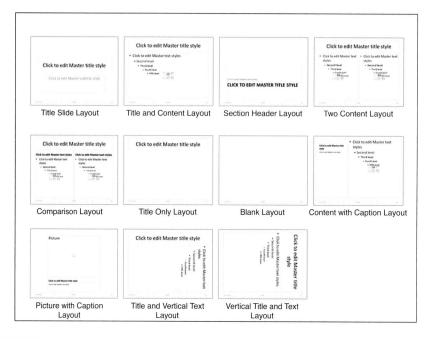

FIGURE 5.1

The default Blank template includes 11 slide layouts.

In most countries, only nine of these layouts show up in the New Slide or Layouts gallery. The two vertical slide layouts are included for right-to-left language formats (such as Chinese or Japanese). Only those users who have enabled a right-to-left language see these two layouts in the galleries. Keep these layouts in the template you're building if a chance exists it might be used globally.

This chapter covers all the default layouts, uses for each, and suggestions for reconfiguring and reformatting them. You also learn what changes to make to the layouts for the Tutorial template.

NOTE

Save your file often during the build process. For now, you can save the file in .PPTX format. We recommend saving subsequent versions of the file in progress so you can avoid hours of rework if you make a mistake. Establish an easy-to-recognize file naming convention for your work in progress, such as mcmahontate-v1.pptx, mcmahontate-v2.pptx, MTtemplateA.pptx, or MTtemplateB.pptx, and keep your files organized in well-defined folders. One of the last steps in the finalization process is to save your file as a template (.POTX).

OVERVIEW OF SLIDE LAYOUTS

We recommend including all the default layouts with new templates to prevent problems for users. When copying slides from other presentations, PowerPoint applies the corresponding slide layout from the new template. If any layouts have been deleted, PowerPoint applies a different existing layout from the template. Users must manually reconfigure those slides.

Each slide layout includes a different configuration of placeholders. You can reformat and resize these placeholders however you like, but don't delete any of them. If you do delete them, there will be problems when you copy slides into presentations that include the deleted placeholders, much like there are problems when there's a missing slide layout. PowerPoint applies the same layout type to a copied slide; but if a placeholder is missing, content appears in another placeholder or is positioned elsewhere on the slide.

The date, footer, and slide number placeholders appear on all default slide layouts. However, they do not show up in slide editing mode until you use the Header & Footer dialog to apply them to your slides. Don't delete these placeholders either, or users will have problems when copying slides from other presentations. If you don't want the footers to show up on a specific layout you can turn them off. As you edit a slide layout, uncheck the box next to Footers on the Slide Master tab, as shown in Figure 5.2.

FIGURE 5.2

To turn footers off of any slide layout, uncheck the box next to Footers on the Slide Master tab.

Although inserting new placeholders on a slide layout is possible, creating custom slide layouts for this purpose is best. Adding placeholders to the default layouts causes more complications when copying slides to and from presentations based on your new template. See Chapter 6, "Custom Slide Layouts," for more information about inserting placeholders on custom slide layouts.

You can rename the slide layouts, but leaving the default names is better to prevent confusion for those who might already be working with similarly named layouts. If you choose to rename any of them, keep the new names brief and descriptive. You want to make it easy for others to choose the correct layout from the galleries.

Slide layouts can be reordered, if desired. Move the most commonly used layouts to the front of the group so they show up first in the galleries. There are a few key things to consider when reordering. Keep the Title Slide layout first in line. Moving this layout to another position can cause problems when users click the New Slide button. Also, note that the second layout is inserted when users click the top of the New Slide button.

A little-known feature of slide layouts can be one of the most helpful for template users. You can enter custom prompt text in any placeholder. Instead of leaving the default, "Click to add text," replace it with more descriptive prompts to guide users as they create new slides. The Tutorial template slide layouts include a few basic examples of custom prompt text. Instructions follow each section of this chapter.

Most of the slide master settings are automatically applied to placeholders on the slide layouts. A few placeholders require formatting changes such as line spacing, font color, and font size. Do not use Format Painter or the eyedropper tools to pick up and apply settings from one placeholder to another. These tools can introduce random formatting issues on slides, such as a bullet character that mysteriously appears on subtitles or captions. Manually editing placeholder formatting is best.

TITLE SLIDE LAYOUT

The Title Slide layout is typically used for the first slide in a presentation. This layout includes two placeholders: one for titles and another for subtitles. Title slides are often displayed on the screen while an audience is entering a meeting room. They can be used to introduce new speakers and topics, as well as for closing slides. Because title slides have less content, you can increase the size of placeholder text. Graphics or logos can be made more prominent. Some template designs feature a unique background for the Title Slide layout.

Figure 5.3 shows the default Title Slide layout for the Tutorial template in progress. Notice that the Title placeholder has picked up the same left paragraph alignment as the slide master. The subtitle placeholder is still center-aligned; change this to match the alignment of the title placeholder. The line spacing on the subtitle is the same as the first-level text in the body placeholder on the slide master. You might want to edit the line spacing on the subtitle.

The gradient-filled rectangle and logo are in place as you formatted them on the slide master. As mentioned in Chapter 4, any shapes, pictures, or logos placed on the slide master appear on every slide layout. You can customize individual slide layouts by hiding these graphics as needed.

If you followed along with the steps in Chapter 4, you have completed formatting the slide master for the Tutorial template. The formatting you applied to the slide master is reflected in all the slide layouts.

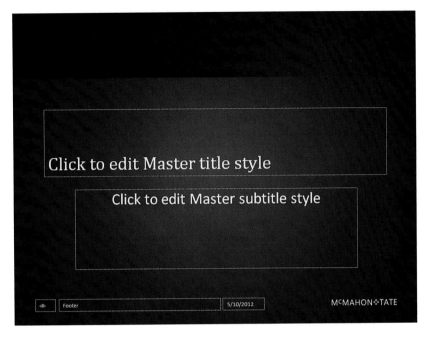

FIGURE 5.3
The Title Slide layout in the Tutorial template requires some formatting adjustments.

TUTORIAL

To continue formatting the Tutorial template, select the Title Slide layout from the thumbnails pane.

1. Right-click on the slide background and select Format Background. In the Fill dialog, select the box next to Hide Background Graphics and click Close. (Do *not* click Apply to All.) This hides the rectangle at the top and the logo at the bottom.

2. Select the slide master and copy the gradient-filled rectangle from the top of the slide.

3. Select the Title Slide layout again and paste the rectangle. Make the rectangle height taller (3.08 inches) and move it down on the slide. The top of the rectangle should meet the second horizontal guide from the top, at 2.25 inches. Select Arrange and Send to Back.

4. Select the Title placeholder and change the font size to 44 points. Resize the placeholder width to 8 inches and the height to 1.5 inches. Align the placeholder to the center of the slide. Move the placeholder up so the top edge meets the horizontal guide set at 1.75 inches. Change the placeholder prompt text to "Type Presentation Title Here."

5. Select the Subtitle placeholder and change the font size to 24 points. Edit the line spacing to 0 points before paragraph. Change the paragraph alignment to Left. Resize this placeholder to fit below the title placeholder. The new dimensions should be 8 inches wide by 0.83 inches tall. Move the Subtitle placeholder below the Title placeholder so the top edge is just above the middle guide. Change the placeholder prompt text to "Type Speaker Name and Title Here."

6. On the Slide Master tab, uncheck the box next to Footers. Turning the footers off on the Title Slide means that users don't have to worry about selecting the Don't Show on Title Slide option in the Header-Footer dialog.

7. On the Insert tab, click Picture. Locate and select the McMahon Tate logo, MT_logo_white.png, and click Insert. Resize the logo to 3.85 inches wide (the height automatically changes to 0.58 inches). Reposition the logo in the lower-right corner, with the bottom edge resting on the horizontal guide at 3 inches and the right edge on the right vertical guide at 4.50 inches. Figure 5.4 shows the completed Title Slide layout.

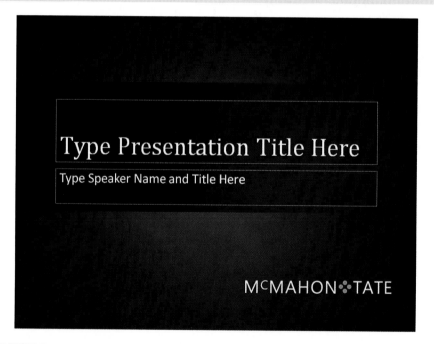

FIGURE 5.4

The finished Title Slide master includes larger graphics and a larger title font size.

TITLE AND CONTENT LAYOUT

The Title and Content layout is used to build the majority of slides in a typical presentation. As you can see in Figure 5.5, the placeholders on the Title and Content Layout are automatically formatted the same as the slide master. The only difference is the body placeholder, which becomes a content placeholder on this layout.

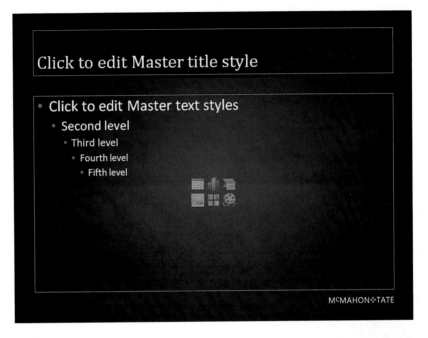

FIGURE 5.5

The Title and Content layout is identical to the slide master.

Aside from bulleted text, users can insert various types of graphics and data on the content placeholder. In slide editing mode, a user can click the appropriate icon to insert a table, a chart, a SmartArt diagram, a picture, clip art, or a video. Inserted content is sized to fit the width, or both the width and height of the body placeholder. This helps to maintain consistent size and positioning throughout a series of slides.

Do not make any changes to the placeholders on this slide layout. If you need to make adjustments, go back to the slide master and change the settings there.

TIP

If you accidentally make changes to the placeholders on the Title and Content layout, they become disassociated from the slide master. Don't despair! It's fixable. Open a new Blank presentation and copy the Title and Content layout into your template. It picks up the slide master formatting automatically. Delete the broken layout and rename the new one from 1_Title and Content to just Title and Content.

The footer placeholders appear at the bottom, as formatted on the slide master. For the Tutorial template, uncheck the box next to Footers (on the Slide Master tab) to turn them off for this layout.

SECTION HEADER LAYOUT

The Section Header layout is used for divider or transition slides. This layout is similar to the Title Slide layout, as it includes a title and subtitle placeholder. The primary difference in the default configuration is that the subtitle is on top of the title placeholder. They don't have to remain this way; change the position and formatting for both placeholders as you prefer.

The title placeholder on this layout has a Bold font style applied and is formatted with All Caps. If you're not using Bold or All Caps font styles in your template design, turn these settings off in the Font dialog. Select all the text inside the title placeholder, right-click, and select Font to open the Font dialog.

Figure 5.6 shows the updated Section Header slide layout in the Tutorial template.

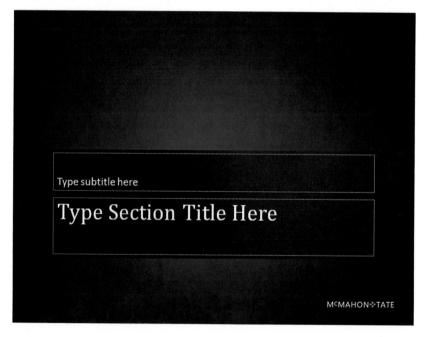

FIGURE 5.6

The Section Header layout in the Tutorial template features a larger gradient-filled rectangle behind the text placeholders.

TUTORIAL

To format the Section Header for the Tutorial template, use the following steps:

1. Right-click the slide background and select Format Background. In the Fill dialog, select the box next to Hide Background Graphics and click Close. (Do *not* click Apply to All.) This hides both the rectangle at the top and the logo at the bottom.

2. Go back to the slide master and copy both the gradient-filled rectangle and the logo.

3. Return to the Section Header slide layout and paste the rectangle and logo. Select Arrange and Send to Back.

4. Make the rectangle height taller (2.58 inches) and move it down on the slide so the top of the rectangle is about 0.5 inch above the middle guide.

5. Select the Subtitle placeholder and edit the line spacing to 0 points before paragraph. Resize the placeholder width to 8 inches and height to 0.9 inches. Align to the center of the slide and move the placeholder down so that it's positioned below the top edge of the gradient-filled rectangle. Change the placeholder prompt text to "Type subtitle here."

6. Select the Title placeholder and click the Bold font style button on the Home tab to remove the bold setting. Press the Ctrl+T to open the Font dialog. Uncheck the box next to All Caps and click OK. Resize the placeholder width to 8 inches and the height to 1.35 inches. Align the placeholder to the center of the slide. Move the placeholder below the subtitle. Change the placeholder prompt text to "Type Section Title Here."

7. On the Slide Master tab, uncheck the box next to Footers.

TWO CONTENT LAYOUT

The placeholders on the Two Content layout can be used for two columns of bulleted text or any other content type. Some presenters use this slide layout to insert text in one placeholder and a picture or diagram in the other.

The placeholders on this layout reflect any formatting changes made to the slide master. The only exception is content placeholders' height and position in relation to the slide master body placeholder. You have to manually adjust these settings on the Two Content layout. Use the guides to quickly adjust the top and bottom of the placeholders to their proper position. The placeholders are the same width and positioned equidistant from the slide edges. If you make any adjustments to the placeholder width, check to make sure they are equal in size and evenly spaced on the slide.

The content placeholder font size is the same as the slide master, which might be a bit large for two columns of text. Reduce the font size as needed to accommodate more text. Figure 5.7 features the Two Content layout, updated for the Tutorial template.

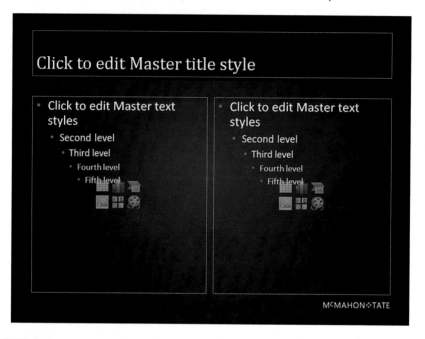

FIGURE 5.7

The Two Content layout is useful when including different types of content on one slide.

TUTORIAL To format the Two Content layout in the Tutorial template:

1. Select both content placeholders so you can edit them at the same time. Drag one of the top sizing handles down to meet the horizontal guide at 1.75 inches. Drag a bottom sizing handle down to meet the horizontal guide at 3 inches.

2. With both content placeholders selected, click the Decrease Font Size button on the Home tab.

3. On the Slide Master tab, uncheck the box next to Footers.

COMPARISON LAYOUT

The Comparison layout is very similar to the Two Content layout. The only difference is the additional text placeholders above each content placeholder. These text placeholders are intended for headings.

Like the Two Content layout, the placeholders on this slide pick up the settings from the body placeholder on the slide master. The difference in the Comparison layout is that the font sizes are automatically reduced. You can make them smaller, if you prefer.

The text placeholders (for headings) are formatted with a Bold font style. Keep or change this style to suit your template design. These placeholders are aligned to the bottom; change this to middle alignment if you like. Making these placeholders tall enough to accommodate two lines of text is a good practice. Like subtitles, these header placeholders pick up the line spacing from the first line of body text on the slide master. You should change this to 0 before and 0 after.

The height and position for all placeholders (except the title) must be adjusted to match the body placeholder on the slide master. Use the guides to help you properly resize the placeholders and maintain consistency throughout the layouts.

TUTORIAL

To format the Comparison layout in the Tutorial template, follow these steps:

1. Select both text placeholders (for headings) and uncheck the Bold font style on the Home tab. Change the text alignment to Middle. Drag a bottom sizing handle to make the placeholders a bit taller. (Actual height in the Tutorial template is 0.82 inches.) Move the placeholders down about 0.25 inches. Change the placeholder prompt text to "Type heading here."

2. Move the top of the content placeholders down so they don't overlap the headings placeholders. Also make them shorter so they align with the body placeholder guides. See Figure 5.8 for an example of the completed Comparison layout.

3. On the Slide Master tab, uncheck the box next to Footers.

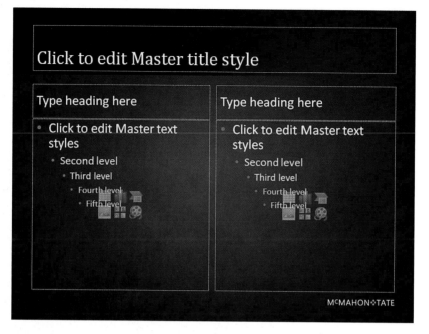

FIGURE 5.8

The Comparison layout includes two content placeholders and two placeholders for headings.

TITLE ONLY LAYOUT

You can use the Title Only layout for slides that require a title, but the content doesn't fit in any of the other layouts' placeholders. This might be a set of three or four pictures, for instance, or perhaps a graphic diagram made with PowerPoint shapes.

The title placeholder on this layout is identical to the one on the slide master. There is no need to make changes to the text formatting or position.

If you want to provide more space for content, you can remove the logo by hiding the background graphics. Remember to copy the gradient-filled rectangle from the slide master and paste it back onto this layout.

TUTORIAL   To change the Title Only layout for the Tutorial template, uncheck the box next to Footers on the slide master tab.

BLANK LAYOUT

The Blank layout comes in very handy for large screen captures, a handful of pictures, or whenever you have content that requires more slide space. Keeping the Blank layout very simple is best. Remove any additional graphics, lines, or logos.

TUTORIAL

To format the Blank layout for the Tutorial template:

1. Select the box for Hide Background Graphics in the Format Background dialog.

2. Uncheck the box next to Footers on the Slide Master tab.

CONTENT WITH CAPTION LAYOUT

The default Content with Caption layout, pictured in Figure 5.9, features a smaller title place-holder, a large content placeholder, and an additional text placeholder intended for captions. This slide layout is helpful for slides that include a larger chart or table, for instance, along with a caption that further describes that content.

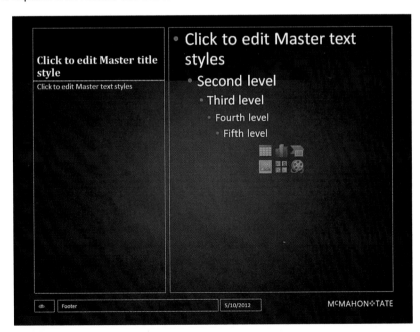

FIGURE 5.9
The default arrangement for the Content with Caption layout can be improved with a few adjustments.

This slide layout is considerably different from the slide master. The title placeholder is positioned in the upper-left corner and has a much smaller font size than the slide master title. The caption placeholder is formatted at 14-point font size, which is quite small and potentially harder to read when projected. It also picks up the line spacing attributes from the slide master, which might or might not be appropriate for the caption font size you use. The content placeholder picks up the basic text formatting from the slide master, but the font sizes are larger.

You do not have to keep the placeholders in this configuration. Adjust any or all of them to better suit your template design. Consider keeping the content placeholder a bit larger than the caption placeholder, because the content should be the main focus on a slide.

The title placeholder on the Content with Caption layout (and the Picture with Caption layout, which is discussed in the next section) is a complete departure from those throughout the rest of the template. Although this might be appropriate for a casual or personal presentation, it would probably look odd in the middle of a corporate presentation. For our corporate clients, we usually format and position the title placeholder on the Content and Picture with Caption layouts so they match the rest of the template.

TUTORIAL

To format the Content with Caption layout (shown in Figure 5.10) for the Tutorial template, do the following:

1. Select the caption placeholder and change the font size to 20 points. Drag the top sizing handle down to meet the horizontal guide at 1.75 inches so it's positioned at the same vertical place as other body and content placeholders throughout the template. Drag the bottom sizing handle down to the horizontal guide at 3 inches. Edit the placeholder width to 3.25 inches. Change the placeholder prompt text to "Type caption text here."

2. Select the content placeholder and click the Decrease Font Size button on the Home tab. Resize the height of this placeholder to match the caption placeholder. Change the placeholder width to 5.5 inches and move the placeholder so the right edge meets the right margin guide.

3. Select the title placeholder and turn off the Bold font style. Change the font size to 32 points. Use the guides to quickly resize the placeholder to match the title on the slide master.

4. On the Slide Master tab, uncheck the box next to Footers.

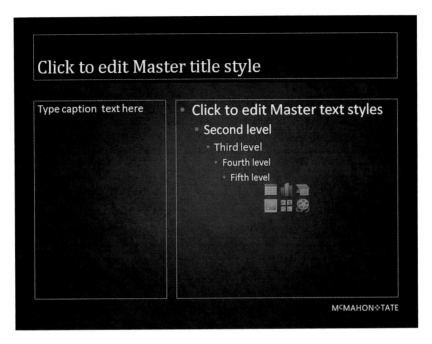

FIGURE 5.10

The Content with Caption layout in the Tutorial template is similar to the Title and Content layout.

PICTURE WITH CAPTION LAYOUT

Figure 5.11 shows the Picture with Caption layout in the Tutorial template prior to editing. This layout includes a rectangular picture placeholder with small title and caption placeholders stacked directly beneath. This layout is used for slides with one picture, a title, and caption text.

This vertically stacked placeholder configuration is quite different from the others. Although variety can be a good thing in a presentation, a few small changes can make this layout more consistent with the rest of the template. There is room to make all the placeholders larger, and an asymmetrical layout would better suit the horizontal slide.

The picture placeholder is formatted without any embellishments. If this clean style suits your template design, leave the placeholder formatting alone. You can add outlines, shadows, or other effects to the picture placeholder. Any formatting changes you make to the placeholder are applied to pictures on slides that use this layout.

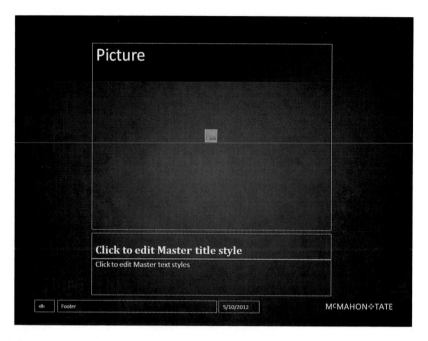

FIGURE 5.11

The default Picture with Caption layout includes three placeholders, stacked on the center of the slide.

Note that outlines added to picture placeholders appear differently on slides than they do on the slide layout. On the slide layout, the outline appears to be centered on the placeholder border. On the slides, though, this outline automatically extends beyond the edges of the picture. Testing any picture embellishments on sample slides before finalizing a template is a must.

TIP

Seeing certain effects applied to the picture placeholder on the slide layout can be difficult. When making formatting decisions like these, seeing how effects look on an actual picture versus the dashed-outline placeholder is better. On a blank slide, insert a new picture and add an outline, shadow, or other simple effect. (A note of caution: Applying too many effects, such as bevels, 3-D rotation, and reflections, makes slides look cluttered and amateurish. Keep it simple.) Adjust the picture settings in slide editing mode until you're satisfied with the results. Write down these settings so you can duplicate them on the picture placeholder on the slide layout.

The picture placeholder is a rectangular shape in the default template. You can change this to any other shape. Select the placeholder; and from the Drawing Tools Format tab, choose Edit Shape, Change Shape, and click to apply another shape from the gallery.

CUSTOM-SHAPED PICTURE PLACEHOLDERS

You can transform a picture placeholder into any of the predefined shapes in PowerPoint. But what if you want a specific shape that doesn't exist in the gallery? You can edit picture placeholders to create very unique custom shapes. There are a couple of ways to accomplish this.

In Slide Master view, select a picture placeholder, click the Drawing Tools Format tab, choose Edit Shape, Change Shape, and choose a shape from the gallery. A rectangle is a good choice to start, but you can select any shape that is closest to your desired final result.

Click Edit Shape again and then click Edit Points. Right-click a point or segment to adjust the placeholder shape. This method works well in both PowerPoint 2007 and 2010.

With PowerPoint 2010, editing picture placeholders is much faster via the Combine Shapes commands. These commands enable you to quickly create custom forms by merging shapes together, intersecting them, or by subtracting one shape from another.

To access this command, you must add it to the Quick Access Toolbar, located above the File tab. To customize the Quick Access Toolbar, do the following:

1. Click the arrow next to the Quick Access Toolbar, and then under Customize Quick Access Toolbar, click More Commands.

2. In the PowerPoint Options dialog box, in the Choose Commands From list, select All Commands.

3. In the list of commands, click Combine Shapes, and then click Add. Figure 5.12 shows the Combine Shapes commands added to the Quick Access Toolbar.

FIGURE 5.12

The Combine Shapes commands must be added to the Quick Access Toolbar before you can use them in PowerPoint.

Again, you must change the shape of the picture placeholder prior to editing. With the picture placeholder selected, click the Drawing Tools Format tab, choose Edit Shape, Change Shape, and choose a shape from the gallery.

Next, draw shapes that you will add to, or subtract from, the picture placeholder shape. Figure 5.13 shows circles positioned at each corner of the picture placeholder, prior to subtracting.

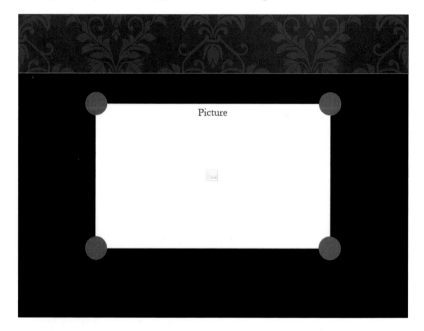

FIGURE 5.13

Four circles are positioned on the corners of the picture placeholder.

Select the picture placeholder, select one of the new shapes, and choose either the Shape Subtract or Shape Union command from the Quick Access Toolbar. Repeat this step for all other shapes. Figure 5.14 shows example slides featuring custom picture placeholders created using the Subtract command.

FIGURE 5.14

A custom-shaped picture placeholder was used to create these example slides.

Sometimes the caption placeholder doesn't suit your template needs. You can easily format it with up to nine levels of bulleted text. To do so, type prompt text into the caption placeholder. This creates the first text level. Press Enter and then click the Increase Indent button on the Home tab of the Ribbon to create the second-level text. Type "Second Level," press Enter, and click the Increase Indent button again to create the third level of text. Apply bullets and format as desired.

TUTORIAL

To format the Picture with Caption layout (shown in Figure 5.15) for the Tutorial template, use the following steps:

1. Select the title placeholder and turn off the Bold font style. Change the font size to 32 points. Use the guides to quickly reposition and resize the placeholder to match the title on the slide master.

2. Select the caption placeholder and change the font size to 20 points. Resize the placeholder width to 3.25 inches and height to 4.75 inches. Move the placeholder to the right side of the slide, aligning it to the guides in place. Change the placeholder prompt text to "Click to enter caption text."

3. Select the picture placeholder and fill with the third Theme color (Brown, Background 2). This makes it easier to see the placeholder and shadow. Resize the placeholder height to 4.75 inches, keeping the width at 6 inches. Move the placeholder to the left edge of the slide, aligning the top and bottom to the guides in place. On the Picture Tools Format tab, select Shape Effects, Shadow, and choose Inner, Inside Diagonal Top Right. Change the font size to 24 points and change the paragraph alignment to Center.

4. On the Slide Master tab, uncheck the box next to Footers.

FIGURE 5.15

The Picture with Caption layout in the Tutorial template features a larger title to match the slide master, a larger picture placeholder, and a placeholder for captions to the right.

TITLE AND VERTICAL TEXT LAYOUT

As mentioned earlier, the Title and Vertical Text layout is used for right-to-left languages. It does not appear in the gallery unless a user has one of these language types enabled.

This layout is identical to the Title and Content layout, except that the text in the body place-holder is rotated to the right. The placeholders should be sized and positioned properly, so there is no need to make any changes to the layout. Figure 5.16 shows the Title and Vertical Text layout in the Tutorial template.

TUTORIAL   To format this layout for the Tutorial template, on the Slide Master tab, uncheck the box next to Footers.

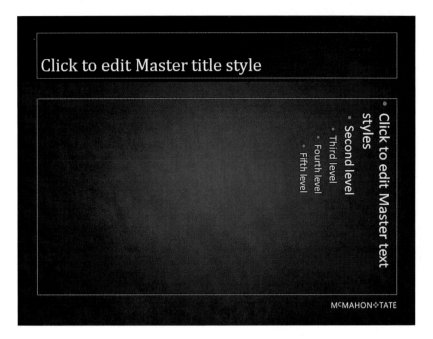

FIGURE 5.16

The Title and Vertical Text layout in the Tutorial template is preformatted with rotated text in the body placeholder.

VERTICAL TITLE AND TEXT LAYOUT

The Vertical Title and Text layout is also used for right-to-left languages and does not appear in the gallery unless a user has one of these language types enabled.

As you can see in Figure 5.17, text is rotated in both the title and body placeholders on this layout. These placeholders require a bit of resizing to mimic positions on the slide master.

For the Tutorial template, the gradient-filled rectangle at the top should be hidden, and a new, rotated rectangle positioned on the right side behind the title placeholder. Figure 5.18 shows the completed Vertical Title and Text layout in the Tutorial template.

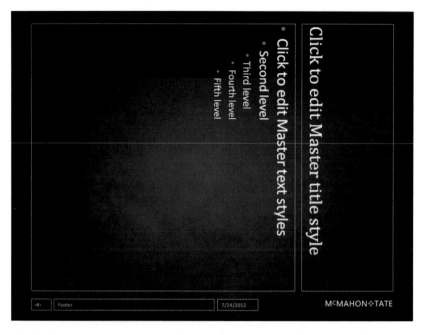

FIGURE 5.17

Both placeholders included rotated text on the Vertical Title and Text layout.

FIGURE 5.18

The Vertical Title and Text layout in the Tutorial template requires a few modifications to the background graphic and placeholders.

TUTORIAL

To format this layout for the Tutorial template, use the following steps:

1. Right-click the slide background and select Format Background. In the Fill dialog, check the box next to Hide background graphics and click Close. (Do *not* click Apply to All.) This hides both the rectangle at the top and the logo at the bottom.

2. Go back to the slide master and copy both the gradient-filled rectangle and the logo.

3. Return to the Vertical Title and Text slide layout and paste the rectangle and logo. Select Arrange and Send to Back.

4. Select the rectangle and change the gradient angle to 90°. Change the dimensions of the rectangle to 2.3 inches wide and 7.5 inches high. Align the rectangle with the right edge of the slide.

5. Resize the title placeholder width to 1.7 inches and height to 6.33 inches and move the placeholder to align with the guides at the top and right side.

6. Resize the body placeholder width to 6.75 inches and height to 6.33 inches. Move this placeholder to align with the guides at the top and left side.

7. On the Slide Master tab, uncheck the box next to Footers.

CREATING CUSTOM SLIDE LAYOUTS

Custom slide layouts are one of the most versatile components in a PowerPoint template. With custom slide layouts, you can provide a variety of preformatted slide designs while maintaining consistent elements such as colors, fonts, and placeholder structure. All slide layouts help to eliminate some of the guesswork during presentation development. Custom layouts go a step further than the default layouts by offering placeholder configurations specifically designed for your company's presentation content.

Custom slide layouts populate the New Slide and Layout galleries, along with the default layouts. Although you can include as many custom layouts as you like, not going overboard is best. Too many layouts can be overwhelming and confusing to users. If you have to scroll a few times within the gallery to see all the options, you probably have too many. A sufficient number of layouts (including default layouts) in a corporate template is 12 to 16. Figure 6.1 shows the Layout gallery with 12 layout choices. Exceptions exist for this number of layouts, especially when you have justifiable reasons to include more.

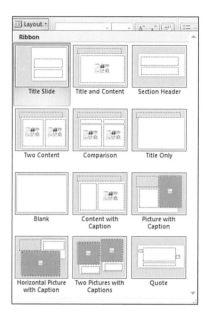

FIGURE 6.1

The Layout gallery displays all the layouts available in a template. Limiting the number of layouts is best, so users don't have to scroll multiple times to view them all.

WHEN TO INCLUDE CUSTOM LAYOUTS

We mentioned in Chapter 5, "Formatting the Default Slide Layouts," that you should keep all default layouts in a template to prevent problems when copying slides to and from other presentations. We also warned against adding or removing placeholders on the default layouts for similar reasons. Every slide is associated with a specific slide layout. When you copy a slide into a different template, PowerPoint recognizes and applies the same layout type. The default slide layouts include a set number of placeholders. If you add or remove any of these placeholders, users will have problems when copying or pasting slides. When a placeholder is missing, content is sometimes forced to populate a different placeholder or it might appear elsewhere on the slide. You can end up with bulleted text inside of the title placeholder. Imagine how long manually reformatting a presentation with that kind of mix-up would take.

This is where custom slide layouts come in handy. Create a custom slide layout any time you want to add or delete a placeholder on a default layout.

Perhaps your template design calls for a subtitle on the Title and Content layout. Start by duplicating the Title and Content layout, and then add and format a new text placeholder for the subtitle. Adjust the body placeholder as needed and rename the new slide layout. Figure 6.2 shows a custom layout added to the Tutorial template that includes an additional placeholder for subtitles.

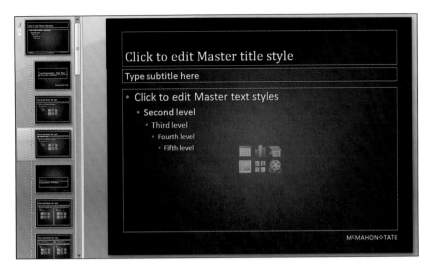

FIGURE 6.2

Create a custom slide layout when you want to add a subtitle placeholder to an existing layout.

Some template designs call for a picture on the title slide. If you want users to be able to easily change this picture to suit their presentation content, the slide layout should include a picture placeholder. Figure 6.3 shows an example custom layout in the Tutorial template. To create this custom layout, duplicate the Title slide layout, add and format a picture place-holder, and rename the new layout.

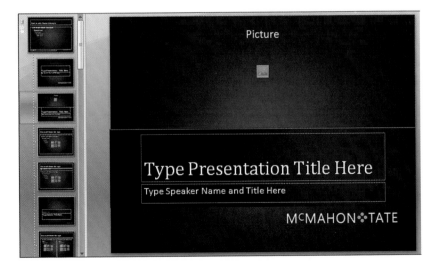

FIGURE 6.3

Insert a picture placeholder on a duplicate Title slide layout to allow users to easily add their own picture.

You might need a layout with multiple placeholders—for instance, two, three, or more pictures. Add a custom slide layout, formatted to include all the placeholders you need. Figure 6.4 features an example custom layout in the Tutorial template that includes additional placeholders for pictures and captions.

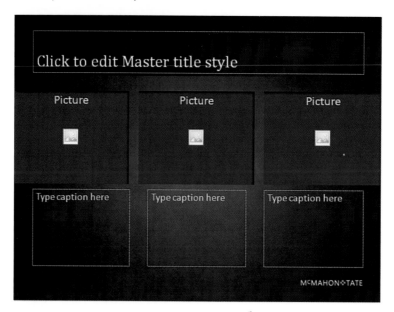

FIGURE 6.4

Add a custom slide layout when you want to include multiple picture and caption placeholders.

CUSTOM SLIDE LAYOUT EXAMPLES

Limitless possibilities exist for custom layouts. You can insert multiple placeholders, and then format, resize, and reposition them as you want. These layouts should serve a specific purpose though. Don't include a custom layout just because you can or just because you like it! Too many custom layouts can be confusing, and your efforts are wasted if the layouts won't be used at all.

Before you develop a new template, reviewing a variety of recent presentations is best. This is an important part of the template design process. (To learn more, see Chapter 10, "Designing a Template.") Take note of slide concepts and configurations that are most common. Is there a particular type of slide that users are struggling to format manually? Do the presentations always end with a company logo slide, a thank-you slide, or a call to action? Figure 6.5 shows a thank-you slide layout that was designed for the CoreMedia corporate template.

Other common slides include quotations (see Figure 6.6), executive biographies, and product features and benefits. When you provide preformatted layouts for slides like these, you make creating consistent-looking presentations easier for others.

FIGURE 6.5

The thank-you slide layout in the CoreMedia template was created using a custom slide layout.

FIGURE 6.6

Consider including a custom slide layout with space for a quote and attribution.

REPOSITIONABLE QUOTATION MARKS

Large, graphical quotation marks, like those shown in Figure 6.6, can be a great addition to a custom slide layout. You can add text boxes directly onto the layout, typing (or inserting as symbols) left and right quotation marks into each text box. The downside to this method is that you can't move the symbols in slide editing mode to better align them with the quoted text.

Fortunately a workaround exists that involves pictures and placeholders. Placeholders can be repositioned anywhere on a slide. When you fill a placeholder with a *picture* of a quotation mark, you can move the mark on the quote slide wherever you like, as shown in Figure 6.7

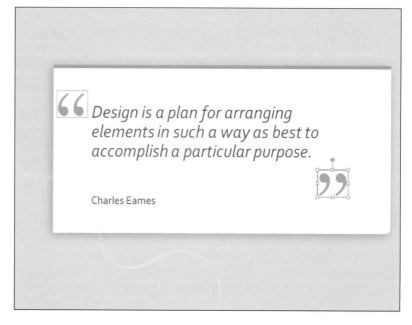

FIGURE 6.7

Placeholders with pictures of quotation marks can be repositioned on the slide as needed.

To create moveable quotation marks, do the following:

1. On the slide layout, type left and right quotation marks into two text boxes, using a very large font size. Change the font if you prefer another design for the quotation marks. Right-click the textbox and choose Save As Picture. Save each quotation mark as a separate picture. (.PNG format works best.) Delete the textboxes.

2. Insert a text placeholder on the layout, remove all bullet symbols, and delete all sublevels of text. Change the font size to 1 point, making it almost imperceptible in the textbox.

3. With the text placeholder selected, open the Format Shape dialog, select Fill, Picture or Texture Fill, Insert from File, and select one of the quotation mark pictures. Select the box next to Tile Picture as Texture. If the picture is too large, reduce the Scale X and Scale Y percentages under Tiling options.

4. Resize the placeholder as needed so that it encompasses just one full quotation mark.

5. Duplicate this "text placeholder" and change the picture fill to your other saved picture.

6. Reposition both quotation marks on either side of the quote text placeholder.

Case studies are another common type of slide used often in marketing presentations. If your company presents case studies, include a custom layout that makes filling in pertinent information easy. See Figure 6.8 for an example case study slide layout.

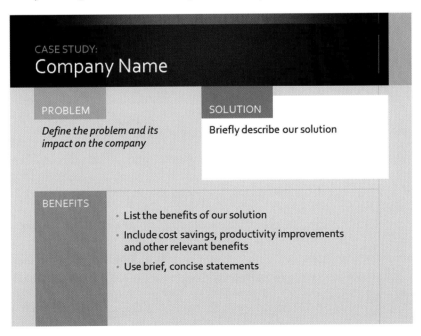

FIGURE 6.8

Use a custom slide layout that includes placeholders for information specific to each new case study.

CREATING A CUSTOM SLIDE LAYOUT

The two ways to add a slide layout are to either insert a new layout or duplicate an existing one. From the Slide Master tab, click the Insert Layout button to add a custom slide layout. The new custom layout includes only the title and footer placeholders as formatted on the slide master. This might be all that you need prior to inserting and formatting placeholders.

Most of the time, your custom slide layout will be very similar to an existing one. Starting with a duplicate of the existing layout saves you time and reduces the likelihood of creating errors you'll need to correct later. Right-click the layout thumbnail you want to copy and choose Duplicate Slide Layout.

Either way you begin, the next step to creating a custom layout involves inserting and formatting placeholders. From the Slide Master tab, click Insert Placeholder and select a placeholder type. On the slide layout, click and drag to define the approximate size of your new placeholder. Make any adjustments necessary. Remember to use the guides that you defined on the slide master to help align and position new placeholders. This helps to maintain consistency throughout the template.

Although you can choose from eight different types (as shown in Figure 6.9), remember that a content placeholder is universal—it's not limited to just one type. By using content placeholders instead of single-use placeholders, you can make your slide layouts more flexible to accommodate a variety of graphics, text, charts, and media. Creating a custom slide layout with a specific-use placeholder, such as a table, chart, or SmartArt, is unnecessary if the Title and Content layout (or other layout) can be used to achieve the same results.

Text placeholders are preferable when formatting a subtitle, caption, or other small textbox on a custom slide layout. When you insert a text placeholder, the text levels are formatted to match the slide master body placeholder. For captions, headings, or subtitles, you should remove all bullet characters and indents and make the font size the same for all levels. You can delete the prompt text for the second through fifth levels.

As a time saver, you can copy and paste placeholders from one slide layout to another. This is helpful when you've manually formatted a placeholder; perhaps you included an outline, shadow, or other effects. When you copy and paste the placeholder into a new layout, any custom formatting carries over.

CAUTION

Do not use the Format Painter or eyedropper tools (Pick Up and Apply Style) to copy and paste formatting from one placeholder to another. This technique can lead to formatting bugs that don't show up until you create new slides. For example, if you use the Format Painter to copy styles to and from a subtitle placeholder, you might see a bullet character appear when typing the subtitle on the slide. Making manual formatting changes to placeholders is best.

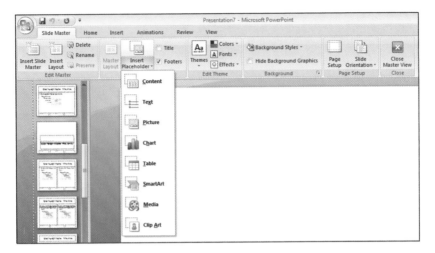

FIGURE 6.9

You can insert eight different placeholder types on slide layouts.

RENAMING SLIDE LAYOUTS

When you use the Insert Layout button, the new layout is named Custom Layout Layout. Add another and it is called 1_Custom Layout Layout. If you duplicate an existing slide layout, the new layout is named the same as the original, with a 1_ preceding the name.

These nondescript names do no one any favors. You should always rename custom layouts to be more descriptive. Keep the names brief so that users can see the entire label in the galleries.

You can rename the default slide layouts to be more descriptive of the types of slides your company uses. For instance, the Section Header layout could be labeled Transition Slide. Use discretion when renaming the default layouts because new names might confuse others if they've become accustomed to the original set of names.

To rename a layout, right-click a thumbnail in the Slide Layout pane and choose Rename Layout. Type a new name for the layout and click Rename.

REORDERING SLIDE LAYOUTS

As mentioned in Chapter 5, you can reorder slide layouts. This includes any new, custom slide layouts. Move the most commonly used layouts to the front of the group so they show up first in the galleries. Remember to keep the Title Slide layout first in line to prevent problems when users click the New Slide button.

WHEN TO USE MULTIPLE SLIDE MASTERS

As mentioned at the end of Chapter 4, most templates do not require additional slide masters. Custom slide layouts enable you to add as many unique configurations as you need. You can also change the background and placeholder arrangement on the default layouts. This layout customization should suffice for most templates, but in certain instances, multiple slide masters can come in handy.

A second slide master can be helpful for separating common layouts from those used less frequently. In the galleries, slide layout thumbnails are grouped underneath a slide master title. You can use a second (or third) slide master to divide the gallery into smaller groups of layouts, making it easier for others to find the layout they need. As you can see in Figure 6.10, there are 10 commonly used slide layouts for CFA Institute, as well as an additional 19 alternative title slides, dividers, and table of content layouts. With the addition of a second slide master, all the additional layouts are separated from the core content layouts. Template users can quickly locate common layouts and still have access to the wide variety of alternate designs.

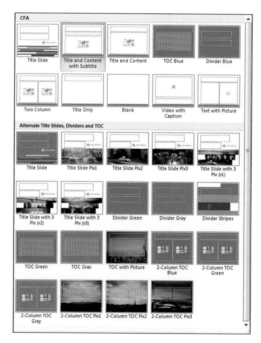

FIGURE 6.10

The template for CFA Institute features two slide masters to help divide the slide layouts within the galleries.

If your template calls for two (or more) distinctly different backgrounds or a duplicate set of layouts each with a unique logo, you should consider using multiple slide masters.

The most common use for multiple slide masters is to provide an identical set of light and dark slide layouts. This makes converting slides for presenting in various lighting situations easier. Dark presentation backgrounds are best for formal venues where lights are dimmed and the screen is backlit. Lighter backgrounds are better suited for web-based presentations or well-lit environments. Figure 6.11 shows both light and dark layouts in the Tutorial template, created with two slide masters.

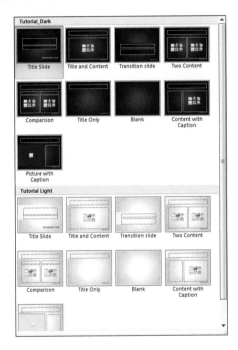

FIGURE 6.11
Use multiple slide masters to provide both light and dark slide layouts within the same template.

CREATING MULTIPLE SLIDE MASTERS

If the template slide masters and layouts will have identical arrangements, completing one set first and then making a copy is best. In the Thumbnails pane, right-click the slide master and choose Duplicate Slide Master. This creates a copy of the slide master and all of its associated slide layouts. Select the new slide master and make changes appropriate to the alternative design.

Background styles and light or dark colors play an important role in this situation. If you followed the steps to create the Tutorial template, you chose a dark background style on the slide master. This forced the default text color to be Light 1 (white).

To convert the new (duplicate) slide master into a light version, you should first apply a light background style. This automatically converts the text color to Dark 1 (black).

A few other changes might be necessary to complete the inverted slide master and layouts. For the Tutorial template, these changes include a lighter background picture and a lighter gradient fill on the rectangular title shapes.

Remember to rename the alternative slide master appropriately.

IN THIS CHAPTER

- Applying theme settings to notes and handout masters
- Formatting placeholders on the notes master
- Formatting placeholders on the handout master

FORMATTING NOTES AND HANDOUT MASTERS

PowerPoint's notes pages and handouts are used in a variety of situations, such as backup information for a speaker or leave-behind information for an audience. Most people forget about formatting the notes and handout masters when they develop a PowerPoint template, which is unfortunate because it's a missed opportunity to provide continuity between a presentation and the printed materials generated from it. In this chapter you learn how to give your notes and handout pages a bit of panache.

APPLYING THEME COLORS, FONTS, AND EFFECTS

The notes and handout masters do not automatically pick up the theme settings you've applied to the slide master. To manually apply these to the notes and handout masters, follow these steps:

1. On the View tab of the Ribbon, click the Notes Master button to open Notes Master view.

2. On the Notes Master tab of the Ribbon, click the Colors button and apply a theme color set (see Figure 7.1).

3. Click the Fonts button and apply a theme font set.

4. Click the Effects button and apply a theme effects set.

5. Repeat steps 1–4, substituting the handout master for the notes master.

Of course, if you want your notes and handout masters to match your slides, choose the same colors, fonts, and effects sets that you used on the slide master.

FIGURE 7.1

Use the Colors, Fonts, and Effects buttons to apply theme settings to the notes and handout masters.

ADJUSTING THE NOTES MASTER

After you've applied matching colors, fonts, and effects sets, you're ready to resize and reposition elements on the masters. The default notes master is shown in Figure 7.2. Formatting objects on the notes master is essentially the same as formatting objects on a slide or slide master.

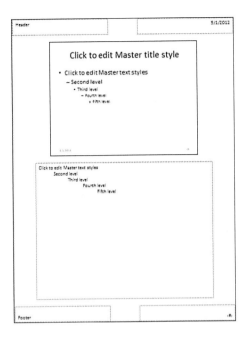

FIGURE 7.2

The default notes master has one large slide thumbnail with another placeholder for text.

FORMATTING THE PLACEHOLDERS

Notice that the slide image is relatively large on the notes master page. Often you can get away with a smaller slide image, which leaves extra room for speaker notes or other information. To resize the slide image placeholder, select it, press Shift, drag the corner to shrink or enlarge the thumbnail, and then drag it to the appropriate position. Remember also that notes pages are typically printed, so leave enough margin on each edge so that information isn't cut off.

Next, resize and position the four header and footer elements. Move them into position just as you would on a slide master or layout, and format them just as you would a typical placeholder or textbox. Populate the header and footer placeholders with information in the following manner:

1. On the Insert tab of the Ribbon, click the Header and Footer button.

2. In the Header and Footer dialog, click the Notes and Handouts tab.

3. Select the appropriate boxes and add information as desired (see Figure 7.3).

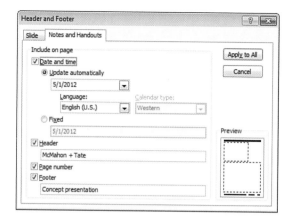

FIGURE 7.3

The Header and Footer dialog includes an often-unnoticed tab to add header and footer information to notes and handouts pages.

Finally, size and position the text placeholder. You can format this text placeholder just as you would the text placeholder on a slide master: add bullets; adjust indent and hanging indent settings; change line spacing; use bold, italics or color, and so on.

NOTE   *If you add color to text in the placeholder on the notes master, the color shows up when you are in Notes Page view, but it does not show up in the Notes pane in Normal (editing) view. (The formatting is still there; it's just not displayed in the Notes pane.) The same thing also happens with other elements on the notes master. For example, if you add a logo to the notes master, each notes page has a logo, but it does not display in the Notes pane in Normal (editing) view.*

ADDING MORE GRAPHICS

Adding other objects to the notes master is just like adding objects to a slide master. For example, to add a logo, click the Picture button on the Insert tab of the Ribbon, navigate to your logo, and click Insert. Size the logo and drag it into position. To add a rule line to a notes master, select the Line tool from the Shapes gallery on the Home tab, draw the line, drag it into place, and then format it using the tools on the Drawing Tools Format tab.

TIP   *If you've deleted a placeholder from the notes or handout master, you can select the box next to it on the Notes/Handout Master tab of the Ribbon to bring it back.*

You can see the changes we made to the notes master of the Tutorial template in Figure 7.4. You can also download the Tutorial template with customized note and handout masters from http://www.quepublishing.com/title/0789749556.

FIGURE 7.4

Resizing the slide image placeholder creates extra room for text.

ADJUSTING THE HANDOUT MASTER

The handout master works the same as the notes master, with one notable exception: The slide image thumbnails cannot be resized or repositioned. Click the Slides Per Page button, shown in Figure 7.5, to see the different layouts that are applied when users print handouts with the number of slides set to 1/page, 3/page, 6/page, and so on. This helps ensure that any graphics you add to the handout master don't interfere with the slide images in the printed handouts.

Follow the steps from the "Adjusting the Notes Master" section to specify theme colors, fonts, and effects for the handout master. Add graphics and position and format the four placeholders just as you did on the notes master. If you already populated the placeholders with information for the notes master, you see that information appear in the placeholders on the handout master as well.

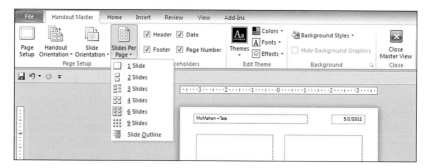

FIGURE 7.5

Use Slides Per Page to see the different handout layouts.

ALTERNATIVE HANDOUT TOOLS

A lot of people want more flexibility from PowerPoint's handouts. Shyam Pillai's Handout Wizard gives you the ability to create custom handout layouts. It's available at http://skp.mvps.org/how/. Bill Dilworth has an add-in that adds functionality to PowerPoint's Send to Word feature. It's available at http://billdilworth.mvps.org/SlideIntoWord.htm.

FORMATTING THE BACKGROUND

Most notes pages and handouts use a white background. The white background isn't really white, of course—it just means that the notes and handouts print on whatever color paper you put in the printer. If you need to specify a different notes page or handout background for some reason, you can select from the Background Styles on the Notes/Handout Master tab of the Ribbon. You can also right-click the workspace and choose Format Background.

CHANGING ORIENTATION

You can change your notes pages or handouts from the default portrait orientation to landscape by clicking the Notes Page Orientation or Handout Orientation button on the Notes/Handout Master tab of the Ribbon. Although we suggest you do this before positioning the placeholders and adding graphics to the master, it's not absolutely critical. If you do change the orientation after you've added graphics, the graphics stretch and you need to readjust the aspect ratio so the objects are not out of proportion. (This is especially important with logos and other pictures.) To do so, use the following steps:

1. Right-click the graphic and choose Format <Object>.

2. On the Size tab of the Format Object dialog, make sure Lock Aspect Ratio is not checked.

3. Input new values into Scale: Height or Scale: Width (or both) so that these percentages are equal, as shown in Figure 7.6.

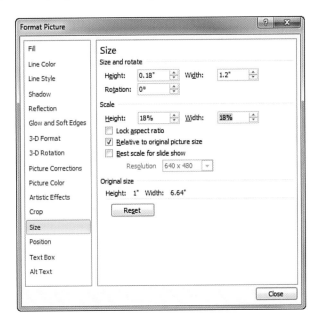

FIGURE 7.6
Keep values for scale height and width the same to ensure that graphics are not stretched out of proportion.

If you need to change the orientation of the slide image placeholder, click the Slide Orientation button on the Notes or Handout Master tab of the Ribbon and select Portrait or Landscape. This doesn't affect the notes page or handout itself; it just changes the orientation of the slide image on the page. We've never had a need to use this so far, but it's good to know it's there if we do!

NOTE

Notes pages and handouts work together. If you change the orientation of one, the orientation of the other changes also. You cannot have portrait notes pages and landscape handouts.

TEMPLATES VERSUS THEMES

You should be aware that notes page and handout masters travel with PowerPoint template files (*.POTX), but they do not travel with Office Theme files (*.THMX).

If you double-click a *.POTX file and begin a new presentation based on that template, any formatting applied to the notes or handout masters remain intact. However, if you apply a *.THMX or *.POTX from the Themes gallery on the Design tab, all custom formatting on the notes or handout masters disappears.

CREATING EXAMPLE SLIDES AND SETTING DEFAULTS

We've seen thousands of templates over the years, which means we've seen a lot of different types of example slides. The best templates give the users some direction, but they stop short of being overwhelming. Let's face it, although they might glance through a 60-slide template, no user is going to actually *read*, much less *retain*, all that information! Most users delete them and only keep a few basic slides to work with. In this chapter, we give you some tips for creating effective sample slides and specifying various default settings that will make your template easier to use.

INCLUDING INSTRUCTIONAL TEXT ON SAMPLE SLIDES

Including sample slides to show users how they can use the template is a great idea. Sample text can include instructions for keeping slides simple, listing capitalization rules, and so on. Figure 8.1 shows a typical instructional slide we use in many templates.

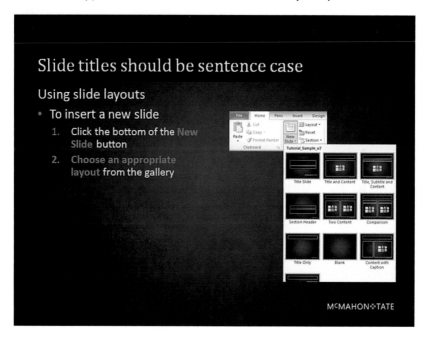

FIGURE 8.1

Sample slide with a screenshot and instructions showing how to use the New Slide gallery. Note the instructional text in the slide title.

Our general rule is to insert one sample slide per layout, but this isn't a hard and fast rule. In fact, this can be overkill if there are many custom layouts. For example, if your template has five alternative title slides each with a different background image or color, there's no reason to include a sample of each. Just include one sample slide with text in the Title or Subtitle placeholder area explaining more title slides are available.

KEEP IT SIMPLE

When creating sample slides and instructional text, our mantra is this: Do not overwhelm the user. A template with 60 sample slides does no one any favors. Although giving the users all the information you think they might need is tempting, it can be confusing and ultimately defeats the purpose.

> Keep your template simple. Include examples of the important things: charts, tables, alternative title slides, and so on. Add instructions for using the New Slide gallery so users know more layouts are available and how to access them. Links to the corporate intranet or to a separate "graphics library" PowerPoint file can be more effective than including multiple slides full of arrows, icons, and logos that users will ignore.

You can usually omit sample slides for the Blank layout, for the Title Only layout, for the Comparison layout, and possibly others, depending on your template, your users, and the sample slide content you want to include. Having 10 or 12 sample slides is reasonable, but if you're pushing 20, it's time to reassess.

IMPLEMENTING OFF-SLIDE INSTRUCTIONAL TEXT

Users often delete sample slides from a template. Because of this, some instructions don't lend themselves well to inclusion on sample slides. This is often the case for instructions that are specific to a slide layout. Especially if the slide layout is infrequently used, users might forget its purpose or specific usage quirks by the time they're ready to use it in a presentation. Or maybe you want to include a note to remind the user to change text in the headers and footers before finalizing the presentation.

Whatever the reason, creating instructions that will stick is easy enough. Simply add a shape with the text instructions off to the side of the slide layout. You can even add screenshots of the interface, if you think that might help the users (refer to Figure 8.1).

We often add specific instructions to the Picture with Caption layout. This one is confusing for users, because the picture placeholder crops the image to fit the placeholder. To help users understand this, we add instructional text on the sample slide itself, but we also add a shape with text off the edge of the slide layout so it's always available when this type of slide is created (see Figure 8.2).

You can also include instructional text shapes off the edges of regular sample slides. Of course, they won't be available every time the layout is used, but sometimes that's okay. In the example shown in Figure 8.3, where there are instructions for using quick styles to format a chart, there isn't a specific layout on which to include these instructions. The hope is that users will notice the instructions on the sample slides and the screenshot visuals will help them remember how to apply the formatting later. You can include text informing users they can delete the instructions if they want.

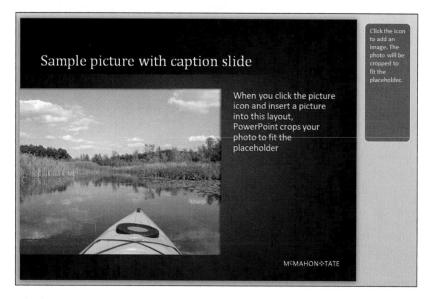

FIGURE 8.2

Instructional text in shapes placed to the side of a slide layout are available every time the layout is used.

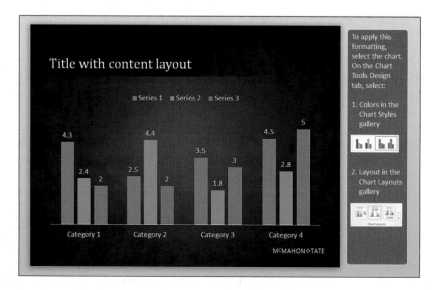

FIGURE 8.3

This instructional text, which also happens to include screenshots, is placed in a shape next to the sample slide.

As another example, you might include a shape off the edge of a sample chart slide that says, "Hide chart gridlines to make data on a chart easier to read. To do so, right-click the gridlines and then click Delete." This is especially useful if the default PowerPoint chart formatting is similar to that specified by your branding. However, in either case, if extensive chart customizations are necessary, you might want to consider chart templates instead. (See Chapter 11, "Understanding Charts and Chart Templates," for more information about chart templates.)

CREATING EXAMPLE CHART SLIDES

Many corporate templates include far too many example chart slides. We have to ask our clients: "C'mon, how many people really use Radar charts? Are they really that important here?" Of course, sometimes the answer is, "We use Radar charts in most of our presentations." If that's the case, then of course include a Radar chart example! But if it isn't, then omit it.

The typical chart samples we include in our templates are a column chart, a line chart, and a pie chart. Occasionally we're asked to include a stacked column chart, and we sometimes include a combo chart (column + line) with instructions because the client uses them frequently and creating them is not intuitive.

You might consider using a Two Content layout to show sample charts, because users don't always realize they can use this to include more than one chart on a slide. The placeholders on the Two Content layout help ensure that the charts are consistently sized.

Really, the goal for example charts is to show users what their charts should ultimately look like. Many of our clients recommend that users duplicate a sample chart slide and simply change the data to create new charts. This is usually the case when either the template is poorly built so charts don't work correctly, or when the desired chart formatting is very different than what PowerPoint creates by default. We think this "duplicate the chart and change the data" method is even more difficult for users than chart templates are! What are the users supposed to do when their chart already exists? As mentioned before, if your corporate branding calls for highly stylized charts that require lots of manual formatting, consider providing chart templates and teaching users how to apply them.

CREATING EXAMPLE TABLE SLIDES

Tables are often highly stylized. Unfortunately, PowerPoint doesn't let you create custom table styles. However, it does enable you to specify one of the stock table styles as the default table for a template.

To specify a default table style, do the following:

1. Insert a table on a slide. You can use the table icon in a placeholder, or you can simply insert a table directly onto a slide.

2. Select the table.

3. On the Table Tools Design tab, right-click a thumbnail in the Table Styles gallery and choose Set as Default (see Figure 8.4).

FIGURE 8.4

You can specify a default table style from the stock PowerPoint table styles.

Now when someone inserts a table in a presentation based on this template, the table uses this style by default. If there's not an exact match, at least try to select one of the stock table styles that's close to the look you want. For example, if you want a table with gray banded rows and a gray header row, but you don't actually have gray as one of the stock table colors to choose from, you can select the table style with the black header row (shown in Figure 8.4) as the default table so the gray banded rows are already set up correctly. Add instructional text explaining how to select the top row and change its color, as shown in Figure 8.5.

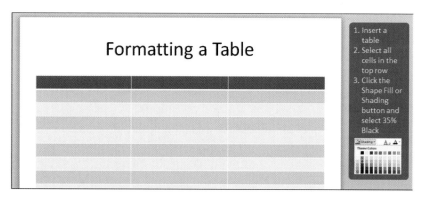

FIGURE 8.5

If necessary, add instructional text to help users format tables.

CAUTION   *If you apply a template or theme from the Themes Gallery on the Design tab of the Ribbon, the default table style is not included.*

OTHER SAMPLE SLIDES TO CONSIDER

Another type of sample slide you might consider including in your template is a color palette slide. This slide usually specifies the actual RGB values for all theme colors and color chips with those theme colors applied. Figure 8.6 shows two examples.

To create a color palette slide, do the following:

1. Create a rectangle.

2. Duplicate the rectangle to create 10 shapes (12 if you want to identify the hyperlink and followed hyperlink colors).

3. Fill each shape with its corresponding theme color.

4. Add outlines to the shapes if desired, and format them with the same color as the shape fill.

5. Apply text formatting for all the shapes in case users copy and paste the shapes to create their own graphics. (You don't want to have white text appearing on a light-colored shape!)

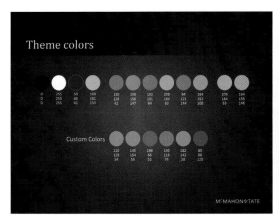 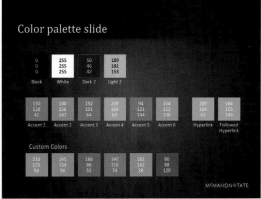

FIGURE 8.6

Two examples of color palette slides.

A graphics palette slide is a handy toolbox to help users maintain style consistency as they develop their own slides. You can even combine it with the color palette slide and include theme color chips, a textbox, sample lines or arrows, alternative shape fill styles, logos, and so on. Include instructions to copy and paste these elements or pick up and apply the formatting to existing objects. Don't go crazy here! You want this slide to include objects that help others, not overwhelm them. If you need to include so many graphics that you're forced to use multiple slides, you should consider linking to the corporate intranet or providing a separate "graphics library" presentation.

A sample slide with multiple logos (partners, competitors, clients, and so on) is approaching the gray area between what to include in the template and what not to include. There's no perfect answer. For example, if your company often uses a logo slide that doesn't change much, then you might want to include it in the template. However, if the logos frequently change, then you should probably consider a different way to provide this slide.

SETTING DEFAULT SHAPES

If you don't specify otherwise, any shape you insert on a slide by default uses Accent 1 for its fill color and a darker shade of Accent 1 for its outline. You can change this by doing the following:

1. Draw a rectangle or other shape on a slide.

2. Format the shape as desired.

3. When the shape is formatted to your satisfaction, right-click it and choose Set as Default Shape (see Figure 8.7).

4. Delete the shape.

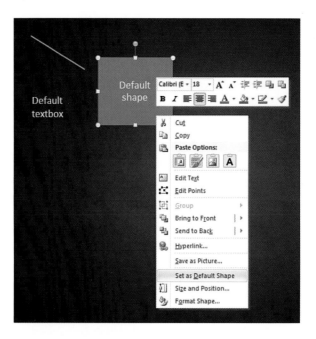

FIGURE 8.7

Set default shapes, lines, and text boxes.

Format the shape fill and the shape outline as well as the font color, size, vertical and horizontal alignment, internal margin, and line spacing. The text automatically picks up the theme body font. It's best not to change this for the default shape.

The default Autofit setting for text is Do Not Autofit. If you prefer, you can change this to one of the other Autofit settings: Shrink Text on Overflow or Resize Shape to Fit Text.

You can follow this same procedure to change the formatting for the default line. Draw a line and format it to your specifications. Right-click the line and choose Set as Default Line.

Finally, create a default textbox. Add a textbox to a slide and format it as desired. Right-click the textbox and choose Set as Default Text Box.

Be careful about using complex shape fills and effects for your default shape. If you choose a gradient, for example, keep it simple and test it on many different shape types, such as star or donut. On slides with multiple shapes, it can be visually overwhelming if everything has a gradient fill. The same caution applies for extreme shadows, reflections, and bevels. Consider using a simple style for your default shape and include more elaborate effects on the graphic palette slide.

CAPS AND JOINS

You might not have realized it, but PowerPoint lines and shapes have cap and join settings as part of their formatting. The three types of line caps are shown in Figure 8.8, and the three types of joins on shapes are shown in Figure 8.9.

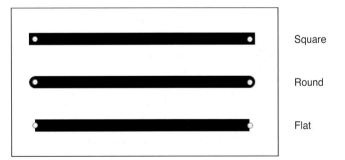

FIGURE 8.8

Three cap styles are available for lines. The "flat" cap actually applies no endcap to the lines.

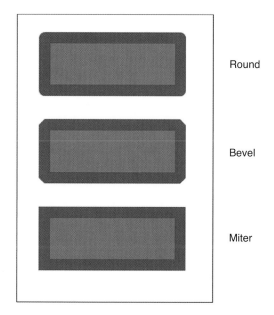

FIGURE 8.9

Three join styles are available for shapes.

To access these settings, do the following:

1. Right-click the line or shape and choose Format Shape.

2. On the Line Style tab, choose the appropriate cap or join type.

Flat caps and mitered joins tend to make things easier to align perfectly.

A FINAL WORD

Remember that a template isn't going to make your users magically create beautiful presentations. In that same vein, sample slides and instructional text are not a substitute for some basic user training. If possible, provide some in-person or online training for users on the fundamentals of how to use your template effectively. Demonstrate how using placeholders can save time and effort, why selecting from the theme colors will help you stay on brand, and so on. Basic functionality training can help users understand how your well-built template makes it easier for them to create consistency throughout their presentations. Plus, creating those "Aha!" moments can be very rewarding, too.

FINALIZING YOUR TEMPLATE

The steps you perform to finalize your template will probably vary from project to project. A number of little things can help users and contribute to consistency, but they'll fall through the cracks unless you make it a point to address them. When we are finalizing our client templates, we refer to a multiple-page checklist before sending the template out the door. This chapter shares and discusses items from our checklist. These steps are also included in the Appendix, "Key Steps to Building a Template."

REVIEW SLIDES AND SLIDE MASTERS

You've probably already made most of the changes to the slide masters and layouts that you need to, but double-checking things such as line spacing, all nine levels of bullets on the master and layouts, and the related settings mentioned in this section doesn't hurt.

CREATE TEST SLIDES

As you finalize a template, testing and reviewing all the slide layouts is important. If your sample slides do not represent every layout, create additional dummy slides to use as you review. This also gives you a chance to review the prompt text that appears in the placeholders. You should probably delete these additional slides before delivering the template to your client or before distribution to end users.

SLIDE MASTERS AND LAYOUTS

Double-check each slide master and all layouts in the template. Make sure names are short but descriptive and that they're in the order you want them to appear in the New Slide gallery. Remember that the Title Slide should be first in each list of layouts.

Also check the Preserved status. This setting ensures a master and its layouts remain in the template even if the presentation no longer includes any slides based on that master. To access this setting, right-click the slide master and choose Preserve Master. If a master is preserved, you see a small pin next to it in Slide Master view (see Figure 9.1).

FIGURE 9.1

A thumbtack icon indicates the slide master will remain in the template even if no slides are based on that master.

THEME COLORS, FONTS, AND EFFECTS

Hover your mouse cursor over the Colors, Fonts, and Effects buttons on the Design tab so you can see what theme colors, fonts, and effects are applied to the template. If any colors have changed as you've developed the template, review those RGB values to confirm you're using the correct colors.

For the Tutorial template, the color and font theme names should be Tutorial, and the effects theme name should be Module.

CHECK SHAPE DEFAULTS

By default, any shape you insert on a slide uses Accent 1 for its fill color and a darker shade of Accent 1 for its outline. But as you learned in Chapter 8, "Creating Example Slides and Setting Defaults," you can also specify your own default formatting for shapes, lines, and textboxes. For example, you might want to create default shapes that don't have outlines so that users have one less thing to worry about formatting if they change a fill color. Or you might decide to make the text in your default textbox exactly match the formatting of the top level of text in your template's content placeholder because users who don't know better often tend to use textboxes instead of placeholders when creating slides.

TUTORIAL

To set up default shape, line, and fill formatting for the Tutorial template, do the following:

1. Insert a rectangle onto any slide in the Tutorial template file. Leave its fill as Accent 1 and remove its outline. Leave the font color white (Light 1) and the size and face 18-point Calibri (body).

2. Click the Paragraph dialog launcher on the Home tab and change the line spacing to Multiple at 0.9 to match the template placeholder text (see Figure 9.2).

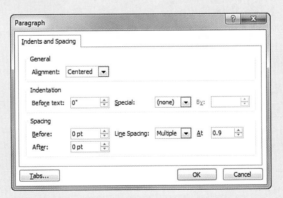

FIGURE 9.2

Change the paragraph options before creating a default shape or textbox.

3. Right-click the shape and choose Set as Default Shape (see Figure 9.3).

4. Insert a line onto any slide in the Tutorial template. Right-click the line and choose Format Shape.

5. In the Format Shape dialog on the Line Color tab, choose White (Light 1) Darker 35%. On the Line Style tab, choose Width 1.5 pt. Change the join type to Miter.

6. Right-click the line and choose Set as Default Line.

7. From the Shapes gallery, insert a textbox and type a bit of text. Leave the text white, Calibri, 18 points.

8. Click the Paragraph dialog launcher and change the line spacing to Multiple at 0.9 to match the template placeholder text (refer to Figure 9.2).

9. Right-click the line and choose Set as Default Text Box.

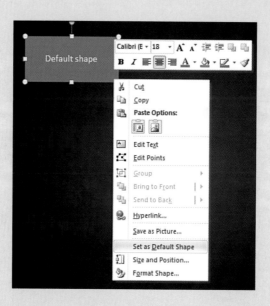

FIGURE 9.3

Right-click to set a default shape, line, or textbox.

VIEW IN SLIDE SHOW MODE

PowerPoint is, after all, a presentation application, so be sure to test the file in Slide Show view before finalizing it. The following sections cover a few things to remember as you check the slide show.

TRANSITIONS

We usually apply a fast fade transition to all slides, occasionally applying a more dramatic transition to the title or section header slides. Sometimes a client prefers that no transitions be applied. Either way, you want to check to ensure that no stray Vortex transition appears when you least expect it.

ANIMATIONS

Check to ensure that graphics and other objects you copied don't have unexpected animation effects applied to them.

LEGIBILITY AND VISIBILITY

Make sure text is readable. To test, create a sample slide for each layout and populate it with dummy text for each level of text. Look specifically at contrast and font size.

TIP *A quick way to add text in PowerPoint 2010 is to type* =lorem() *into a placeholder. This populates the placeholder with ersatz Latin known as Lorum Ipsum text. It's been used by the printing industry since the 1500s to let you see how text will look without being distracted by real content.*

Check the contrast and quality of all images. Take a hard look at any logos and other cutout graphics to ensure that they are not ragged and no small bits of color are around the edges.

Also look closely at the perimeter of the slide to confirm that images and graphics extend all the way to the edge (if they are supposed to). A tiny pixel-wide slice of contrasting color showing up along one of the sides of a projected slide is not uncommon. If you see this, head to the slide layout and use the alignment tools to align the graphics to the edge of the slide. Sometimes this works better than placing the graphic "by the numbers" in the Size and Position dialog boxes.

HIDDEN SLIDES

Make sure there are no hidden slides in the template. Users sometimes don't realize a slide is hidden and might not understand why it doesn't display when they run the slide show or upload the file to webconferencing software. If you do opt to include hidden slides, be sure there is a good reason.

OPTIMIZE FILE SIZE

Check the size of the template file as part of the finalization process. You want to keep the template reasonably small because the file size will only become larger as users build presentations. Sharing large files can be problematic, so keep the template file as small as possible while retaining image quality.

FIX OVERSIZED IMAGES

Wanting to use very high-resolution images in a template or presentation is natural, but they are really not necessary. In fact, oversized images are usually overkill because your template or presentation is limited to the resolution of the projector or monitor that displays it. See Chapter 4, "Formatting the Slide Master," for information on correctly sizing images for your template. If you've followed those recommendations but your file size still seems large, double-check any images used for the slide backgrounds to ensure they're not larger than they need to be.

GET RID OF EXTRA FONTS

Extraneous fonts can also affect your file size. If you suspect unnecessary fonts are bloating your template, check for them using the following steps:

1. On the Home tab, click the arrow next to the Replace button and choose Replace Fonts.

2. In the Replace drop-down list, review the list of fonts included in the presentation.

3. If you see unnecessary fonts, choose a replacement font from the list in the With drop-down list.

Sometimes you see a common font such as Arial or Wingdings when your presentation uses only Calibri. If you're not able to replace the font using the Replace Fonts dialog, then these fonts are probably assigned to the bullet characters on levels 6 through 9 of the bulleted text. If this is the case, check all levels of bullets on the slide master and change them to the appropriate font.

CAUTION

Double-byte fonts can be difficult to get rid of. When you try, you receive a warning that says, "You selected a single-byte font to replace a double-byte font." If this happens, you need to locate each object that uses the double-byte font and choose another font (preferably one of your theme fonts) from the Font drop-down list on the Home tab. Alternatively, you might be able to get rid of the font using the free Starter Set add-in from PPTools. Download the tools and read the instructions at http://www. quepublishing.com/title/0789749556.

TEST PRINT

In this age of digital distribution, it's easy to forget that folks sometimes do need to print their slides. Make sure you check the most common print scenarios as you finalize your template so you can avoid any obvious pitfalls.

CREATE PDFS

The ability to create PDFs was introduced in PowerPoint 2007 and is still available in PowerPoint 2010. In 2007, it's available as an option when you do a Save As; look for the PDF or XPS options. In 2010, choose File, Save & Send, Create PDF/XPS Document. Use this feature to create a PDF of your sample slides to ensure the template creates good-quality PDFs.

If you're creating a template for users who are accustomed to printing to a third-party PDF driver, also test the template with it if possible. Note that many third-party PDF creation utilities have trouble reproducing PowerPoint's gradients and transparencies, and PowerPoint's own PDF creation tool often performs better. Users are often not aware it exists, so you might consider including information about it in your instructional slides or off-slide text.

SPECIFY BLACK AND WHITE SETTINGS

PowerPoint has a little-known option to specify Black and White or Grayscale settings for objects on the slides or masters. These settings apply *only* when printing in black and white or grayscale; they do not affect color in any way whatsoever. Change the settings for objects on the slide master and slide layouts to globally apply them to your template.

To access the settings, choose View, Grayscale (or Black and White). This gives you a pre-view of what your slides will look like when you opt to print Grayscale or Black and White in the Print dialog (see Figure 9.4). Grayscale prints the slides in shades of gray, whereas Black and White is starker and omits most object fills. Black and White also drops out any slide background fills that you added using Format Background, Picture, or Texture Fill. (Pictures placed on a slide master or layout are treated just like other objects in Grayscale or Black and White view.)

NOTE *No way exists to create a black-and-white or grayscale PDF using PowerPoint's PDF/XPS tool.*

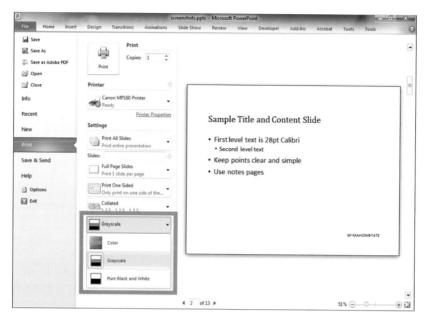

FIGURE 9.4

You can opt to print in either black and white or grayscale in the Print dialog.

You can select any object and change its black-and-white or grayscale setting by clicking one of the options on the Ribbon, as shown in Figure 9.5. After making any changes, be sure to check in both Black and White and Grayscale view because the setting applies to both views. (In fact, depending on the template, there might not be a whole lot of difference between Black and White and Grayscale views.)

TIP

Unfortunately, the default Black and White and Grayscale settings cannot be changed on either charts or SmartArt diagrams. This can be especially problematic with charts on slides that use a dark background style because the axes won't print. If this scenario is problematic for you, consider applying a light gray axis to the charts in Color view. It will look light enough on the dark background when presented in color and will give you a light gray axis in Black and White and Grayscale views for printing purposes.

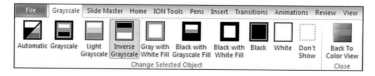

FIGURE 9.5

Choose an option on the Ribbon to change the Grayscale setting of an object.

TUTORIAL

To change the Grayscale settings for the Tutorial template, do the following:

1. Switch to Slide Master view and then choose View, Grayscale. The slide backgrounds become white, and all graphics also become white.

2. Select the gradient at the top of the slide master. On the Grayscale tab, choose Don't Show.

3. Select the logo in the lower-right corner and choose Inverse Grayscale.

4. On the Title Slide, Section Header, and Vertical Title and Text layouts, select the logo and set it to Inverse Grayscale.

SETTING UP TO SAVE

You might not realize it, but a PowerPoint file remembers the view you were in when you saved it. If you've ever opened a presentation or template and it's been zoomed in very close so that you have to zoom out to see the entire slide, then you've experienced this already. It's annoying. Make life easier for your users by double-checking a few things related to the view before you save.

1. Make sure you are in Normal (editing) view, not in Slide Master or another view.

2. Decide whether the Slides pane and the Notes pane should be opened or closed. Size them appropriately by dragging their frames.

3. Click the Fit Slide to Current Window button, pictured in Figure 9.6, so the slide is not zoomed in or out too far. This button is next to the zoom tools in the lower-right corner of your screen.

FIGURE 9.6

Fit Slide to Current Window fits your slides to the current workspace.

4. Turn Snap to Grid on or off. Some people find that resizing and aligning graphics is easier with this option turned on. Others would rather not use Snap to Grid. If you can, find out what the majority prefers before changing this setting.

5. Make sure any guides are positioned appropriately in case a user opts to display them. Remove any extraneous guides that you might have added while constructing the template.

VERIFY ADMINISTRIVIA

As you put the final touches on the template, don't forget to deal with things related to spelling, accessibility, and file formats.

SPELL-CHECK AND PROOFREAD

It should go without saying, but we're saying it anyway: Don't forget to carefully proofread your template. However, don't rely only on spell-check because it doesn't check things such as prompt text and text in sample graphs. Misspelling something in a template is embarrassing, so double-check everything! Look at the text on the slide masters and layouts as well as the prompt text that appears in the slides based on those layouts.

TIP *Proofing your own work is difficult, so if you can, have a colleague review the template. Before you roll it out to a large group of users, have a small group thoroughly test the template to ensure everything is working properly.*

INSPECT DOCUMENT

Run the Inspect Document tool to strip any leftover comments or document properties that remain in the template. Be careful not to remove presentation notes if they're included for instructional reasons. The Inspect Document tool is on the File tab under Info, Check for Issues in PowerPoint 2010 and on the Office Button in the Prepare section in PowerPoint 2007.

CHECK ACCESSIBILITY

Workplace fairness laws are making accessibility more and more important to build into business documents. In PowerPoint 2010, you can run the Check Accessibility tool to ensure that you haven't included objects that will be difficult for users with disabilities to access. You might need to go back and add descriptive text to objects on the sample slides or slide layouts. These descriptions can be added in the Alt Text tab of the Format Shape dialog in PowerPoint 2010 (see Figure 9.7) and on the Alt Text tab of the Size and Position dialog in PowerPoint 2007.

The Check Accessibility tool is not available in PowerPoint 2007. In PowerPoint 2010, you can find it on the File tab under Info, Check for Issues.

FIGURE 9.7
Enter descriptive text in the Alt Text dialog to make accessing content easier for users with disabilities.

SEEING DOUBLE?

Have you ever pasted a slide into a presentation and gotten two logos? Or have you ever applied a theme to a presentation twice and later discovered that you have multiple layers of graphics on the slide backgrounds?

These issues are related to an XML attribute known as userDrawn. It indicates that someone (you) intentionally added a graphic to a slide master or layout. Assuming you don't want to inadvertently lose that graphic, the userDrawn tag is added automatically to instruct PowerPoint not to delete it.

This tag is also added to custom layouts, which is one reason you sometimes end up with extra "orphaned" layouts after you paste slides into a new presentation.

Fixing this issue is an ambitious effort and requires a bit of XML-editing knowledge. For specific instructions, see http://www.quepublishing.com/title/0789749556.

SAVE AS TEMPLATE (.POTX)

Until now, we've been saving the "template" as a .PPTX file, which is a typical PowerPoint file that opens in Normal (editing) view. This is strictly for ease of use while working on the template. Although you can apply or use a .PPTX as a template, distributing a .POTX to users is generally safer. This is because when a user double-clicks a .POTX file, it opens a new file that is *based on* the template rather than opening the actual .POTX file itself. Distributing a .POTX file prevents users from inadvertently messing up the template.

With the old file format used by PowerPoint 2003 and prior, you could create a template from a .PPT file by renaming it with a .POT extension. This no longer works in PowerPoint 2007 and newer; you must actually save the file as a template in those versions.

To save the Tutorial template as a template file, click File, Save As to open the Save As dialog. In the Save As Type drop-down, as shown in Figure 9.8, choose PowerPoint Template (*.POTX). Your tutorial template is finally complete.

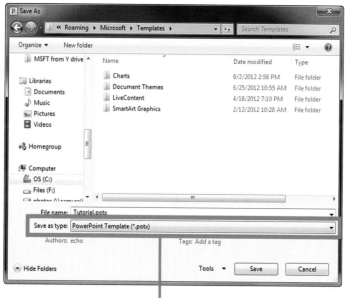

Save As Type dropdown

FIGURE 9.8

Select PowerPoint Template (.POTX) in the Save As dialog to save your presentation file as a template.*

NOTE

When you save your .PPTX file as a .POTX, PowerPoint automatically takes you to the folder where template files are stored, which is usually something like C:\Users\ UserName\AppData\Roaming\Microsoft\Templates. If this happens, simply navigate back to your working folder and save the .POTX there.

IN THIS CHAPTER

- Questions to ask before designing
- Reviewing brand guidelines
- Sketching concepts
- Assembling digital assets
- Designing in PowerPoint
- Projecting to test

DESIGNING A TEMPLATE

In this book, we teach you the steps to building a successful PowerPoint template. However, the first step to a truly successful template begins long before the build stage. We're talking about design—both visual *and* functional design. This means developing a template that not only looks fabulous, but also works well for everyone who will use it.

Generally speaking, the more you prepare during the design phase, the more useful your template will be. This preparation involves asking and answering many questions about how it will be used. Most importantly, you need to know who will use the template, what type of slides they generally present, and how presentations will be delivered.

EVALUATE THE USER BASE

Some templates are designed and built for a single presenter. Others are developed for a one-time event with multiple presenters. Also, don't forget the most challenging and complex type: templates for the masses—those designed for an entire company or organization, for hundreds or even thousands of people with varying PowerPoint skill levels. As you're designing, keep these people in mind. What can your template provide that will help them create better presentations? Should you include more layouts or more instructional prompt text to guide new users?

REVIEW COMMON SLIDE TYPES

A slick design serves little purpose if others struggle to use it. All template elements, including the background design, colors, layout structure, placeholder formatting, and slide layout assortment, should serve to help people as they build slides. Your goal is to make it easier for them by taking out some of the guesswork as they assemble and develop content.

Before you begin designing, get a good sense for what type of slides will be created with the new template. Gather many recent presentations and conduct a review of common slide content and layouts. No rule exists for how many presentations you should review; just be sure the sampling covers a broad range of slides from various content creators.

You can print the slides as handouts, if you like. Cut apart the slide thumbnails and arrange them into groups of similar layouts. Figure 10.1 shows a small sampling of printed and grouped slide types from CoreMedia presentations. As you review, consider how the old template was used. What worked well and what needs improvement? Are the placeholders formatted to accommodate enough text or other content? Does it appear that users struggled to apply colors and fills correctly and consistently? Does enough slide real estate exist for complex charts or diagrams? Were all the slide layouts used? Do you see a group of slides that would benefit from a preformatted custom layout? Patterns will emerge that can help you decide which layouts to include in the new template.

As you're grouping similar slide types and determining slide layout structure, remember that content placeholders are multipurpose. They can any hold any type of content: text, charts, tables, and so on. With content placeholders, slide layouts can serve more than one purpose.

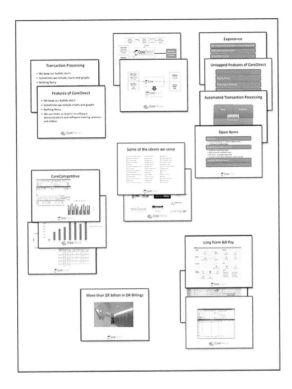

FIGURE 10.1

A review of recent presentations can help you determine which layouts to include in the new template.

DETERMINE PRESENTATION DELIVERY METHODS

Presentations are delivered in many ways and in vastly different environments. They are shown during one-on-one laptop meetings, in web conferences, in boardroom sessions, and often in large auditoriums where they're projected onto massive screens. Think about the differences in lighting, screen size, audience size, and monitor or projection quality in each of these situations. Chances are slim that just one template design will work for every environment.

Consider providing alternative templates for specific presentation conditions. For example, a white background might look great on a laptop or in an ambient-lit boardroom. However, in a darkened ballroom, that same white background will be too bright and difficult to look at for a length of time. Some companies provide light and dark template designs, both in 4:3 and widescreen aspect ratios. Others have internal and external template designs, with varying degrees of graphic enhancement. Ask questions about various delivery methods early on in the template design process.

REVIEW BRAND GUIDELINES AND COLLATERAL MATERIALS

Brand guidelines define a company's graphic standards. They help to maintain a consistent visual identity throughout all communication materials. Branding information typically includes details about logo usage, colors, fonts, photo styles, and any other graphic elements to be used in collateral designs. As an important part of company communications, presentation templates should also be designed to maintain the brand. Quite often, an updated branding package leads to the request for a new PowerPoint template.

Typical branding documents include layout and design standards for printed materials and website pages. In this case, your job is to review the standards and apply the design elements that are appropriate to the presentation template.

Some documents include basic guidelines for presentation templates. Be aware, though, the template designs might have been created using software other than PowerPoint. Re-creating the specs exactly might not be feasible. Use your best judgment when building the template and setting up the placeholders. Determining appropriate font sizes, spacing, and bullet characters in PowerPoint is best.

CORPORATE FONTS

Most companies define their corporate font (or fonts) in the brand guidelines. Once again, this typically applies only to print materials. You might find a reference to a screen font or even an alternative font suggested for presentations. Be careful selecting just any font for the template! Refer to the section "Choosing the Right Fonts" in Chapter 3, "Getting Started: Set Up a Theme," for guidance on choosing fonts that work properly for all template users.

CORPORATE COLORS

The color theme is one of the most important parts of a template. A branding document should include specs for all corporate colors, including the RGB values that you need to build a color theme. Figure 10.2 shows an example color palette from the fictitious McMahon Tate brand guidelines. The brand guide might also include a suggested hierarchy for color use for primary, secondary, and even tertiary levels. Keep in mind that even though a particular set of colors, or order of colors, works for print or web purposes, it might not work well for PowerPoint charts and graphics. Some color values might be too light or too dark relative to the others. Your task as a template designer is to determine which colors to apply to the six accents in your color theme and what order to put them in. Because projected colors are quite different from printed colors, you might need to make adjustments to the values provided. Tweak the color saturation and luminosity settings in PowerPoint and project the new colors to check the adjustments.

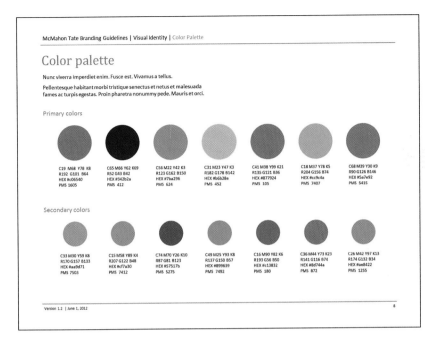

FIGURE 10.2

Brand guidelines specify a company's color palette and include values for different color models. Refer to the RGB values when formatting theme colors.

NOTE

Your corporate color palette might extend beyond the number of colors allowed in a theme. You can program a set of additional, custom colors to appear in the color gallery. You need the hex values for all custom colors to program them in XML. See Chapter 13, "Editing PowerPoint and Theme File XML," for instructions.

CORPORATE LOGOS

No company brand is complete without a logo. Finding at least one or two pages in the guidelines devoted to the corporate logo is a given. Some of the logo guidance will apply to the presentation template. Pay attention to logo variations, such as horizontal or stacked versions. When should each be used in a design? Is there an example of a reversed logo that can be used on dark backgrounds? Figure 10.3 features an example logo page from our fictitious company's brand guidelines.

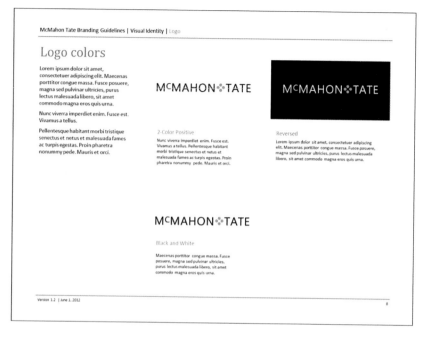

FIGURE 10.3

Refer to brand guidelines for logo variations, colors, and correct usage.

Some companies go overboard with logos and trademarks on their presentations and templates. Striking a balance here is best. For live presentations, including a logo on every single slide is not necessary. A large logo can be prominently featured on an introductory slide and repeated on a closing slide. Let the presentation content remain the focus by losing the small logo in the corner.

> **NOTE**
>
> *We try to steer our clients away from putting a logo on every slide, but we're not always successful. Most often the reason for wanting the logo on every slide is because many presentations are still serving dual purposes: to be delivered in front of an audience and printed as a leave-behind. Do whatever you can to discourage this practice. A presentation designed for visual support is not the same as a document developed for reading. The two should be addressed individually.*

DESIGNING WITHOUT FORMAL GUIDELINES

If the company (or person) you're designing for does not have formal brand guidelines, refer to other collateral materials for graphic cues. Review the website, brochures, and any other printed materials. Look for common design elements, colors, and graphic styles that you can apply in the new template to help them maintain a consistent look for their communications.

When designing for a specific event, such as a conference or awards banquet, you need to work with the team responsible for the event materials. Take a look at invitations, posters, or the event website for design ideas that you can translate into the event template. Request a copy of the event logo for use on specific slide layouts. Knowing some specifics about the presentation venue is also important. Ask about the room lighting for the event so you can plan appropriately for light or dark backgrounds. Ask about the projection aspect ratio so you can size the new template accordingly. If the presenter will have a widescreen projector, find out whether to use 16:9 or 16:10 for your page setup.

SKETCH BASIC DESIGN CONCEPTS

Get out a paper and pencil and start putting together rough ideas for slide designs and layouts. This preliminary, brainstorming step enables you to quickly try out several ideas before spending too much time and effort in PowerPoint. Don't get hung up on details when sketching. Figure 10.4 includes a few quick slide ideas that were sketched on a blank hand-out page. You're looking for approximate proportions and sizes—a general idea of where you'll put various elements on different slide types.

FIGURE 10.4

Save time by sketching rough design ideas before diving into PowerPoint.

NOTE *An important reminder for all template designs: Keep it simple! Your company's print materials might feature a detailed illustration or complex graphic. If you must, reserve elements like this for title slides only. A busy, detailed background detracts from any content placed on top. Forget about using faded photos or complex patterns behind or surrounding placeholders. A clean, uncluttered design works best.*

ASSEMBLE DIGITAL ASSETS

You need to gather or prepare logos, backgrounds, and any other graphic elements for use in PowerPoint. Make sure you have RGB values to set up the theme colors.

LOGO(S)

Request or convert any logos that you'll need for the template. .EMF and .WMF files work well for most logos, because you can resize and recolor these vector formats in PowerPoint. You can also use .PNG files for logos, because this raster format does not lose quality when compressed and details hold up at smaller sizes. If you need both large and small versions of a logo, you might have to save .PNGs in two different sizes. For more details, see the "Which File Format Should You Use for Logos?" sidebar in Chapter 4, "Formatting the Slide Master."

BACKGROUNDS, PICTURES, AND GRAPHICS

If your template design calls for picture- or texture-filled backgrounds, you probably need to resize images for PowerPoint. Your template page size dictates the dimensions for the background image. See the "Resize and Format a Picture for Your Background" section in Chapter 4 for more information about image dimensions and file format.

CAUTION *Stock images are often provided as .JPEG files. Many of these images are saved with an embedded color profile that PowerPoint has trouble reading. When you import a picture with this color profile, a dark line appears at the top and left sides of the picture.*

To fix this issue, open the stock image in Adobe Photoshop, select File, Save As, and uncheck the ICC Profile setting. Click Save to overwrite the file.

Or you can use our preferred method: Simply save the file as a .PNG, which doesn't embed the color profile.

Your designs might include accent graphics that have been created in another program, such as Adobe Illustrator. You can export these graphics for use in PowerPoint. As we've mentioned, a .PNG file is a good format to use for detailed, multi-color images that you won't need to recolor in PowerPoint. However, if the graphics consist of shapes filled with a single color (not gradients), you can export them as .EMF files. Import the shapes into PowerPoint where you can ungroup them and recolor as needed. This technique enables you to fill shapes with theme colors and even add gradients, shadows, or other effects.

RGB VALUES

A critical step in the template design process involves defining the theme colors. These colors influence the appearance of all content created with a template. If you are working on a corporate template, start by noting the RGB values for the company's primary colors.

Chapter 3 offers a couple of ideas for testing all proposed theme colors. Remember that accent colors you define, including corporate-mandated colors, must contrast with the background(s) and look pleasant as a set. If one accent color is much lighter or darker than the rest, that data series (or fill color) stands out. As you can see in Figure 10.5, the dark color for the second data series draws your attention away from the other series. Consider choosing accent colors that are similar in intensity. As mentioned earlier, you might need to make adjustments to the RGB values provided.

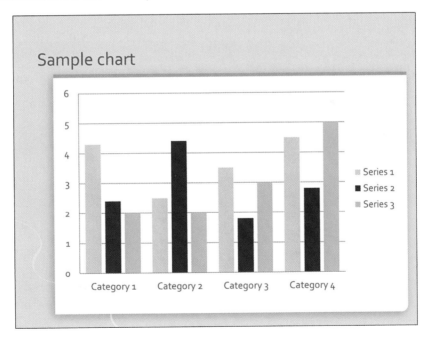

FIGURE 10.5

An accent color that is much darker or lighter than the rest can look highlighted or draw attention away from the other colors.

SELECTING ACCENT COLORS THAT WORK WELL TOGETHER

When developing a color theme from scratch, you can use the following technique to help you choose accent colors of similar intensity.

1. Set up a slide with your proposed template background color or picture fill. Draw a rectangle and fill it with a solid color and no outline. Edit the fill color until you're satisfied that it works for your design.

2. Duplicate the rectangle five times (for a total of six filled shapes).

3. Select the second filled shape. From the Home tab, choose Shape Fill, More Fill Colors. On the Custom tab, change the Color model to HLS. Click the arrows next to Hue to change this value only while maintaining the color's saturation and luminosity. Increase and decrease the hue from 0 to 255 (see Figure 10.6) until you're satisfied with the second fill color.

4. Repeat for all remaining shapes.

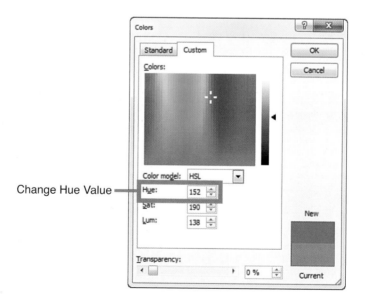

FIGURE 10.6

To choose another color with the same intensity, switch from RGB to the HSL color model and increase or decrease the Hue setting.

DEVELOP DESIGNS IN POWERPOINT

Working directly in PowerPoint gives you the most accurate representation of what the template will look like when it's complete. You don't have to format the slide master and layouts at this point; you can work in slide editing mode to mock up designs.

For a preliminary design review, you'll want to set up a few common slide types. These could include a title slide, a title and content slide, a section header, a sample chart slide, and perhaps a picture with caption. Format the backgrounds and position accent graphics and logos as needed. On a title and content slide, format the text placeholder to show the proposed body font, bullet characters, indents, and line spacing. Include a sample chart with at least a few data series to demonstrate how accent colors will appear next to each other. You might also want to include another colorful slide example for further review of the theme colors.

As you're developing the sample slides, set up guides to help you maintain consistency among different types of layouts. Position guides around the slide perimeter for margins. Insert horizontal guides to align the top and bottom of content placeholders. You can keep the default vertical and horizontal guides in place as they help to quickly identify the slide center.

PROJECT TO TEST

Your preliminary template designs are complete and they look great on your desktop monitor, but you're not finished yet. The proposed designs and colors will only be successful if they work well for all presentation delivery methods. In most situations, this means a projected slide show.

Before you build a template, you should project sample slides for a thorough review of colors, contrast, and legibility. Not all projectors are equal; they vary between models and even individual machines. So if at all possible, reviewing with the projector likely to be used for presentations is best.

If necessary, make changes to the designs and project them again for another review.

PRESENT TEMPLATE DESIGNS FOR FINAL APPROVAL

Gather key decision makers and review the preliminary template designs. Take notes and make any changes, if necessary, for the next review round.

For the final review, you should prepare sample designs for each layout. Mock up slides showing various types of content (charts, pictures, tables, and so on). Thoroughly review all template elements and get final approval for slide layouts, background designs, placeholder formatting, fill styles, and theme colors before you begin building.

Take the time to design and review before you build a template. It might seem like a lot of preliminary work, but it can save you hours of rework later.

11

UNDERSTANDING CHARTS AND CHART TEMPLATES

Many corporations stipulate very intricate styles for their graphs. Unfortunately, you cannot specify the look for a default chart in a PowerPoint template, and extremely stylized charts are often difficult for a typical user to replicate. This is where chart templates come in.

Chart templates were introduced with Office 2007 and are also available in Office 2010. They can be very helpful for users by making it easy to maintain branding standards without a lot of work. As a developer, though, you should be aware that chart templates have some quirks. This chapter covers the chart template issues you need to be aware of and provides strategies to overcome them.

ABOUT DEFAULT CHART SETTINGS

When you create a chart on a PowerPoint slide, it is based on a group of default settings that include things such as the data series formatting, the font color and size, and the dummy data that's included in the Excel spreadsheet. These default settings cannot be controlled (see Figure 11.1).

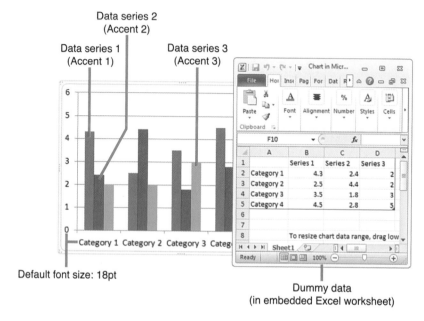

FIGURE 11.1

Settings in PowerPoint's default charts cannot be changed.

However, if you change any of your theme settings (colors, fonts, and effects), the default chart reflects those changes. For example, the data formatting in a default chart is based on your color theme: The first data series uses the Accent 1 color, the second data series uses Accent 2, the third uses Accent 3, and so on. So, technically speaking, you *could* change the default colors of a chart, but you would have to change your whole color theme to do so.

Some other settings simply cannot be changed. For example, the font size for a default chart is always 18 point. Regardless of what size font you've declared in the body text placeholder, the title placeholder, or even in a chart placeholder on the slide master or layouts, when you first create a chart on a slide, the text size defaults to 18 points. Period. You can do nothing about it.

These hard-coded settings usually leave your users with a lot of work to do to get from that default chart to your corporate-branded chart. Many of them won't have the time to spend to go through these motions, and many more of them won't have the knowledge necessary to manipulate the chart extensively. As a user, it's a tough position to be in.

WHAT'S A DEFAULT CHART?

By "default chart," we mean the chart you create by doing either of the following:

- Clicking the Chart button on the Insert tab of the Ribbon

- Clicking the chart icon in a content or chart placeholder

The chart that appears is the default chart.

Don't despair! All is not lost! Depending on the look you want for your charts, creating a template with color and effects themes to support the look you want might be possible. Creating it can be tricky, but if the design is fairly simple, it's completely doable.

THEME MATRIX FOR DEFAULT CHARTS

As with most other Office objects, such as shapes and SmartArt diagrams, the options in the Chart Styles gallery are based on a matrix of subtle, moderate, and intense effect settings. (See Chapter 3, "Getting Started: Set Up a Theme," for definitions and examples of effect settings, and read Chapter 12, "Using the Theme Builder Utility to Customize Your Theme," to learn how to edit effects settings.) These combinations are represented in the Chart Styles gallery (see Figure 11.2).

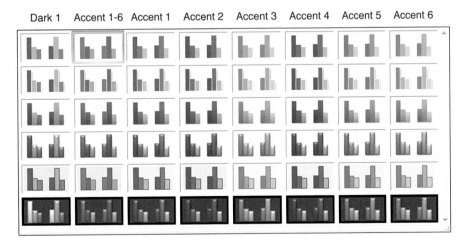

FIGURE 11.2

Each option in the Chart Styles gallery (on the Chart Tools Design tab) uses colors from the color theme and a combination of effects from the effects theme.

The Chart Styles gallery offers users a number of options to select from when creating charts. The various settings PowerPoint uses to populate this gallery are described in the following pages.

Although the chart styles become more intense as you travel down the columns in the Chart Styles gallery, some settings are the same on all chart styles. Refer to Table 11.1 for a listing of these common chart settings.

Table 11.1   Origin of Common Default Chart Settings

Chart Element	Default Setting
Font size	18 point
Font color	Dark 1 or Light 1
Font face	Body font
Gridlines weight	Subtle line weight
Gridlines line color	Variation of Dark 1 or Light 1
Axis* weight	Subtle line weight
Axis* line color	Variation of Dark 1 or Light 1

Tickmarks are considered part of the axis.

When you hover on the thumbnails in the Chart Styles gallery, you'll notice that the styles are named, beginning with Style 1 in the upper-left corner and continuing through Style 48 in the lower-right corner. Unfortunately, you cannot rename, remove, add to, or otherwise alter these styles or this gallery.

Style 2 in the first row of the Chart Styles gallery is the default chart that is inserted on a slide (see Figure 11.3). As with all chart styles, it uses the default settings listed in Table 11.1 for the font, axes, and gridlines. Chart styles in this top row of the gallery also use the subtle fill specified in the theme, but there is no border on the data series. The chart styles in this row apply no theme effects.

Using a new, blank presentation, which is based on the default Office Theme, you can apply a chart style from each row of the Chart Styles gallery and see how the different theme settings are applied to each element in the chart. See Table 11.2 and Figures 11.3 through 11.8 to see the theme settings in action.

Table 11.2   Relationships Between Theme Settings and Data Series Elements

	Border Color	Border Weight and Type*	Fill Style	Effects Style
First row (Style 2)	None	None	Subtle	None
Second row (Style 10)	Light 1 / Dark 1	Subtle	Subtle	Subtle
Third row (Style 18)	None	None	Intense	Moderate
Fourth row (Style 26)	None	None	Intense	Intense
Fifth row (Style 34)	Variation of Accent (data) or Dark 1 (chart area)	Subtle	Subtle	None
Sixth row (Style 42)	None	None	Intense	Intense

Solid, dashed, and so on

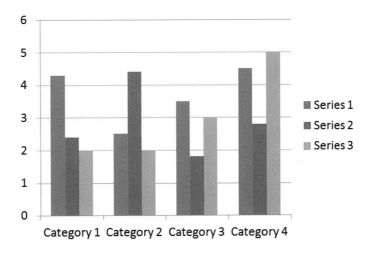

FIGURE 11.3

The fill style of data series in the first row of the Chart Styles gallery is based on the Subtle fill from the theme.

Like the chart styles in the top row of the Chart Styles gallery, those in the second row also use the subtle fill for data series. In addition, they place a border on each data point. This border is based on the Light 1 color and the subtle line weight. These chart styles also use the subtle theme effects, which is the slight shadow you can see behind each data point in Figure 11.4.

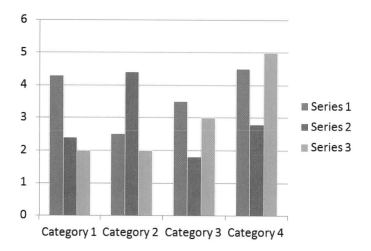

FIGURE 11.4

Styles in the second row of the Chart Styles gallery use the subtle fill for data series, but add a border based on the Light 1 color and subtle line weight as well as subtle effects.

The third row of the Chart Styles gallery gives the data a fill based on the intense fill style and applies any moderate effects. Seeing it is a bit difficult in Figure 11.5, but the moderate effects in the Office Theme consist of a slight shadow that has been applied behind each data point.

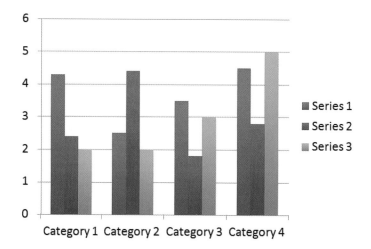

FIGURE 11.5

Third-row chart styles use the intense fill for data series, which is represented here as a gradient that is darker on the bottom and lighter on the top. Moderate effects are also applied.

Charts in the fourth row use the intense fill for data series, represented in Figure 11.6 as a gradient that is darker on the bottom and lighter on the top. Intense effects—in this case a bevel and a very slight shadow—are also applied. This style has no border added to the data series.

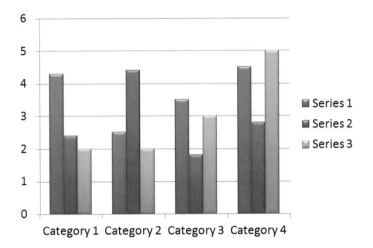

FIGURE 11.6

Chart styles in the fourth row use the intense fill and intense effects.

The fifth row of chart styles uses the subtle fill and no effects on the data series (see Figure 11.7). All borders on the chart are based on the subtle line style and weight. One exception is the border color on the data series; it is a variation of the accent color, which cannot be changed. The plot area defaults to a shade of gray, while the chart area uses the subtle fill style and Light 1 or Dark 1 as the basis for its color. (You might not notice that the chart area is filled unless the slide background has a pattern or image—or if your subtle fill style is not a simple solid fill.)

The sixth and last row of the Chart Styles gallery, as shown in Figure 11.8, is identical to the fourth row, adding Dark 1 for the chart area fill and a variation of that for the plot area fill. The chart styles in the fifth and sixth rows are used more often in Word than they are in PowerPoint.

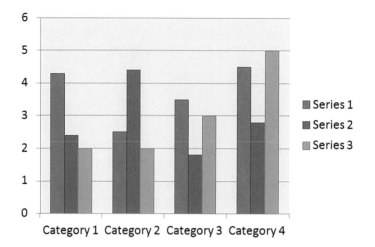

FIGURE 11.7

Chart styles in the fifth row use the subtle fill for both the data series and the chart area.

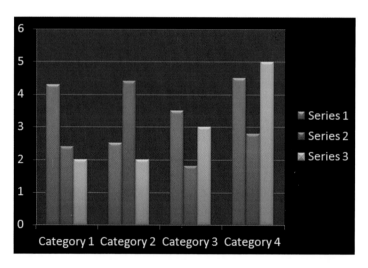

FIGURE 11.8

The last row of chart styles uses the intense fill for data series and intense effects, just like the fourth row of the Chart Style gallery does.

DON'T FORGET LINE CHARTS

Line and other types of charts generally use the same settings in the Chart Styles gallery as column charts do. Of course, line charts have an actual data series line rather than a column, and they can also have data point markers. Line charts have an additional quirk: The thickness of the data series line is based on a *multiplier* of the Subtle line weight. See Table 11.3 to identify these settings.

For example, the default chart (Style 2) in a new, blank presentation uses a 2.25-point line for its data series. This is based on the Subtle line thickness setting in the theme (.75) and a multiplier of 3. (for example, $3 \times .75 = 2.25$). Charts in the fourth row of the Chart Styles gallery have data series lines that are 5.25 points thick. This is based on a subtle line weight setting of $.75 \times 7$.

Table 11.3   Line Weight Multiplier for Line Charts

	Data Marker Line Style	Data Marker Fill Style	Effects Style	Line Weight Multiplier	Thumbnail
First row (Style 2)	Subtle	Subtle	None	3× subtle line weight	
Second row (Style 10)	Subtle	Subtle	Subtle	5× subtle line weight	
Third row (Style 18)	Subtle	Intense	Moderate	5× subtle line weight	
Fourth row (Style 26)	Subtle	Intense	Intense	7× subtle line weight	
Fifth row (Style 34)	Subtle	Subtle	None	5× subtle line weight	
Sixth row (Style 42)	Subtle	Intense	Intense	5× subtle line weight	

If you are struggling to envision which setting PowerPoint uses for a particular chart part, create a theme that uses outrageous colors and specifications for the various subtle, moderate, and intense settings. Then create a slide with the appropriate type of chart and apply the different chart styles to see how the theme affects it. You can download our version of an outrageous theme for testing from http://www.quepublishing.com/title/0789749556.

ARGH! WHY DO MY DATA SERIES KEEP CHANGING COLORS?

You might have noticed that sometimes when you add data to a chart, the colors of the existing data change and become a bit darker when you add the sixth data series. An example of this is shown in Figures 11.9 and 11.10. If you continue to add data series to your chart the colors of the existing data points continue to change as well, becoming lighter and darker color values of Accents 1 through 6.

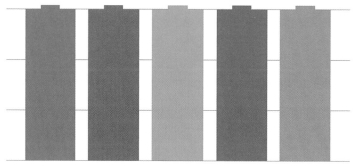

FIGURE 11.9

Five data series in a chart and the colors exactly match the theme's Accent colors, which are represented by the small boxes at the top of each column.

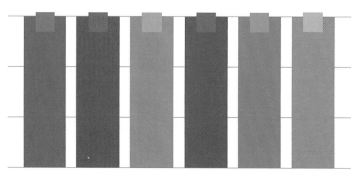

FIGURE 11.10

Add a sixth data series and all the colors become a bit darker and no longer match the theme accent colors, which are represented by the small boxes at the top of each column.

Believe it or not, this is not a bug; it is how charts are designed to work in Office 2007 and 2010. PowerPoint is trying to be helpful by adding contrast to the colors. If you look at one of the chart styles that uses only one accent color (rather than the default multi-colored chart style), as shown in Figure 11.11, you can probably see how it can, indeed, be helpful.

This feature can be especially maddening if your branding guidelines expect charts to maintain exact brand colors. If this situation happens too often for your liking, you might want to consider providing chart templates for your users.

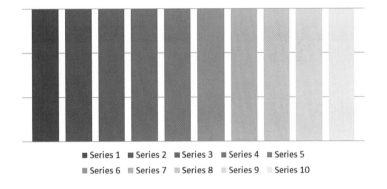

Series 1   Series 2   Series 3   Series 4   Series 5
Series 6   Series 7   Series 8   Series 9   Series 10

FIGURE 11.11

This chart (Chart Style 3) is based only on Accent 1. Here you can see how the automatic adjustment of existing data colors can be helpful.

CHART TEMPLATES TO THE RESCUE

Setting up a theme to accommodate very stylized charts is sometimes impossible, especially if you need the theme to behave a certain way for elements such as shapes and SmartArt. This is where chart templates come in. (If you're ambitious, read Chapter 12 to learn how to customize the subtle, moderate, and intense effect settings using the Theme Builder.)

Chart templates let you apply custom settings to a chart all at once, saving you the trouble of manually applying settings to a chart every time you create one. Think of them as custom chart styles.

The most important thing to understand about chart templates is that their formatting is not tied to your theme. If you base a chart on a chart template, its formatting won't change if you apply different theme colors, fonts, or effects to the presentation or paste the slide into another presentation. This is known as *absolute formatting*, and it can actually be a good thing.

NOTE   *When you insert a chart, it picks up your theme formatting by default. Sometimes the theme formatting isn't exactly what you need, so you apply custom formatting. Maybe you change the font size, remove gridlines and tick marks, and reposition the legend. Maybe you even go so far as to change some of the series colors. You can now save this as a chart template so you can apply all that formatting to other charts with one click.*

CREATING A CHART TEMPLATE

Creating a chart template is extremely easy. To do so, follow these steps:

1. Create a chart.

2. Format it to your liking.

3. On the Chart Tools Design tab, click the Save As Template button. (The Save Chart Template dialog box opens to the folder where chart templates are stored.)

4. Type a name for the chart template and click Save.

AVOIDING CHART TEMPLATE GOTCHAS

The most difficult part of creating chart templates isn't actually difficult at all. It is really just a matter of being aware of the idiosyncrasies of chart templates.

GOTCHA #1: CHART TEMPLATES AREN'T THEMED

As mentioned earlier, chart template formatting is not themed. Even if you select one of the theme accent colors as a data series fill, after you save that chart as a chart template, any link to your theme breaks. If you apply a chart template, the format of the resulting chart is considered absolute formatting and will not change if you apply a different template, theme, or color theme to that slide.

Be especially wary of this if you need to use chart templates on both light and dark slide backgrounds. The chart font color from a chart template does not change. You need to create one chart template with a light font designed for a dark background and another with a dark font to be used on a light background.

GOTCHA #2: THE AXIS SCALE IS PART OF THE CHART TEMPLATE

When we say that chart templates include all the chart formatting, we aren't kidding! Chart templates include *all* the chart formatting, even things you might not expect such as number formats, axis scale settings, and so on.

When you create chart templates for your users, carefully consider whether the value axis scale should be fixed or automatic. If it is fixed, think about what those settings should be.

For example, we often create a series of chart templates with different axis settings, as shown in Figure 11.12. One usually has an axis with a minimum of 0, a maximum of 100, and the number format set to percentage (with 0 decimal places) because many clients want charts that show percent to always go to 100% regardless of the data. Another chart template usually has an axis with all of its scale settings automatic and a number format set to Number with one decimal place. A third also has an automatic axis scale but a number format of Number with zero decimal places. Yet another has no axis at all because the data is represented using data labels.

GOTCHA #3: THE DUMMY DATA CANNOT BE CHANGED

You cannot use your own dummy data in a chart template— it will always revert to Microsoft's dummy data (refer to Figure 11.1). Yes, it's annoying. As you can see on the upper-left image in Figure 11.12, the percentage axis has a fixed scale from 0 to 100, yet the data is very tiny, and you can hardly see the columns. There's nothing you can do about this, so don't waste your time trying.

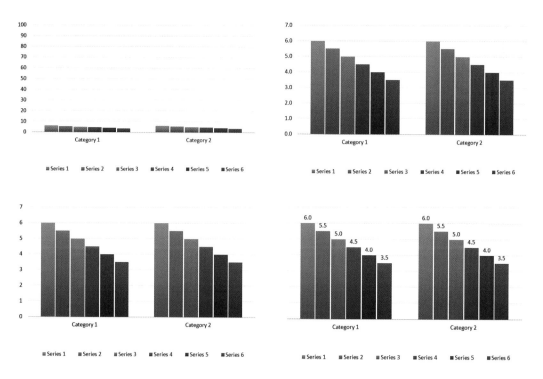

FIGURE 11.12

Clockwise from upper left are examples of four axis styles used in chart templates: Fixed at 100%, Automatic with one decimal place, no axis at all, and Automatic with whole numbers.

GOTCHA #4: THE THUMBNAILS AREN'T DETAILED

Chart template thumbnails are not detailed. In fact, they will often look identical, especially if the data point fill colors are the same and the only difference is the axis scale. In addition, the thumbnails reflect the theme colors used on the slide, not necessarily the colors used in the chart template.

Also, if you create the chart templates in PowerPoint 2007 (shown in Figure 11.13), the appropriate light or dark background in the thumbnail displays. If the chart template is created in PowerPoint 2010 (see Figure 11.14), these thumbnails will look identical.

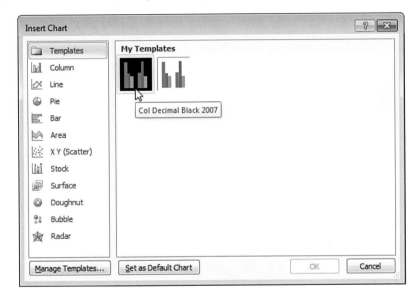

FIGURE 11.13

These chart templates were created in PowerPoint 2007, which maintains dark and light slide backgrounds as part of the chart template thumbnails.

GOTCHA #5: NAME MATTERS

Even though the name doesn't display in the Chart Templates dialog box, the name does matter. Chart templates are displayed in alphabetical order in the dialog, and the name of the chart will display as a tool tip when you hover your mouse over each thumbnail, which you can see in Figures 11.13 and 11.14.

Consider how to name your chart templates to the best advantage. You might want to prepend the name with Column or Line to signify the chart type, or you might decide that is not necessary because the chart type generally shows up well in the thumbnail.

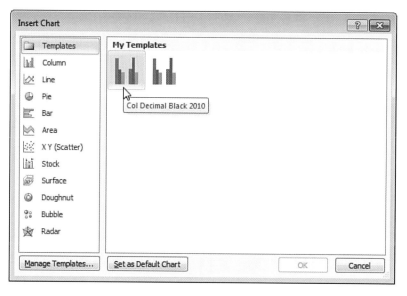

FIGURE 11.14

These chart templates were created in PowerPoint 2010. The one on the left is designed to work on a dark slide background, but you cannot tell this from the thumbnail image alone.

GOTCHA #6: NO SUBFOLDERS ARE ALLOWED

You might think you can help your users know which chart templates to use by putting them in separate folders. This would be a good idea, except for that fact that it doesn't work! In PowerPoint (and Word and Excel, for that matter), look for chart templates in the C:\Users\ *UserName*\AppData\Roaming\Microsoft\Templates\Charts folder, and any subfolders there are simply ignored.

GOTCHA #7: YOU DIDN'T FORMAT ENOUGH SERIES

When you create a chart template, be sure to add and format more data series than you expect users will need. Even though all the series data doesn't show in the default charts or templates, the formatting will still be included when a user applies the chart template. (We generally recommend at least 6 for a column chart and 8 or 10 for a line chart (see Figure 11.15), but feel free to set up more if you think it's necessary.) This is because the chart template needs formatting to have something to apply to a chart. Consider this: If your user has a chart with five data series, but you only set up four series in the chart template, then what is PowerPoint supposed to do with that fifth series when the user applies the chart template?

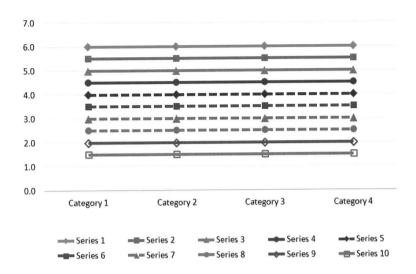

FIGURE 11.15

This line chart has 10 data series. We recommend you set up at least 8 series in a chart template to accommodate charts like this.

USING CHART TEMPLATES

To use a chart template effectively, it's best to apply it to an existing chart. To begin, insert or select a chart on the slide, and then do the following:

1. On the Chart Tools Design tab, click Change Chart Type.

2. In the Change Chart Type dialog, click the Templates folder.

3. Select the appropriate chart template and click OK.

We don't recommend inserting a new chart based on a chart template. Even though you've created a chart template that includes formatting for extra data series, the default chart you insert only shows three of these. When you add more data series, PowerPoint automatically fills those with current theme colors—it does not recognize the custom formatting from the chart template. To correct this, you must reapply the chart template. It's easier to edit all of your data on a default chart and *then* apply the chart template.

TIP   *Every time you add data to a chart, you must reapply the chart template.*

DISTRIBUTING CHART TEMPLATES

Unfortunately, chart templates are not part of either the Office Theme (.THMX) or the PowerPoint Template (.POTX). Chart templates are separate files with the extension .CRTX, and they live on each user's computer.

The Office applications all look for chart templates in this folder: C:\Users*UserName*\ AppData\Roaming\Microsoft\Templates\Charts (%AppData%\Microsoft\Templates\Charts).

To distribute chart templates to users, you can give them the .CRTX files and instruct them to save the files in that folder. (If they do not see a Charts subfolder in the Templates folder, they can create one.)

In many situations, you can also ask the IT staff to add the .CRTX files to that folder or see whether they will add the .CRTX files to the image they use to set up new systems.

An alternative distribution method is to send the user slides with sample charts that are formatted and ready to be saved as chart templates. Instruct the user to do the following to save the chart templates on their system:

1. Select the chart.

2. On the Chart Tools Design tab, click the Save As Template button (the Save Chart Template dialog box opens to the appropriate folder).

3. Type a name for the chart template and click Save.

These are the same steps that you would use to create a chart template based on the sample chart, but this method allows each user to save the chart template on her computer without having to poke around in the innards of her computer to find the appropriate location.

You might also have noticed a button in the Insert Chart and Change Chart Type dialogs that is named Set as Default Chart (refer to Figure 11.14). This button allows the user to select any chart type—including any chart template—as the default chart. Once set, the Insert Chart dialog box opens to the specified chart type when the user inserts a chart. Note that this setting does *not* travel with the PowerPoint template; it is specific to each user's computer.

The Manage Templates button, which is shown Figure 11.14, simply open the C:\Users\ *UserName*\AppData\Roaming\Microsoft\Templates\Charts folder, so you can add, delete, rename, or otherwise manage the templates in this folder.

IN THIS CHAPTER

- Installing the Theme Builder utility
- Understanding the process for customizing a theme
- Using the colors and fonts tab of the Theme Builder
- Customizing fill, line, effects, and background styles

12

USING THE THEME BUILDER UTILITY TO CUSTOMIZE YOUR THEME

You don't have to use the Theme Builder to create an Office theme or PowerPoint template. You can always choose from the stock set of theme colors, fonts, and effects that are available in the drop-down lists on the Design menu to tweak your themes and templates. You can even create and apply your own color theme or font theme directly in the PowerPoint interface.

The tricky part occurs when you want to create your own theme effects because you cannot do this in PowerPoint: You must use the free Theme Builder utility to create or edit theme effects and background styles. Working with the Theme Builder can be frustrating, but mastering it is also immensely rewarding. This chapter gets you started on that journey to conquering the Theme Builder utility.

NOTE

In case you've forgotten, the Theme Effects controls the options available to your users in various quick-style galleries: Shape Styles, Chart Styles, Table Styles, and SmartArt Styles. You can read more about theme effects in Chapter 3, "Getting Started: Set Up a Theme."

DOWNLOADING AND INSTALLING THE THEME BUILDER UTILITY

The first step to getting started is to download and install the Theme Builder utility and other required files. Install them in this order:

.NET Framework (3.0 or a later version)

Primary Interop Assemblies (or PIAs—for Office 2007 or 2010 as appropriate)

Theme Builder utility

.NET FRAMEWORK 3.0

Check to see whether you have at least .NET Framework 3.0 before installing the Theme Builder utility. If you have a newer version of .NET Framework (.NET Framework 4, for example) installed already, that is fine. You can get the latest .NET Framework installation files at http://www.microsoft.com/download/.

PRIMARY INTEROP ASSEMBLIES

You also need to install the appropriate Primary Interop Assemblies (PIAs) for your version of Office before installing the Theme Builder utility.

If you are using Office 2007, download and install these PIAs: http://www.microsoft.com/download/en/details.aspx?id=18346.

If you are using Office 2010, download and install the Office 2010 PIAs: http://www.microsoft.com/download/en/details.aspx?id=3508.

THEME BUILDER UTILITY

The Theme Builder utility seems to be in a perpetual beta state. It's been available since sometime in 2007, and it's not been updated since April 2009. Regardless, it works fairly well and should let you do what you need to do. Download it here: http://openxmlthemebuilder.codeplex.com/releases/view/91466. If you're unable to access it from this link, head to the book website for updated information: http://www.quepublishing.com/title/0789749556.

GETTING STARTED WITH THE THEME BUILDER

The Theme Builder utility is not a PowerPoint add-in; it is a stand-alone program. After you've installed the Theme Builder utility, you see it as Theme Builder in the list of programs on your Windows Start button.

Click the application name in the Windows Start menu to open the Theme Builder utility. Accept the EULA, and the interface opens with no theme in place, as shown in Figure 12.1.

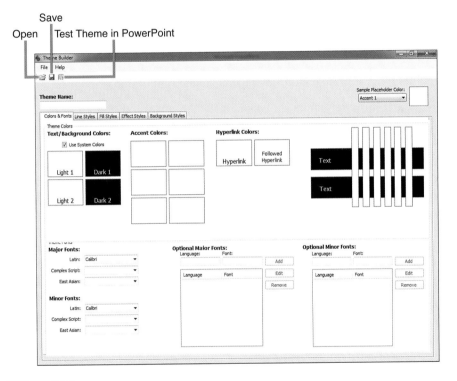

FIGURE 12.1

When the Theme Builder opens, it opens to a completely blank theme with none of the elements populated.

DON'T OVERWRITE THE THEMES THAT SHIPPED WITH OFFICE

Notice that the toolbar beneath the File and Help menus in the Theme Builder utility, as shown in Figure 12.1, consists of three buttons: Open, Save, and Test Theme in PowerPoint. This toolbar cannot be edited, so you're stuck with those three options.

Editing an existing theme is easier than starting one from scratch. However, take note of those three buttons, especially Save. It's not *Save As*, it's *Save*, and it cannot be changed on the toolbar.

Because of this, clicking that Save button and overwriting an existing theme is extremely easy. To prevent this from happening, before you start working with the Theme Builder utility, make a copy of the .THMX files that shipped with Office (either 2007 or 2010) and use the copies to study, experiment with, and base your own themes on.

The themes that ship with Office 2010 are housed in C:\Program Files\ Microsoft Office\Document Themes 14. (For Office 2007, the default folder is named Document Themes 12.) Simply copy that folder and paste it somewhere you can easily access. We also recommend you rename the copied folder, so it's obvious to you later that these are not the actual theme files you see in the Office interface.

Don't worry about copying the Theme Colors, Theme Effects, and Theme Fonts folders that are inside the Document Themes folder because you don't need them. The XML files inside these folders are where PowerPoint gets the default list of colors, fonts, and effects you see in the drop-down lists in the Themes group on the Design tab, as shown in Figure 12.2. Your custom .THMX and .XML files go into a different folder. Read Chapter 14, "Deploying Your Template or Theme," for more information.

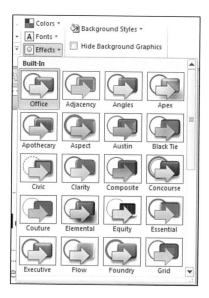

FIGURE 12.2

The stock theme colors, fonts, and effects that ship with Office are in the drop-down lists on the Design tab.

Choose File, Open to navigate to and open a.THMX file.

You might notice that there is no .THMX file called Office Theme, which is the name of the theme a new, blank file is based on in PowerPoint—and in Word and Excel, too. The Office Theme doesn't show up as a separate .THMX file. But, as you know, all PowerPoint files and templates are based on a theme. If you don't apply a specific theme to the PowerPoint file, then it is based on the basic Office Theme.

CREATING AN OFFICE THEME TO USE AS A STUDY GUIDE

Creating your own default Office Theme .THMX file to work with is easy enough. To do so, follow these steps:

1. Open PowerPoint. It opens to a new, blank presentation. (If you already have PowerPoint open, you can choose File, New, Blank Presentation to open a new blank file.)

2. Choose File, Save As.

3. In the Save As Type dialog, as shown in Figure 12.3, choose Office Theme (.THMX) from the Save As Type drop-down list, which automatically takes you to the proper folder to store your custom themes in. If it doesn't, you can navigate to the appropriate folder: C:\Users*UserName*\AppData\Roaming\Microsoft\Templates\Document Themes.

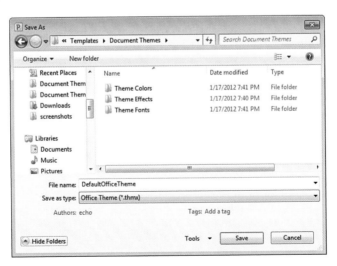

FIGURE 12.3

When you choose Office Theme (.THMX) in the Save as Type drop-down list, PowerPoint automatically takes you to the correct folder in which to store custom themes.

4. In the File Name box, type a name for the theme. We used DefaultOfficeTheme in Figure 12.3. The .THMX extension is appended automatically to the filename, so you don't have to type it.

Now you have a theme based on the default Office Theme. You can open it (or any of the other themes) in the Theme Builder utility and study its settings.

The Theme Builder remembers the last place it opened a theme, and the next time it is launched, the File, Open command targets that same location. This can easily cause confusion, so be sure to pay attention when opening files in the Theme Builder.

THE PROCESS TO BUILD A NEW THEME

Creating a basic theme is fairly straightforward. You open a new, blank file in PowerPoint and apply (or create and apply) theme colors and fonts. That part is easy. You can also select theme effects, which determine the look of the graphics in files based on your theme. That part is also easy.

After you've selected the different theme colors, fonts, and effects, you can format the slide master. Select a background style (which is discussed in Chapter 4, "Formatting the Slide Master") and apply any graphics to the slide master and layouts. Format the placeholders. Add custom layouts and format them. Finally, save the file as a PowerPoint Template (.POTX) and as an Office Theme (.THMX). Done.

The tricky part is when you want to create custom effects or custom background styles for the theme. Then the process can become rather circular, especially because it's so much easier to edit an existing theme than it is to start from scratch.

THE PROCESS TO CUSTOMIZE A THEME

If you like one of the existing Office themes and just need to tweak its effects or background a little then you can open it in the Theme Builder utility and start editing. As mentioned earlier, working with a copy of the theme is best so you don't overwrite the original by mistake.

We find that there is usually a stock Office theme that has effects or a set of background styles that is *almost* right for our purposes. In those situations, using that theme as the basis for building the new theme is the easiest path. Figure 12.4 shows a high-level overview of the basic steps.

Throughout the rest of this chapter, we expand on each of these steps in turn, concentrating on the steps that use the Theme Builder.

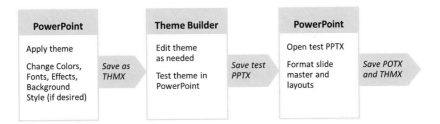

FIGURE 12.4

These are the key steps in the theme customization process.

USING THE THEME BUILDER UTILITY TO CUSTOMIZE A THEME

As outlined in the preceding section, the first part of the process occurs in PowerPoint and is straightforward. You will perform basically the same steps you would use to create a theme in PowerPoint when you don't need to edit the graphic effects theme or background styles.

1. Open PowerPoint to a new, blank presentation.

   If PowerPoint is already open, you can choose File, New, Blank Presentation. A presentation based on the default Office Theme opens.

2. In PowerPoint, apply an existing theme that has a similar effects theme or background style to the one you want to create.

   To apply an existing stock theme to the new, blank presentation, click a thumbnail in the Themes gallery on the Design tab, as shown in Figure 12.5. Stock themes (from C:\Program Files\Microsoft Office\Document Themes 14) display here, as do custom themes and templates that are in the C:\Users*UserName*\AppData\Roaming\Microsoft\Templates\Document Themes folder. Of course, if you want to work with the settings used in the default Office Theme, you can skip this step.

More button

FIGURE 12.5

Click the More button to expand the Themes gallery.

3. In PowerPoint, apply a font theme.

    We recommend that you start with one of the built-in font themes so the definitions for other script fonts are included in your theme. (See the "Editing Fonts" section later in this chapter to learn more about this.) Choose one that is similar or identical to the fonts you intend to use. For example, if you plan to use a serif heading font and a sans serif body font, select a built-in font theme that uses a serif heading and a sans serif body font.

    To apply a stock theme font set, simply select it from the Built-in section of the Fonts drop-down on the Design tab. This is, of course, an optional step. If the theme already uses fonts you like, you can leave those. You will be able to edit the theme fonts later in the Theme Builder utility.

4. In PowerPoint, apply theme colors.

    See Chapter 3 for instructions to create your own theme colors. To apply a theme color set, simply select it from the Colors drop-down on the Design tab. This step is also optional. If the theme uses colors you like, you can leave them. You can also edit the theme colors in the Theme Builder utility.

5. In PowerPoint, save the theme file.

    Choose File, Save As. In the Save As Type dialog, as shown in Figure 12.3, choose Office Theme (.THMX) from the Save As Type drop-down. This automatically takes you to the proper folder where you store your custom themes so they display in the Themes gallery on the Design tab. If it doesn't, you can navigate to the appropriate folder: C:\Users*UserName*\AppData\Roaming\Microsoft\Templates\Document Themes.

    In the File Name box of the dialog, type a name for the theme. The .THMX extension is appended automatically to the filename, so you don't have to type it.

6. Now open this newly created .THMX file in the Theme Builder utility.

    Go to the Windows Start menu and open the Theme Builder utility. Choose File, Open, navigate to the .THMX file you created and click the Open button.

USING THE COLORS AND FONTS TAB OF THE THEME BUILDER

Creating and applying theme fonts and colors in PowerPoint is generally easier, but you can still edit your colors and fonts in the Theme Builder if you want.

The Colors and Fonts tab of the default Office Theme is shown in Figure 12.6. The color grid on the far right is simply a representation of the accent colors (vertical bars) and dark/light combinations (horizontal bars and text). Checking the colors for contrast and visibility on this tab is useful.

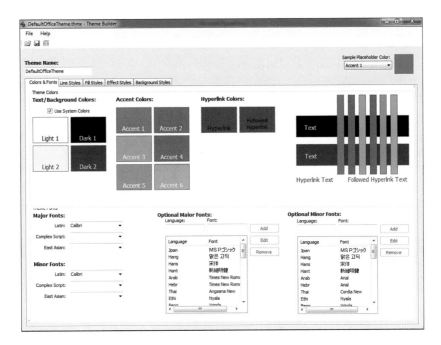

FIGURE 12.6

Here you can see the default Office Theme opened to the Colors & Fonts tab of the Theme Builder.

EDITING COLORS

To change any of the colors in the color theme, click its preview rectangle in the Theme Builder. This opens a color dialog, as shown in Figure 12.7, where you can choose another color from the basic colors palette or create a custom color. Click OK to apply the color you've created or selected.

Note in Figure 12.6 that the Use System Colors box is checked. This is the case for most of the stock templates that shipped with Office 2007 and 2010. The Use System Colors setting syncs the Light 1 and Dark 1 colors to the system setting on the computer the theme is viewed on. Because the Windows system colors are black and white 99.99% of the time, this means the light and dark colors are white and black 99.99% of the time. Uncheck this box to define specific colors (including black and white). See Chapter 3 for more information on defining theme colors, and don't forget that chart fonts and SmartArt fonts specifically are based on the Light 1 and Dark 1 color values.

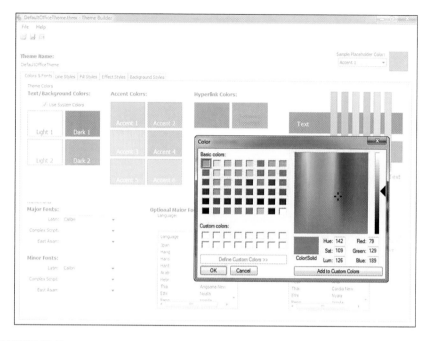

FIGURE 12.7

Clicking a color rectangle in the Colors & Fonts tab of the Theme Builder utility opens this Color dialog, where you can use the slider, palette, RGB, or HSL settings to define a color.

The Theme Builder's color dialog is not designed very well. Before clicking the button to Add to Custom Colors, pictured in Figure 12.7, be sure to select one of the empty cells in the Custom Colors section. Otherwise you'll overwrite any custom color you just created there. Also be aware that there is no undo. If you don't like the color you just chose, you have to reset it manually.

EDITING FONTS

The major and minor Latin fonts are based on the fonts you specified in the Fonts drop-down list on the Design tab in PowerPoint. The major font represents the Headings, and the minor font is the Body font. If you began with a built-in font theme that isn't exactly what you wanted, select the appropriate Latin fonts.

If you need complex script or East Asian fonts available in your theme, select them on the Colors & Fonts tab as well. (You might see these listed in the Theme Builder if your version of Office is for a language that uses a complex script or an East Asian font or if you have enabled multiple editing languages that use these fonts.)

The optional major (Headings) or minor (Body) fonts for other languages are simply a list of which fonts to use when applying your theme to non-Latin languages (such as Japanese or Arabic). Starting with an existing theme (or font theme) pre-populates this list.

If you want to change one of these combinations of optional major or minor fonts, select it and click Edit. To add an optional major or minor font, type the language and the font name in the boxes provided, and then click Add when the button becomes available.

NOTE *You should probably enter Slide Master Name in the Theme Name box shown in Figure 12.6. When you use the Test Theme in PowerPoint option in the Theme Builder, whatever is in that box becomes the name of the slide master in the test file.*

Click the Save icon or choose File, Save (or press Ctrl+S) to save the theme.

CAUTION *Remember, Theme Builder utility has no "undo" option. If you have unsaved edits and open a different theme, you don't get a prompt saying you're about to lose those edits.*

PARTS OF THE THEME EFFECTS STYLES

The next steps involve editing the theme effects styles in the Theme Builder, but before you can do that with any confidence, you must understand the different parts and how they're put together to create theme effects.

TIP *Two very helpful files are available in the Theme Builder. Click the Help menu to access the Theme Creation Guide and the Document Themes SDK. These documents are chock-full of information about themes and the Theme Builder.*

Theme effects are made up of a matrix of lines, fills, and graphics effects styles in varying degrees of subtle, moderate, and intense. This matrix is shown in Figure 12.8.

These elements are combined to create the shape styles you see in the various quick-style galleries throughout PowerPoint, Word, and Excel: Shape Styles, Chart Styles, SmartArt Styles, and the Table Styles labeled Best Match for Document. Figure 12.9 shows the Shape Styles gallery.

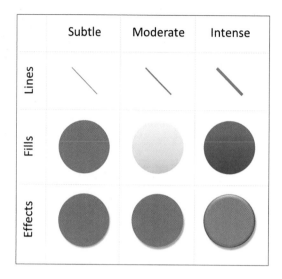

FIGURE 12.8

An effects theme defines the varying degrees of intensity for lines, fills, and graphic effects.

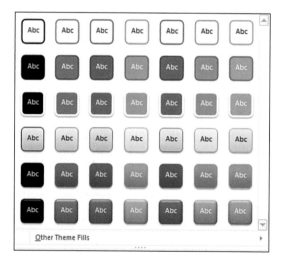

FIGURE 12.9

The styles available in the Shape Styles gallery are based on the subtle, moderate, and intense lines, fills, and effects defined in the theme effects styles.

One of the best ways to see how these styles are derived is to change a value in the Theme Builder utility, and then click the Test Theme in PowerPoint button to see how that setting changes the rounded rectangles on the sample slides. For example, changing the subtle line style from its default setting (see Figure 12.9) to a more visible 10 points lets you see that Styles 4 and 5 use the Subtle line weight, as shown in Figure 12.10.

NOTE

Unfortunately, themes don't combine the subtle, moderate, and intense settings as you might expect. For example, you won't ever see an option on a quick-style gallery that uses the subtle line style combined with the subtle fill style and the subtle effects style.

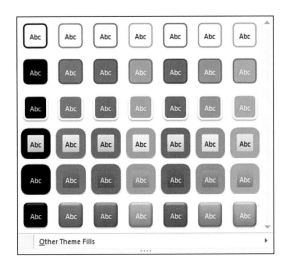

FIGURE 12.10

Changing one element at a time lets you see where that element is used in the theme effects. Here we've changed the subtle line weight to 10 points, which affects styles in the fourth and fifth rows of the Shape Styles gallery.

You don't have to test each and every piece of the effects theme; we've done it for you! Refer to Table 12.1 to see how the parts of the Effects Styles work together to create the styles that are available to users in the Shape Styles gallery on the Drawing Tools Format tab. You can see how the different parts of the theme Effects Styles are applied to the chart's quick-styles gallery in Chapter 11, "Understanding Charts and Chart Templates."

Table 12.1   Effects Theme Settings Used in the Shape Styles Gallery

	Style # (Tooltip Name)	Line Style	Fill Style	Effects Style
Abc	1 (Colored Outline)	Moderate	Light 1	None
Abc	2 (Colored Fill)	Moderate (Note: Line color is a hard-coded variation of the Moderate line color.)	Subtle	None
Abc	3 (Light 1 Outline, Colored Fill)	Intense (Note: Line color is always Light 1.)	Subtle	Subtle
Abc	4 (Subtle Effect)	Subtle	Moderate	Subtle
Abc	5 (Moderate Effect)	Subtle	Intense	Moderate
Abc	6 (Intense Effect)	None	Intense	Intense

MODIFYING LINE STYLES IN THE THEME BUILDER

The Line Styles tab of the Theme Builder is shown in Figure 12.11. This tab is where you customize the line colors and weights for each of the subtle, moderate, and intense settings in the theme effects.

Specify a weight for each of the subtle, moderate, and intense lines. Remember that these weights affect all but the last style in the Shape Styles gallery. They are also important in the Chart Styles gallery, especially in regard to line charts because the line thickness in the different line chart styles is based on a multiplier of the subtle line weight. For details, see Table 11.3, "Line Weight Multiplier for Line Charts," in Chapter 11.

Use the Style drop-down list to change to different types of dashed or dotted lines; the Compound drop-down list to opt for a single, double, or thick-thin line; and the End Cap drop-down list to define a different type of end for your line.

NOTE   *The most common type of end cap is Flat, which applies no end caps to lines. When you align shapes on your slides, this type of end cap is cleaner and easier to work with than the other two types of end caps.*

You can also choose a Center or Inset alignment for the lines. With a centered alignment, half the line is outside the edge of the object and half of it is inside. With an inset alignment, the whole line is inside the object. This difference is shown in Figure 12.12.

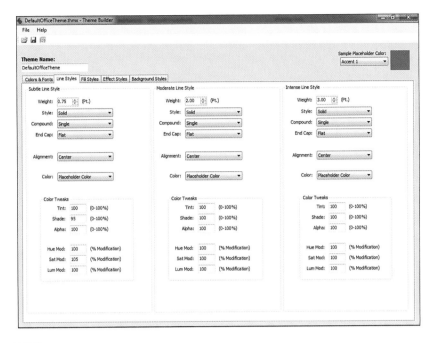

FIGURE 12.11

The Line Styles tab of the Theme Builder is where you can define subtle, moderate, and intense line styles.

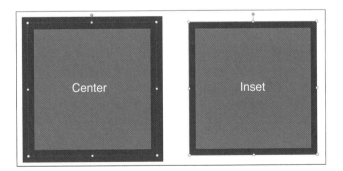

FIGURE 12.12

A line style that uses a center alignment extends beyond the actual edge of the object (left). A line style that uses an inset alignment extends only to the edge of the object (right).

We encourage you to use inset alignment. This setting is helpful when applying outlines to pictures and picture placeholders—especially when these objects are aligned with other objects on the slide master or layout. A center alignment tends to cause pictures and picture placeholders to become a little larger to accommodate the half of the line width that extends beyond the edge of the object; an inset alignment won't do this.

DEFINING COLORS IN THE THEME BUILDER

The Color drop-down of the Line Styles tab defaults to the Placeholder Color. This means that the line color uses your theme colors (mostly the accent colors, but occasionally the dark and light colors) in the various Quick Style galleries. Choose Custom from the drop-down and then click the color rectangle that appears if you want to define a specific color that this line style should always use.

You can further tweak the line color in the Color Tweaks section of the Line Styles tab. Because the Theme Builder is working with six different accent colors, you must define color changes by percentages rather than specific RGB values.

TIP

For example, if you want the line color in the Quick Styles galleries to be exactly the same color as the accent colors in your theme, then specify a value of 100 (100%) in each of the Tint, Shade, Alpha, Hue Mod, Sat Mod, and Lum Mod fields. If you want the line color to be a bit darker than the accent colors in your theme, lower the Shade value. You might also want to increase the Sat Mod (saturation) or Lum Mod (luminosity) when darkening the shade to help preserve the vibrancy of the theme color.

The existing stock themes use this Shade or Tint plus Sat Mod/Lum Mod tweaking technique frequently, especially for fill colors; reviewing them can help you get a better grip on how to handle this technique effectively in your own themes. Refer to Figure 12.11 to see that the Subtle line color has been tweaked in this manner, and see Table 12.2, which further defines each of the color tweak options.

Table 12.2   Explanation of Color Tweak Options in the Theme Builder

Color Tweak Setting	Definition	Notes
Tint	Adds white to a color	100 tint means 100% color Lowering the tint lightens the color
Shade	Adds black to a color	100 shade means 100% color Lowering the shade darkens the color
Alpha	Transparency	100 alpha means 100% opaque Lowering alpha increases transparency 0 alpha = 100% transparent 70 alpha = 30% transparent 100 alpha = 0% transparent

Color Tweak Setting	Definition	Notes
Hue Mod	Defines the color on the color wheel	You probably don't want to change the hue. Changing this gives you a different color altogether.
Sat Mod	Saturation (affects the purity of the color)	A Sat Mod of 300 means the color saturation is increased threefold. Saturation > 100 makes the color brighter; saturation < 100 makes it less vivid.
Lum Mod	Luminosity, Brightness (measures how far a given hue is from white)	Luminosity > 100 lightens the color (a luminosity of 255 = white)
		Luminosity <100 darkens the color (a luminosity of 0 = black)

NOTE

Style 2 in the Shape Styles gallery in PowerPoint has a line color a bit darker than the actual accent color. The line color on this style will be darker than the fill no matter what your theme settings are. Even if you set all color tweaks in the Moderate line style to 100, the line will still be darker. This is because the line color tweaks for Style 2 are built into the Office interface and cannot be changed. (You can change the other settings in the Moderate line style, and they will still be applied to this Style 2.)

MODIFYING FILL STYLES IN THE THEME BUILDER

Figure 12.13 shows the Fill Styles tab of the Theme Builder. These settings affect the fills of objects such as shapes, charts, SmartArt, and Best Match tables on your slides. You can set three types of fills: solid, gradient, and image. It doesn't sound like very many, but honestly, the possibilities are endless!

The Line, Fill, Effect, and Background styles generally become more intense as you move left to right from subtle to moderate to intense. For example, the subtle fill style is almost always a solid color. The moderate fill might be a gradient, and the intense fill style should be the most visually intense of the three. It might be another gradient, or it might be a duotone image or tile.

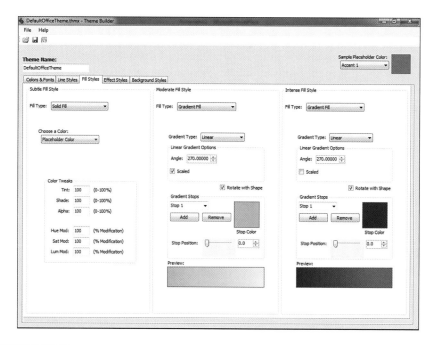

FIGURE 12.13

The Fill Styles tab of the Theme Builder utility lets you choose a Solid Fill, a Gradient Fill, or an Image Fill. Pictured here is the Fill Styles tab from the default Office Theme.

SOLID FILLS

The Solid Fill color should be set to Placeholder Color so the theme uses the theme accent colors to fill objects. If you choose any other option from the Color drop-down, every object in the Quick Styles galleries uses the same color!

Working with the color tweaks for a Solid Fill Style is exactly the same as working with the color tweaks for a Line Style. Refer to Table 12.2 for details. Remember, if all color tweak settings are 100, the fill colors that rely on this Fill Style are exactly the same as your theme accent colors.

GRADIENT FILLS

Gradient fills can be Linear, Radial, or Rectangular, and the color stops are set the same way regardless of the type of gradient.

TIP   *Keep your fills simple and remember a little goes a long way. Defining a gradient or image for your subtle fill style could drive your users crazy!*

A "stop" indicates a color change in the gradient. Most of the Office gradients have two or three stops, but you'll occasionally run into one that has more. To edit an existing stop, choose it from the drop-down in the Gradient Stops section of the Fill Styles tab in the Theme Builder. (The Gradient Stops section appears when you select Gradient Fill as the Fill Type, as pictured in Figure 12.13.)

After you've selected the appropriate stop from the Gradient Stops drop-down, click the Stop Color preview rectangle to open the Edit Color and Tweak dialog, as shown in Figure 12.14, where you can edit the fill color. As with line colors, gradients are created from variations to a single theme accent color, which are defined in Table 12.2. If you look at color settings in existing themes, you'll see that they frequently use a combination of Tint or Shade plus Sat Mod tweaks. This technique is a way to lighten or darken a color while maintaining its vibrancy.

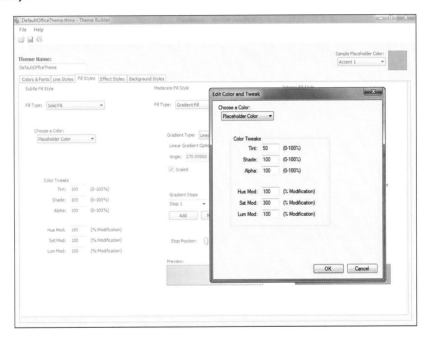

FIGURE 12.14

Use these settings to edit fill colors. Lowering the Tint value lightens the color. This can sometimes wash out the color; increase Sat Mod (saturation) to help maintain its vibrancy.

Add a stop by clicking the Add button. Delete a stop by selecting it in the drop-down and then clicking Remove. Reposition a stop by selecting it, and then moving the Stop Position slider, typing in the box, or using the spinner arrows. The gradient Preview rectangle updates to reflect the change.

You can select a different accent color from the Sample Placeholder Color drop-down to see how these settings look with the rest of the theme accent colors. The same settings apply to all accent colors, not specifically to any one individual color.

When Rotate with Shape is checked, the gradient also rotates when you rotate a shape filled with this gradient. When unchecked, the gradient stays in the same place when the shape is rotated.

TIP *Don't hesitate to copy settings from a theme that has a background style, fill style, or effect that you like. Open it in the Theme Builder utility, go to the appropriate tab and write down the settings you want to use. Then input those in your own theme.*

Linear Gradient Options

The Angle in the Linear Gradient Options setting of the Fill Styles tab specifies where Stop 1 begins, as shown in Figure 12.15. To begin the gradient on the left edge of a shape, use an Angle value of 0. To begin at the upper-left corner, use 45, and for the top, use 90. Checking the Scaled option lets the angle of the gradient adjust when the shape it's been applied to has an aspect ratio other than 1. Unchecking the Scaled option forces the exact angle to be maintained at all times. You can see these two settings applied to shapes in Figure 12.16.

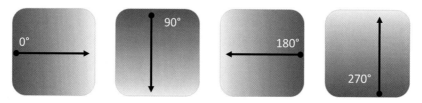

FIGURE 12.15

The angle in a linear gradient represents degrees of position. It simply defines where Stop 1 begins. From left to right, we have Angle 0 (left edge), Angle 90 (top edge), Angle 180 (right edge), and Angle 270 (bottom edge).

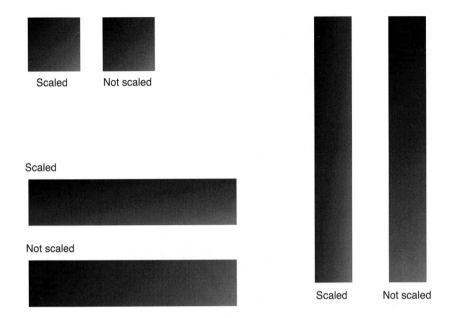

FIGURE 12.16

When the aspect ratio is 1 (the height and width of a shape are equal), you cannot tell the difference between a scaled and an unscaled gradient. When the aspect ratio is not 1, you can more easily see a difference.

Radial and Rectangular Gradient Options

Choosing either a Radial or Rectangular Gradient Type opens another set of positioning options, pictured in Figure 12.17. These settings are based on a quadrant, and they define where in a rectangle Stop 1 of the gradient falls. A setting of 50 in each left, right, bottom, and top quadrant places Stop 1 smack dab in the middle of the shape, as shown in Figure 12.18. A setting of 0 indicates an edge, so if you have Left set to 0, Stop 1 originates exactly on the left edge. If you give all four quadrants a value of 0, the shape looks like a solid color.

When the values are greater than 50, the quadrants push against each other. Negative numbers move Stop 1 off the edge of the slide. Thinking of the quadrants as having a push-pull relationship where their total value equals 100 seems to work in most cases.

Tweaking gradient angles, stop colors, and positions can take quite a bit of trial and error, but don't get discouraged. As you study the stock themes and become more familiar with the settings typically used in them, creating the gradients you want gets easier and faster.

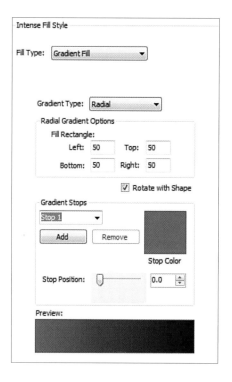

FIGURE 12.17

Use the gradient options pictured here to position your gradient. Setting all quadrants (left, right, top, and bottom) to 50 places Stop 1 of the gradient in the middle of any shape that uses this fill.

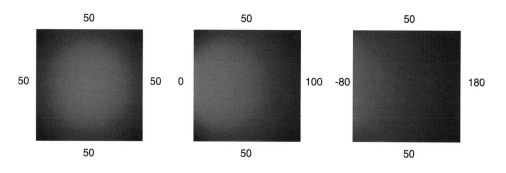

FIGURE 12.18

Adjusting the fill rectangle settings moves the origin of radial and rectangular gradients. Here is an example of settings that will move the gradient origin to the left.

Image Fills

The Theme Builder also offers an opportunity to use image fills for one or more of the Fill Styles. To add an image, select Image Fill from the Fill Type drop-down and then click the preview rectangle that displays below it. This opens the Find an Image dialog, where you can navigate to the image you want to use. .JPEG/.JPG or .PNG are both good formats for this purpose, although .PNG does not maintain its transparency because it gets converted to .JPEG.

Select the Apply Duotone Recoloring check box, and the Duotone Properties become available. Click the preview rectangles to define Colors 1 and 2. These two colors must be different from each other in order for the details of the image to render well. A good example of this is the Paper theme, as shown in Figure 12.19.

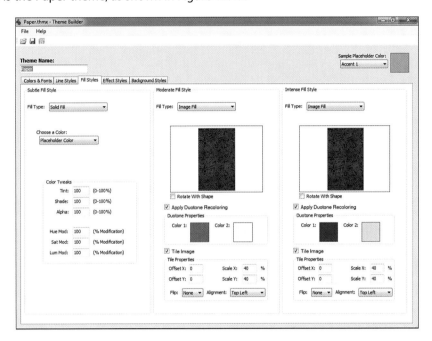

Moderate Tiled Duotone Fills

Intense Tiled Duotone Fills

FIGURE 12.19

When you apply duotone recoloring to a fill, use a grayscale image. Duotone colors 1 and 2 should be quite different from each other, as you can see in the Paper theme.

When you're working with duotone recoloring, use a grayscale image with enough contrast that the recolored image does not look flat. If there's not enough contrast in the image, it will look flat no matter how different Color 1 is from Color 2.

NOTE   *The Moderate fill style uses Dark 1 text, so it must be light enough for this color to be legible. Likewise, the Intense fill style must be dark enough for Light 1 text to be read.*

Obviously, select the Tile Image option to tile the image. If this option is not selected, the image stretches inside shapes and charts. You can adjust the X and Y offsets to change the starting point of the tiled image and use the Scale X and Y settings to change its horizontal and vertical proportion. Alignment defines where the image is anchored within the object it fills, and Flip mirrors the image along the X axis, the Y axis, or both. Rotate with Shape works just as it does for gradient fills.

If you're using tiled image fills, be sure to test them on a few different shapes (rectangle, rounded rectangle, triangle, and circle are generally sufficient) and in a couple of chart styles to ensure that the fill looks good in all situations. You might also want to explore creating seamless tiles to use for image fills.

TIP   *If you're using the image fill to create a pattern (for example, stripes or checks), a pure black-and-white image with no grayscale gives you the cleanest results.*

ADDING EFFECT STYLES IN THE THEME BUILDER

The Effect Styles tab of the Theme Builder is where you add and define the settings for Outer or Inner Shadows, Glows, Reflections, and Soft Edges. You also control the 3D properties to create bevel and lighting effects here.

Although this tab is even less WYSIWIG (What You See Is What You Get) than the others (if that's even possible!), the settings in the Effect Styles dialog correlate with the settings on the Format Shape dialog in PowerPoint. Because of this, creating the shape in PowerPoint first is actually the easiest way to determine the settings you need to enter into the Effect Styles tab in the Theme Builder utility.

To compare these settings, create a shape in PowerPoint and format it. Then right-click the shape and choose Format Shape to see the specifics of the settings for that format.

SHADOW SETTINGS

In the Effects Styles tab of the Theme Builder utility, click the Add Effect drop-down list and select Outer Shadow. Click the Add button to add this effect, and then select the effect in the list on the left and click the Edit button to see its settings.

As an example, Figure 12.20 shows you the same shadow settings in both the Edit Outer Shadow dialog from the Theme Builder and the Shadow tab of the Format Shape dialog in PowerPoint.

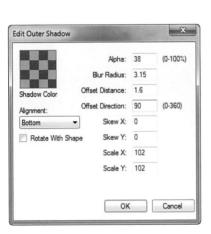

FIGURE 12.20

Comparing shadow settings in the Theme Builder utility (left) and in PowerPoint (right).

 NOTE   *Alpha in the Theme Builder is the opposite of Transparency in PowerPoint: 0% Alpha = 100% Transparent and 100% Alpha = 0% Transparent.*

Use this same technique to determine the settings for any of the effects you want to add here.

3D AND SCENE PROPERTIES

Although they are typically used only in the intense effects, you can enable 3D and scene properties for any of the subtle, moderate, or intense styles. To do so, simply select the box labeled Enable 3-D and Scene Properties.

As with the other effects, you can format a shape in PowerPoint and refer to its 3-D Format and 3-D Rotation specifications as a guide to those settings in the Theme Builder utility.

For example, review the two dialogs for the Intense effects style in Austin.THMX, as shown in Figure 12.21. Although the options are in a different order, they are all present. Most are even relatively easy to decipher!

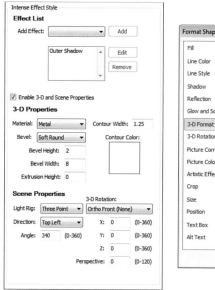 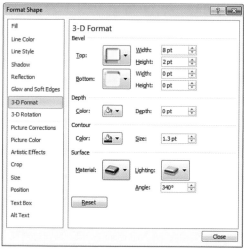

FIGURE 12.21

3-D settings in the Theme Builder utility (left) and in PowerPoint (right).

For the few items that might be confusing, note that Extrusion Height (Theme Builder) is the same as Depth (PowerPoint dialog). Contour Width is the same as Contour Size, and in the Contour Color options, you can select either Placeholder so the contour color reacts to the theme or Custom to force a specific color.

In PowerPoint, click on the Material and Lighting buttons to open those galleries, and then hover over each option to see what it is called; this gives you a better idea of what the Material and Light Rig settings represent in the Theme Builder utility. The same goes for the Bevel type. Also note that the 3-D Rotation options at the lower right of the Theme Builder utility dialog refer to the settings found on the 3-D Rotation tab of the Format Shape dialog in PowerPoint.

EDITING BACKGROUND STYLES IN THE THEME BUILDER

Recall from Chapters 2 and 3 that slide background styles are based on Light 1, Light 2, Dark 1, and Dark 2 theme colors. As you've probably guessed, they are also based on subtle, moderate, and intense styles. In fact, the Theme Builder options for each of the background styles are identical to those used for fill styles: solid color, gradient (linear, radial, or rectangular), or image. To edit them, follow the instructions for fills explained earlier in this chapter.

Background fill styles in the stock Office themes are most often gradients or solid colors. Really, the only reason to use an image as part of the background style is if you want a duotone effect to be applied to the picture or pattern, as shown in Figure 12.22. If you don't need the duotone effect, take the simpler route—just fill the background of the slide master or layout with the image.

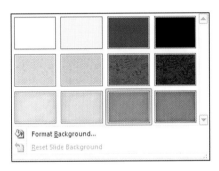

FIGURE 12.22
Background styles let you apply duotone recoloring to background images.

You'll occasionally see a duotone pattern fill in a background style. You might think these are done with PowerPoint shapes, but no, this is also accomplished with an image. For best results, the pattern image is generally black and white with no shades of gray. Module.THMX, pictured in Figure 12.23, uses a duotone pattern image for its intense background style. Again, if you don't need the duotone recoloring, there's not much reason for you to worry about setting this up as a background style; just fill the slide master or layout background with the image and tile it (or not) as necessary.

There's also nothing to stop you from leaving the background styles in the theme alone and simply applying a gradient (or other fill) directly to the slide master or layout. However, you must first choose one of the existing styles from the Background Styles gallery to ensure that chart and SmartArt text is visible. This is key!

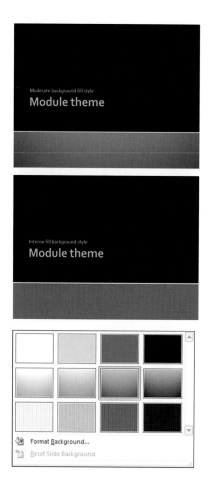

FIGURE 12.23

The Module stock theme uses a gradient for its moderate background fill style (top) and a duotone pattern image for its intense fill style (center). Select these from the Background Styles dialog (bottom).

Let us reiterate this: Even if you override the background style (by manually applying your own fill directly to the slide master or layout), the selected background style still affects the underlying structure of the file. If the background fill you plan to apply is on the dark side, choose one of the dark background styles so it forces light text by default; if you plan to apply a light fill, choose one of the light background styles to force dark text. If you need a refresher on this, refer to Chapter 3.

Whether you leave the built-in background styles or apply a fill directly to the slide master or layout, you're not locked into a basic boring look. Don't forget—any graphics you add to the slide masters and layouts sit on top of the slide backgrounds.

As an example, look at the Title Slide layouts in Module.THMX, pictured in Figure 12.23. The layout on the left uses the moderate background fill style overlaid with a large black rectangle and a thin white line. If you selected one of the intense styles from the bottom row of the Background Styles dialog, you would get a stripe pattern on the bottom of that slide instead of the gradient. It's a quick and easy way to change the look of a presentation.

FINISHING THE THEME

Congratulations! You've customized your theme, and now you're ready to test and finalize it in PowerPoint.

TESTING IN POWERPOINT

After you've tweaked the various settings in the Theme Builder utility, you can see what the theme looks like by clicking the Test Theme in PowerPoint button. This opens a new presentation with the theme applied.

The test presentation includes a sample slide based on each layout as well as two slides, as shown in Figure 12.24, with shapes representing each row of the Shape Styles gallery so you can see how the subtle, moderate, and intense effect styles affect shapes. We recommend adding charts and SmartArt to the content placeholders and applying moderate and intense quick styles to them so you can see how changes to the theme settings affect those objects as well. Be sure to check the Background Styles gallery on the Design tab to see how those settings are represented.

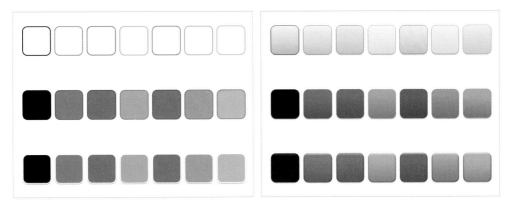

FIGURE 12.24

Clicking the Test Theme in PowerPoint button produces a sample presentation that includes these two slides where you can see how the theme's Effects Styles settings affect shapes.

If you want to change anything, do so in the Theme Builder utility and continue testing until everything is to your liking. PowerPoint continues to use the same sample presentation it created, so any content (charts, SmartArt, and so on) you added to the sample presentation updates when you reapply the theme using the Test Theme in PowerPoint button.

When the theme is satisfactory, click Test Theme in PowerPoint one last time to ensure that all changes have been captured, and then save the PowerPoint file. Do not simply save the .THMX file from the Theme Builder utility! Doing so might cause your theme to not have a preview image, so you will see a big red X instead of a thumbnail representation in the Themes gallery on the Design tab in PowerPoint, as shown in Figure 12.25. Instead, save the sample PowerPoint file as a .PPTX (presentation) file for now.

FIGURE 12.25

Saving the theme directly from the Theme Builder utility might result in a red X instead of a nice thumbnail preview.

CREATING THE THEME AND TEMPLATE FILES

Using the .PPTX file you just saved, format the slide master and layouts. Apply background styles and add any graphics you want. Format and position all placeholders and create any custom layouts you want to add.

We recommend you test all layouts before you finalize them by applying each one to a sample slide. Add dummy text and other content (SmartArt, tables, charts, photographs, and so on) in relevant placeholders to ensure that these elements also look—and work—as you expect them to. You should also add any other final touches, such as specifying the default shape, line, and textbox settings; selecting the default table style; and inserting slide number, date, and footer text. For specifics, see Chapter 9, "Finalizing Your Template."

TIP   *Type* `=lorem()` *into a placeholder or textbox to quickly generate dummy text known as* lorem ipsum *text. This fake Latin is useful for testing font and bullet formatting.*

When you've finished tweaking all the details and you're ready to finalize, remember that the Office Theme and PowerPoint template are very closely related, so you should save them at the same time.

First save the file as a PowerPoint template. Choose File, Save As, and in the Save As Type drop-down select PowerPoint Template (.POTX). Name the file and click Save.

Next save the theme file. Go to the File menu in PowerPoint, click Save As, and choose Office Theme (.THMX) from the Save As Type drop-down. Give the theme a name and click Save.

NOTE

The following are saved with a PowerPoint Template (.POTX) or presentation (.PPTX) file, but not with an Office Theme (.THMX): sample slides; default table style; and date, slide number, or footer text. Default shape, line, and textbox styles are saved with both the theme and the template.

Remember, sample slides are not included in the Office Theme (.THMX) file, but they are included in the PowerPoint template (.POTX or.PPTX). What often happens to us is, as we continue to work on the sample slides in the template we find elements we need to tweak that affect the theme. This includes theme colors, fonts, or effects as well as slide masters and layouts and the placeholders on them. If you make *any* changes at all to these elements, you need to save the theme again.

NOTE

To save a table style with the template, expand the Table Styles gallery, right-click a table style thumbnail, and then choose Set As Default. You must choose from a built-in table style; you cannot design your own.

A FINAL NOTE

Sometimes when you're near the end of the theme and template creation process, you'll decide you want to make a tweak to the background or effects styles. As you know, you cannot do this type of editing in PowerPoint itself.

The problem is that at this point you cannot do this type of editing in the Theme Builder utility, either. The Theme Builder strips out custom XML (such as custom slide layouts and colors), so opening the .THMX file in Theme Builder could cause more problems than it solves. Never fear—there's still a way. You can open the theme or template in an XML editor and manually edit the code, thereby avoiding the Theme Builder. You find out how to do this in Chapter 13, "Editing PowerPoint and Theme File XML."

IN THIS CHAPTER

- The basics of editing XML
- Removing most recently used colors in XML
- Adding custom colors in XML
- XML editing tools

EDITING POWERPOINT AND THEME FILE XML

Office 2007 and 2010 files are created using a type of code known as Office Open XML (OOXML). OOXML was developed by Microsoft and has become an Ecma and ISO standard, under constant review for extensions and clarifications to the standard. *XML* stands for Extensible Markup Language and, rather like HTML, after you get the basics down it can be relatively easy to read and understand. What's important to us as PowerPoint users is the fact that, with OOXML, we can open a PowerPoint file and modify things inside it without actually using PowerPoint at all. OOXML enables us to tweak settings we couldn't otherwise edit because PowerPoint itself doesn't provide an interface for them.

Although OOXML can be a bit intimidating at first, it's really not as complicated as it might seem. In fact, mucking around in the PowerPoint XML after you've become familiar with it can be downright fun!

In this chapter you learn about editing PowerPoint's XML to do two typical tasks: remove the most recently used colors and add custom colors to the color galleries.

WHICH FILES ARE XML-BASED?

Office 2007 and 2010 files are XML-based, which means you can access the underlying code. Four-letter Office application extensions that end with an *X* or an *M* (for macro-enabled file) are XML-based.

	PowerPoint	Word	Excel	Theme
XML (2007, 2010) file format extensions	POTX, POTM PPTX, PPTM PPSX, PPSM	DOTX, DOTM DOCX, DOCM	XLTX, XLTM XLSX, XLSM	THMX
Binary (97–2003) file format extensions	POT, PPT, PPS	DOT, DOC	XLT, XLS	

If you save your 2007 or 2010 PowerPoint file as a 97–2003 presentation with a three-letter extension, you can no longer edit it using an XML editor.

WHAT IS XML?

XML-based documents are actually containers for a set of files known as an *XML package*. An XML package is basically the common ZIP format, and the structure of the files inside, which are known as *XML document parts*, is similar to a folder of files that has been "zipped up."

At its most basic level, the OOXML-editing process requires you to open (or unzip) the THMX, POTX or PPTX file to get to the code, known as *XML markup*, inside. See Figure 13.1 for an overview. XML document parts include text files formatted in XML markup that define everything in the PowerPoint file as well as other files that might be in your presentation (.JPG, .WAV, .WMV, and so on).

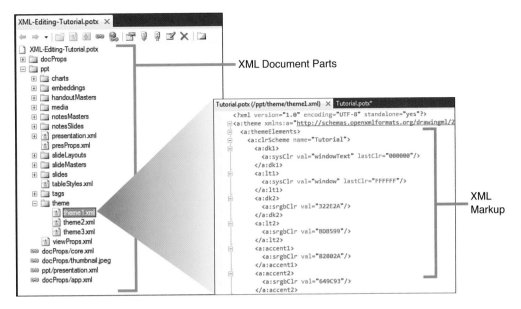

FIGURE 13.1

Opening a POTX file in an XML editor enables you to see the OOXML file structure and XML document parts inside.

BEFORE YOU BEGIN EDITING

You can open and edit XML files a lot of different ways, and a lot of different tools are available to help you with it. Some tools are easier to use than others. This chapter walks you through the process using Microsoft Visual Studio LightSwitch 2011 to edit XML markup. If you're interested in different XML editors, skip to the end of this chapter for a list of other helpful XML-editing utilities.

NOTE *We've provided links to all the software and utilities mentioned in this chapter. Get them at http://www.quepublishing.com/title/0789749556.*

INSTALL VISUAL STUDIO LIGHTSWITCH

Visual Studio LightSwitch is a much lighter, reasonably priced version of Visual Studio. It's perfect for editing XML because it formats the markup in an easy-to-read layout and lets you edit in the same window. Download and install a free 90-day trial from the book website at the link mentioned in the Note.

INSTALL THE OPEN XML PACKAGE EDITOR ADD-IN

After you install Visual Studio LightSwitch, download and install the free Open XML Package Editor power tool for Visual Studio. This add-in lets you open and edit XML-based files directly in Visual Studio LightSwitch without unzipping them first.

DOWNLOAD THE XML EDITING TUTORIAL TEMPLATE

Download the XML-Editing-Tutorial.POTX file from http://www.quepublishing.com/title/0789749556 so you can follow the steps in this chapter. Make a copy of it before you begin editing.

When editing XML, be sure to work on a copy of your file (POTX, PPTX, THMX, and so on), not on the original. This protects you in case something goes wrong and the edited file refuses to open! We also highly recommend copying your file to a working folder, which makes keeping things straight easier.

EXAMINING THE GUTS OF AN XML PACKAGE

Because you installed the Open XML Package Editor add-in, you can skip unzipping the template file and open the POTX directly inside Visual Studio LightSwitch (VSL). Open the template using File, Open File and navigating to the XML-Editing-Tutorial.POTX. (If you prefer to unzip the POTX manually and need instructions, skip to the section about editing XML with Windows, Notepad and Internet Explorer.)

The XML package includes three top-level folders that define everything in the PowerPoint presentation file: docProps, ppt, and _rels. VSL doesn't show you _rels folders by default, but you can click the Show _rels Folders button (see Figure 13.2) to display them.

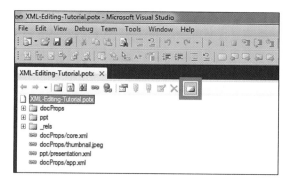

FIGURE 13.2

Click the Show _rels Folders button to see the _rels folders in Visual Studio LightSwitch.

Inside the _rels folder is a .rels file, which defines the relationships between the top-level folders. You see .rels files inside some of the other folders as well; each .rels file defines the relationship between the XML document parts in that folder. Chances are you won't need to edit the .rels files, but they're important because without them the different parts of the XML package (and, therefore, the PowerPoint file) won't work together.

The docProps folder includes three files: app.xml, core.xml, and thumbnail.jpg. The thumbnail image is the slide preview that shows in Windows when you opt to display files as icons. The app.xml and core.xml document parts include settings for the PowerPoint file—author name, number of words, number of slides, presentation format (4 × 3 or 16 × 9, for example), whether it has hidden slides, and so on.

The ppt folder is the main document folder. It contains many subfolders with XML document parts for all components of the PowerPoint presentation file (see Figure 13.3). These folders may change depending on your content. For example, if your PowerPoint file includes a SmartArt diagram, the XML package has a Diagrams folder with XML markup files inside.

FIGURE 13.3

The ppt folder inside an XML package looks like this.

REMOVING THE MOST RECENTLY USED COLORS

When you open a Color Gallery and choose More Colors instead of using one of the theme colors, the color you selected shows up in a section called Recent Colors (see Figure 13.4). We like to remove these from templates before we submit them to our clients. That way, users aren't tempted to choose these recently used colors, which are not themed and might or might not be part of the corporate brand.

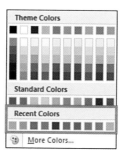

FIGURE 13.4

Colors that show up in the Recent Colors section of the color dialog are not part of the theme color scheme.

One way to remove these is to start a new, Blank presentation, apply the theme, and then paste in the sample slides you've created. Unfortunately, this process is time consuming and leaves much room for error. A better way is to remove the colors by editing the file's XML markup.

For this exercise we're most interested in the files within the ppt folder, specifically the presProps.XML file, which includes (as you might guess) presentation properties and the markup for most recently used colors. In VSL, double-click the presProps.XML file to open it. The file initially opens showing what seems like only one long, wide line of code. Click the Format the Whole Document button on the XML Editor toolbar or press the keyboard short-cut sequence Ctrl+K, Ctrl+D to see the markup in tree view. (See Figure 13.5.)

XML markup uses paired tags to organize, define, and apply everything in the XML package file. Tags are codes that define everything about your file. Each tag is surrounded by brackets (<>). An end tag begins with a slash (/).

For example, the tag `<p:clrMru>`, shown in Figure 13.5, begins the Most Recently Used color section of the markup, and its paired end tag `</p:clrMru>` ends that section. Between those tags you see tags that look like this:

```
<a:srgbClr val="99CC00"/>
```

These tags define the colors that display in the Most Recently Used section of the PowerPoint color gallery. There are ten of them in the XML-Editing-Tutorial.POTX—the same ten colors pictured in Figure 13.4.

Format the Whole Document

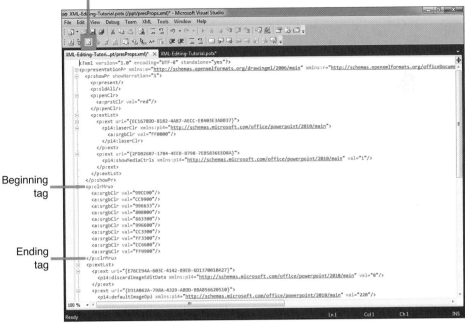

FIGURE 13.5

Most Recently Used colors are listed in the presProps.XML markup.

You might expect RGB values, but what you are seeing is actually a hexadecimal color code (also referred to as hex or HTML colors). Each of these color values is an example of a single line of markup that stands on its own; the slash at the end indicates the end of the tag.

> **NOTE**
>
> *Details such as spaces and capitalization are important in XML markup, so pay attention! Make a mistake with them when editing the XML, and your PowerPoint file might not open.*

To remove the most recently used colors, select all the markup from `<p:clrMru>` to `</p:clrMru>` and press the Delete key to delete the entire tag and its contents.

> **NOTE**
>
> *You can actually delete just the `<a:srgbClr val="99CC00" />` tags in the earlier example and leave the `<p:clrMru>` and `</p:clrMru>` tags intact. The next time you look at the presProps.XML markup in your browser, you see the two `p:clrMru` tags have become one standalone tag: `<p:clrMru />`. This happens because no additional tags are nested between the pair, so PowerPoint "fixes" the XML when it resaves the file.*

When you've finished deleting the `clrMru` tags and the color values inside, save your changes by clicking File, Save. In Windows, double-click the POTX file (or choose File, Open in PowerPoint) to test that your edits were successful and the Recently Used colors section has been removed from the Colors gallery, as shown in Figure 13.6.

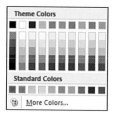

FIGURE 13.6

After editing the XML, the Colors gallery will have no Recently Used section.

ADDING CUSTOM COLORS TO COLOR GALLERIES

Our clients often have more than six colors available in their corporate color palette, so they get frustrated with PowerPoint's six-color limit for accents. In these situations, we often add the extra colors to a Custom Colors section in the color galleries (see Figure 13.7). These custom colors are not theme-aware, and they will do not change if the theme colors are updated, but they are at least available for users to easily select from.

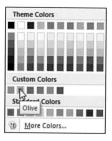

FIGURE 13.7

Custom colors are not themed, but they are certainly handy for users.

Before you begin editing the XML package to add a custom colors section, first you must translate the RGB values into hexadecimal values. Table 13.1 shows our custom colors along with their corresponding RGB and hex values. The RGB values aren't used in the XML markup; they're included only for reference (because most of us are more used to working with RGB values).

Table 13.1   Custom Color Values

Color Chip	Custom Color Name	Hex Value	RGB Value
	Orange	d27d36	R 210 G 125 B 54
	Olive	919a38	R 145 G 154 B 56
	Coral	c64234	R 198 G 66 B 52
	Taupe	8c744a	R 140 G 116 B 74
	Mustard	b68e1c	R 182 G 142 B 28
	Blue	505878	R 80 G 88 B 120

TIP

You can use any color picker that gives you the six-character hex value you need for the XML markup. Create a slide with your colors, open the color picker, hover over the color chip, and read the values in the color picker. Figure 13.8 shows the free Pixeur utility. You can download Pixeur from http://www.veign.com/application.php?appid=107.

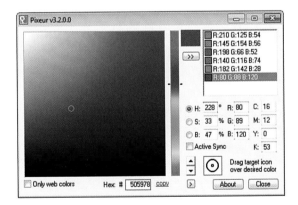

FIGURE 13.8

Pixeur is a handy color picker utility you can use to get the hex value of your colors.

After you have the hex values for your custom colors, you're ready to add them to the XML markup. If you want to continue using the same .POTX file from which you removed the most recently use colors, make a copy of it first in case anything goes wrong while editing.

Open the template in VSL by clicking File, Open File and navigating to the POTX file. Double-click the ppt folder (or click the + next to it) to expand it and then expand the theme folder inside, as shown in Figure 13.9.

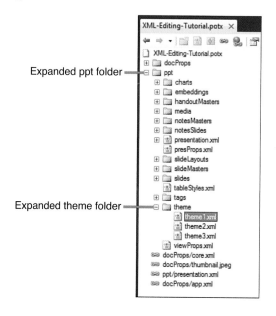

Expanded ppt folder

Expanded theme folder

FIGURE 13.9

Theme1.xml is the theme associated with the slide master. Add custom colors to the theme1.xml document part.

Double-click theme1.xml to open it, and click the button (or use the Ctrl+K, Ctrl+D shortcut) to put the document part into tree view.

SEEING DOUBLE? TRIPLE?

If you see only theme1.xml in the /ppt/theme folder of the XML package, you can move on; however, if you see more than one theme document part in that folder (as shown in Figure 13.9), read on to find out why.

Theme1.xml is the theme applied to the slide master. Theme2.xml and theme3.xml are usually the themes applied to the handout master and notes pages master. (The theme#.xml document parts associated with slide masters are listed first. For example, if you have two slide masters, theme1.xml and theme2.xml are related to the slide masters, and theme3.xml and theme 4.xml are associated with handout and notes pages masters.)

In Visual Studio LightSwitch, you can expand the handoutMasters folder to see that theme3.xml is linked to the handout master. (See Figure 13.10.) Some XML editors don't show this link, and in those cases you must check the rels file to see which theme is associated with the document part. For example, if you were to open the handoutMaster1.xml. rels file, you would see to see a partial line of code that looks like this:

```
Target="../theme/theme3.xml"
```

This also indicates that the handout master uses theme3.xml.

Finally, you won't even see theme.xml files for handout or notes masters in the XML package if you haven't viewed the handout master or notes master in the PowerPoint file! Yes, it's true. You must remember to go to View, Handout Master and View, Notes Master in PowerPoint to force PowerPoint to create those associated theme#.xml files. If you see only theme1.xml in the /ppt/themes folder in the XML package, you know that you haven't yet looked at the handout or notes masters in the presentation or template file.

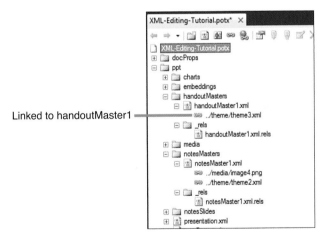

FIGURE 13.10

The link icon indicates that theme3.xml is associated with the handout master and theme2.xml is associated with the notes master.

Scroll to the end of the theme1.XML markup. If you want, you can press Enter a couple of times after the standalone `<a:extraClrSchemeLst/>` tag so you can easily tell where to add your markup. (Although XML markup is picky about spaces within tags, extra spaces between the end of one paired tag and the beginning of another won't hurt anything.)

Input this pair of tags to create the Custom Color section (see Figure 13.11):

```
<a:custClrLst>
</a:custClrLst>
```

Between these tags, enter the following three lines of markup for each custom color (see Figure 13.11):

```
<a:custClr name="Orange">
<a:srgbClr val="d27d36"/>
</a:custClr>
```

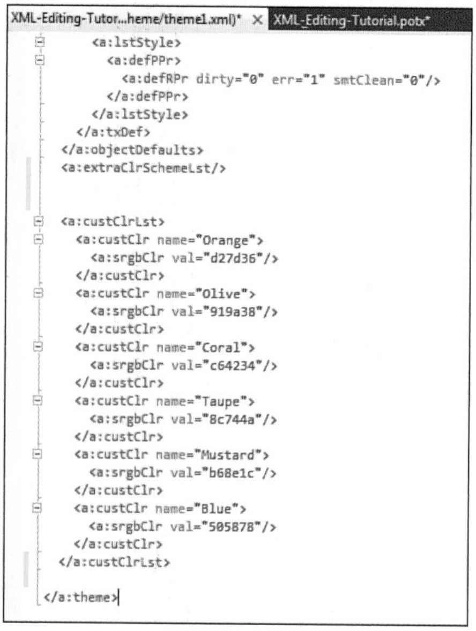

FIGURE 13.11

Add custom colors to the end of the theme1.xml document part.

The *custClr name* will be displayed in a tooltip when you hover your cursor on the custom color chip. (Refer to the example of this in Figure 13.7.) Input the hex value for each color between the quotation marks in the srgbClr val line. Your completed code should look something like Figure 13.11. You do not have to indent or put the markup on separate lines—it's just easier to read and edit if you do.

TIP

When you've typed the ending bracket for the beginning tag, VSL may create the ending tag automatically on the same line. Don't worry, it's just the program trying to be helpful! You can add the custom color markup right there in the same line, or, better yet, press Enter to create some space between the two tags and add the lines of markup there.

VSL similarly adds ending quotation marks to values in the markup. Be watchful, or you could end up with double quotation marks, which will prevent your file from opening.

When you've finished editing the markup, save the file and close Visual Studio LightSwitch. As always, open the file in PowerPoint to ensure your edits were successful.

POKING AROUND IN THE XML

Believe it or not, editing XML is sometimes faster and easier to do than it is to make a change in the Theme Builder, save the new theme, and apply that to a template or presentation you've been working on. Editing XML also enables you to add and change some settings that you cannot change in the Theme Builder or the PowerPoint interface itself. To give you a few ideas, you can use XML to change background style settings or edit the shadow transparency, gradient angles, line weights, and so on for the default shape styles.

TIP   *Don't forget! Opening a default theme and examining its XML markup is a good way to see how the various effects were accomplished.*

CHANGING A BACKGROUND FILL STYLE

We've mentioned a few times that the subtle, moderate, and intense background fills in a theme are based on one color (Dark 1, Dark 2, Light 1, or Light 2).

In Chapter 12, "Using the Theme Builder Utility to Customize Your Theme," we explained how to edit gradient fill stops by tweaking the Tint, Shade, Alpha, Hue, Saturation, and Luminosity settings. To force a gradient stop to be black, you would change the Shade value for the color to 0%; to force a white stop, you would change the Tint value to 0%.

Perhaps you always want your slide background gradients to fade to a specific color—maybe a dark blue or a charcoal gray, for example—instead of fading to a variation of the theme color. This can be accomplished by editing the theme1.xml markup and replacing the code for theme accent colors (`<a:schemeClr val="phClr">`) with one that uses specific RGB values expressed in hexadecimal (`<a:srgbClr val="002060"/>`). Figure 13.12 shows typical moderate background styles in the middle row on the left and customized background styles on the right, where we've specified a dark steel blue for the last stop of the gradient. The markup for these two styles is shown in Figure 13.13.

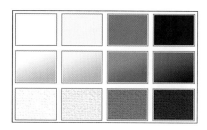 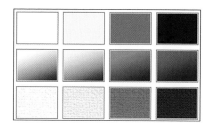

FIGURE 13.12

Typical moderate background styles (middle row, left) use a variation of the same theme color for both stops. The modified moderate background styles on the right have been changed to fade to dark blue.

IDENTIFYING EFFECTS STYLES

The key to editing XML is really about knowing where to look. To edit theme settings, look in the theme1.xml document part. The effects set used in the theme or template begins with a line of code similar to this:

```
<a:fmtScheme name="Module">
```

In this case (see Figure 13.14), Module is the set of effects we applied from the Design tab in PowerPoint when we created the XML-Editing-Tutorial template. If you didn't specifically choose an effects set when you created the file, the default Office theme effects are used, and the line of markup is

```
<a:fmtScheme name="Office">
```

Remember that an effects set consists of a matrix of subtle, moderate and intense fills, lines, and effects. In the theme1.XML markup, you'll see tags for the Fills, Lines and Effects, and there will be definitions and markup for subtle, moderate, and intense settings for each.

TIP

<a:fillStyleLst> begins the fill styles markup, <a:lnStyleLst> begins the line styles markup, <a:effectStyleLst> begins the effect styles markup (shadows, glows, reflections, soft edges, 3D, and lighting settings), and <a:bgFillStyleList> begins the background styles markup.

For an example, look for the `<a:fillStyleLst>` tag (see Figure 13.14), which indicates the beginning of the fill styles. These settings make up the fills in the various PowerPoint galleries used for objects such as shapes, charts, SmartArt, and so on.

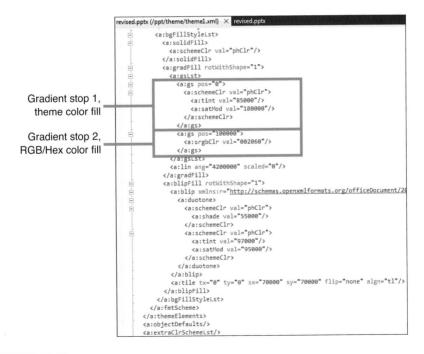

FIGURE 13.13

Markup that uses theme colors looks like that on the top. Markup that uses a specific RGB value, expressed in hex, is shown on the bottom.

There will always be three fill styles: typically a solid fill (subtle), a gradient fill or image fill (moderate), and a gradient or image fill (intense). These are not labeled subtle, moderate, and intense in the XML markup, but that's how they are translated in PowerPoint. In fact, all Effects settings are grouped this way, with markup included for subtle, moderate, and intense line styles, fill styles, effect styles, and background styles. Figure 13.14 shows a solid subtle fill, a gradient moderate fill, and another gradient as the intense fill.

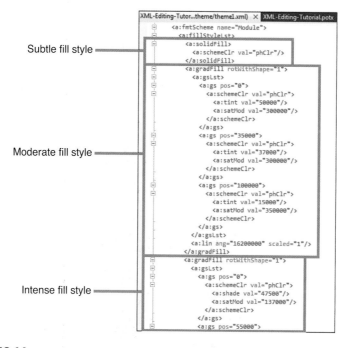

FIGURE 13.14

Subtle, moderate, and intense fill styles are not labeled in XML markup; you just have to know how to identify them.

To help you see when each type of fill starts and stops, look for the paired tags in the markup. For example, in Figure 13.14, you can see `<a:solidFill>` beginning the first (subtle) fill style and `</a:solidFill>` ending it. The next line of markup, `<a:gradFill rotWithShape="1">`, begins the second (moderate) fill style, and `</a:gradFill>` ends it. The following line of markup `<a:gradFill rotWithShape="1">` begins the third and final (intense) fill style. Its ending markup is not pictured, but it also reads `</a:gradFill>`.

NOTE

The XML markup for subtle, moderate, and intense styles changes depending on the design of your template. For example, sometimes the intense fill might have a duotone image, whereas other times it might be a simple gradient or solid.

XML EDITING SOFTWARE

As you know, we've opted to use Visual Studio LightSwitch to edit the XML shown in this chapter. It's one of the few XML editors that enables us to see a tree view of and edit the XML markup in the same window, which is our preferred workflow. It also has that handy-dandy add-in that lets us open XML-based files (PowerPoint, Word, Excel, Themes, and so on) directly, which is so much easier than unzipping the file, extracting the XML document part, and putting it back together (like Humpty-Dumpty!) after editing.

However, there are a number of XML editing tools out there at all different price points, and some are easier to use than others. Following is a list of XML editing options you may want to explore. We've provided links to these at http://www.quepublishing.com/title/0789749556.

WINDOWS, NOTEPAD, AND INTERNET EXPLORER

If you want to go bare-bones basic, you can use the following procedure to edit XML.

1. Enable the file so you can access the XML package. Generally this means renaming the .PPTX file with a .ZIP extension. Of course, this also means you must first have Windows file extensions enabled in order to do so (see sidebar).

2. Copy the XML document part you want to edit from inside the ZIP file. Paste the XML document part into a working folder.

3. Open the XML document part in Notepad and make your edits. The text isn't laid out very nicely so reading and editing the markup in Notepad is difficult. (You can see the tree view of the XML markup in Internet Explorer, but you cannot make edits there.) Save the XML document part.

4. Copy the edited, saved XML document part and paste it back into the .ZIP file.

5. Rename the .ZIP file back to .PPTX.

6. Open the .PPTX file to make sure it has no issues.

ENABLE WINDOWS FILE EXTENSIONS

To rename a PPTX file with a ZIP extension, first tell Windows to display file extensions on all files. Use the following steps to do so in Windows 7:

1. Click the Start button and then click Computer.

2. Click the Organize menu and then click Folder and Search Options.

3. On the View tab, clear the box for the Hide Extensions for Known File Types option. (See Figure 13.15.)

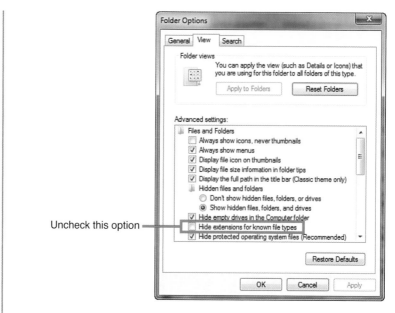

Uncheck this option

FIGURE 13.15

Enable file extensions in Windows to make renaming a PPTX file with a ZIP extension possible.

7-ZIP

Bypass zipping and unzipping altogether with 7-Zip. 7-Zip is a free utility that lets you explore and edit the XML inside an XML-based file without unzipping the file or changing the file extension. In 7-Zip, use File, Open Inside to open the POTX. Right-click the XML document part and choose Edit, and the document part will open in the XML editor you've specified in 7-Zip's Tools, Options, Editor.

XML NOTEPAD

XML Notepad is a free download from Microsoft. XML Notepad shows your code in a tree view that lets you expand and collapse individual sections of markup. We find it a bit difficult to edit XML markup in XML Notepad, but your mileage may vary.

NOTEPAD++

Notepad++ is a free source code editor and Notepad replacement. It also shows code in a tree view, although OOXML is often interpreted as one long line of markup. Still, it's easier than using Notepad because the tags are easier to see. Specify Notepad++ as your XML editor in 7-Zip, and you have a good combination of free XML editing tools.

ALTOVA XML SPY

If you get serious about working in XML, you might decide you need a more substantial XML editor. Altova XML Spy gives you user-friendly views along with a number of tools such as an info pane and autocomplete.

VISUAL STUDIO

If you have a TechNet Plus or an MSDN subscription, or if you're a student, you might have access to Visual Studio. It's extremely expensive and overkill just for editing XML, but if you already have it, it's really fantastic for this task.

VISUAL STUDIO LIGHTSWITCH

Visual Studio LightSwitch is a much less expensive "light" version of Visual Studio, perfect for editing XML. We particularly like it because we can see the tree view and edit the XML in the same window.

OPEN XML PACKAGE EDITOR

If you opt to use either Visual Studio or Visual Studio LightSwitch, download and install the free Open XML Package Editor power tool for Visual Studio . With this add-in installed, you can open and edit OOXML files directly in VS/VSL without unzipping or changing the file extension first.

HOOKED ON XML?

If you're interested in learning more about editing Office Open XML, a lot of information is available on the Microsoft Developer Network (MSDN) site. MSDN has loads of information on this topic, but here are three articles we found to be particularly useful as we began working with the Office Open XML:

- Open XML SDK 2.0 for Microsoft Office—http://msdn.microsoft.com/en-us/library/bb448854.aspx

- Creating Document Themes with the Office Open XML Formats—http://msdn.microsoft.com/en-us/library/cc964302(v=office.12).aspx

- Using Office Open XML to Customize Document Formatting in the 2007 Office System—http://msdn.microsoft.com/en-us/library/dd560821(v=office.12).aspx

Documents, Presentations, and Workbooks: Using Microsoft Office to Create Content That Gets Noticed—Creating Powerful Content with Microsoft Office, by Stephanie Krieger, is another excellent resource for those of you who want to learn more about OOXML.

DEPLOYING YOUR TEMPLATE OR THEME

Most folks we consult with are unclear on the difference between a template and a theme. Additionally, our clients are often confused as to whether colors, fonts, and effects are part of their template or if they must provide their users with both a template and a theme.

Because different types of files show up in different parts of the interface, deployment can become even more muddled, and knowing which files you should roll out is difficult. This chapter covers the set of files you might want to give your users and where those pieces show up in the PowerPoint interface.

THEME VERSUS TEMPLATE

Remember, an Office theme (.THMX) includes a set of colors, fonts, and effects that can be used in Word, PowerPoint, and Excel. An Office theme also includes slide masters and layouts, but it does *not* include any content such as Word macros, Excel formulas, or PowerPoint sample slides.

An application template is specific to Word (.DOTX), PowerPoint (.POTX), or Excel (.XLTX). A PowerPoint template includes the colors, fonts, effects, slide masters, and slide layouts it's inherited from the underlying theme, and it might also include content: (sample slides, header and footer information, and so on). Think of a template as a theme plus some content.

You can deploy only a theme, only a template, or both a theme and a template, depending on what you want your users to have access to.

TEMPLATES: THE ALL-PURPOSE FILE FORMAT

Templates (.POTX) are a special type of file format. They're essentially the same as a PowerPoint file (.PPTX) with some behavioral differences.

When you double-click a .POTX file, it launches PowerPoint and creates a new unnamed document using the contents of the template; it doesn't open the .POTX file itself. This can be helpful because it prevents a user from messing up the actual template. If you want to edit a template file, you must open it from within PowerPoint by selecting File, Open and navigating to the .POTX.

THE THEMES GALLERIES

In PowerPoint, the Themes gallery is on the Design tab. In Word and Excel, it's on the Page Layout tab (see Figure 14.1). To make the theme available in the Custom section of the Themes galleries, place the THMX file here:

Windows 7 and Windows Vista:

C:\Users\<*UserName*>\AppData\Roaming\Microsoft\Templates\Document Themes

(%AppData%\Microsoft\Templates\Document Themes)

Windows XP:

C:\Documents and Settings\<*UserName*>\Application Data\Microsoft\Templates\ Document Themes

(%AppData%\Microsoft\Templates\Document Themes)

The Custom section is created automatically when the first file is placed in the Document Themes folder. You cannot change the name of the custom section.

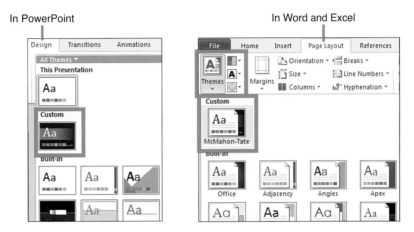

FIGURE 14.1

Themes (.THMX) are available on the Design tab in PowerPoint and on the Page Layout tab in Word and Excel.

PUTTING TEMPLATES INTO THE DOCUMENT THEMES FOLDER

You can put the PowerPoint template (.POTX) into the C:\Users\<*UserName*>\AppData\ Roaming\Microsoft\Templates\Document Themes folder, and it shows up in the Themes gallery the next time PowerPoint is opened. Be aware that if users apply this Themes gallery template to their presentations, it behaves exactly like a theme: All content is omitted (sample slides, header and footer text, and so on).

You can place both the .POTX and the .THMX files in this folder, but we don't recommend it because having two thumbnails that look identical is confusing for users. Stick with one or the other. Also note that any PowerPoint template (.POTX) files placed in the Document Themes folder will not be available for use in Word or Excel; you must place a .THMX file there in order for it to be available in Word and Excel also.

BUILT-IN THEMES

The stock themes that ship with Office display in the Built-In section of the Themes galleries and in the gallery that displays when you choose File, New, Themes. In Office 2010, these files are located in: C:\Program Files\Microsoft Office\Document Themes 14. In Office 2007, substitute Document Themes 12 for Document Themes 14.

NOTE   *If you're using a 32-bit version of Windows, the folder is named Program Files. If you're using 64-bit Windows 7, look for the Program Files (x86) folder instead.*

We're often asked if it's okay to delete all the built-in themes. Although you can delete all the stock themes, colors, fonts, and effects files, you cannot remove the default Office Theme and its related colors, fonts, and effects. These elements are built into each Office application and do not exist in the Document Themes folders.

NOTE   *If you have a mix of .THMX and .POTX files in the C:\Users\<UserName>\AppData\ Roaming\Microsoft\Templates\Document Themes folder, this information might prove useful: In the Custom section of the Themes gallery, all .THMX files display in alphabetical order followed by all .POTX files in alphabetical order.*

COLORS, FONTS, AND EFFECTS XML FILES

For some reason, some users have a hard time understanding that the colors, fonts, and effects sets are built into properly constructed templates and themes, and they don't have to apply these settings separately. Because these elements are inherently part of the template or theme, you don't have to deploy color, font, and effects files separately.

However, in certain situations having access to the new colors or fonts sets is helpful to users. For instance, when working with an existing file, applying new colors is often quicker than taking time to "clean up" slide content after applying an entirely new theme or template. If you think your users will want to apply these settings independently rather than together as part of the theme or template, you can provide the individual XML files for colors, fonts, or effects.

You probably didn't realize it, but when you created new theme colors and new theme fonts, that process generated a *<Colors>*.XML and a *<Fonts>*.XML file. (The actual filename reflects the name you gave the custom Colors or Fonts set.) You can see the results of those XML files in the Custom section of the Colors and Fonts galleries on the Design tab in PowerPoint, as shown in Figure 14.2, and on the Page Layout tab in Word and Excel.

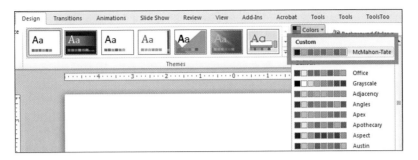

FIGURE 14.2

PowerPoint automatically generates a unique XML file when you save custom theme colors or theme fonts.

These colors and fonts sets do not display on anyone else's computer. When you apply these colors to a theme or template, they become part of the theme or template, but what is displayed in the galleries is a separate file. Provide the XML files to your users to install, and they see the colors and fonts sets in these galleries just as you do. These XML files live here:

Windows 7 and Windows Vista

Colors.XML   C:\Users\<*UserName*>\AppData\Roaming\Microsoft\Templates\
                         Document Themes\Theme Colors

Fonts.XML   C:\Users\<*UserName*>\AppData\Roaming\Microsoft\Templates\
                         Document Themes\Theme Fonts

Windows XP

Colors.XML   C:\Documents and Settings\<*UserName*>\Application Data\Microsoft\
                         Templates\Document Themes\Theme Colors

Fonts.XML   C:\Documents and Settings\<*UserName*>\Application Data\Microsoft\
                         Templates\Document Themes\Theme Fonts

Our clients rarely ask about separate custom effects set files, but you can provide these, too, if you want. As you know, you cannot create a custom effects set from the PowerPoint interface, so providing them is not quite as easy as copying an XML file, but it's not that difficult either.

Make a copy of your theme (.THMX) file. (If you don't have a theme file, open your PowerPoint template and choose File, Save As, Office Theme [.THMX] to create one.) Rename the file from *<MyTheme>*.THMX to *<MyTheme>*.EFTX. Place *<MyTheme>*.EFTX here:

Windows 7 and Windows Vista:

C:\Users*<UserName>*\AppData\Roaming\Microsoft\Templates\Document Themes\ Theme Effects

Windows XP:

C:\Documents and Settings*<UserName>*\Application Data\Microsoft\Templates\ Document Themes\Theme Effects

 NOTE *The Document Themes folder and its subfolders (Theme Colors, Theme Fonts, and Theme Effects) are generated the first time you create a custom theme, color, font, or effects set. You might need to create these folders on your users' machines.*

WHERE TO PLACE POWERPOINT TEMPLATE (.POTX) FILES

As mentioned earlier, if you're not deploying a theme along with your template, you might want to place the .POTX file in the Document Themes folder so that it shows up in the Themes gallery. As we also mentioned earlier, be aware that a template (.POTX) file applied from the Themes gallery behaves like a theme; sample content is not included when you apply it.

If your template includes sample slides and header/footer content, we strongly suggest placing the .POTX file where it retains all of this content. Users see the template in the dialog when they select File, New, My Templates (see Figure 14.3) if you place the .POTX file here:

Windows 7 and Windows Vista:

C:\Users*<UserName>*\AppData\Roaming\Microsoft\Templates (%AppData%\Microsoft\Templates)

Windows XP:

C:\Documents and Settings*<UserName>*\Application Data\Microsoft\Templates

NOTE *Word and Excel templates (.DOTX and .XLSX) placed in this folder show up in the File, New, My Templates dialogs in those respective applications as well.*

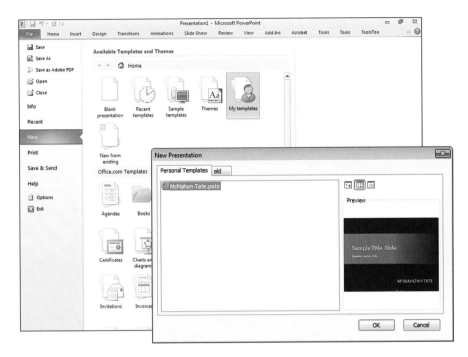

FIGURE 14.3

You can access various PowerPoint templates by choosing File, New.

To create a default template that opens every time you start PowerPoint (as opposed to the familiar blank white template based on the default Office theme), name the template Blank.POTX and place it in the Templates folder:

Windows 7 and Windows Vista:

C:\Users\<*UserName*>\AppData\Roaming\Microsoft\Templates
(%AppData%\Microsoft\Templates)

Windows XP:

C:\Documents and Settings\<*UserName*>\Application Data\Microsoft\Templates

TIP

If your template shows up in the Themes gallery, you can right-click its thumbnail and choose Set as Default Theme.

BONUS INFORMATION! DEFAULT TEMPLATES IN WORD AND EXCEL

To create a default template that opens when you start Word, choose File, Open, click Trusted Templates (Windows XP) or Templates (Windows 7 and Windows Vista), select Normal.DOTM, and then click Open. Apply your theme from the Page Layout tab, make any necessary modifications, and save. Save the Word template to the aforementioned folder and name it Normal.DOTM.

Note that modifying the existing Normal.DOTM is best. Creating your own can destroy the AutoCorrect entries saved in Word's Normal template.

To create a default template that will open when you start Excel, apply your theme from the Page Layout tab in Excel, then save the template to the XLStart folder and name it Book.XLTX. You might also want to include the template used to create new worksheets. This file should contain a single worksheet, should be named Sheet.XLTX, and should also be saved in the XLStart folder. The XLStart folder location might vary, but it's usually located at C:\Program Files\Microsoft Office\Office14\XLStart (Program Files [x86] on 64-bit Windows 7 systems).

WORKGROUP TEMPLATES

Word users especially might already be familiar with workgroup templates. Templates placed in the Workgroup Templates folder become available when you choose File, New, My Templates. The benefit of a Workgroup Templates folder is that all users access templates from a central location. This means you don't have to work so hard to roll out (or update) files to individual users' systems; you can just place the template in the Workgroups folder and be done with it. The drawback is that if the user doesn't have access to the network location that serves as the Workgroups folder, then he does not have access to the template either.

To see what folder has been specified as the Workgroups location, open Word and choose File, Options. At the bottom of the Advanced tab, click the File Locations button. The Workgroup Templates folder is identified here. Copy your PowerPoint template (.POTX) file to that folder.

A Document Themes folder and subfolders are automatically generated in Workgroup Templates when you create a custom theme or colors, fonts, or effects set. You can create these folders manually if necessary. This works just like the Document Themes folder in a

User's App Data folder. Any .POTX or .THMX file placed in this folder appears in the Themes gallery on the Design tab and custom colors, fonts, and effects files placed in the subfolders display in their respective galleries.

OTHER TYPES OF TEMPLATES

If you've created chart templates (.CRTX) for your users, they live here:

Windows 7 and Windows Vista:

C:\Users\<*UserName*>\AppData\Roaming\Microsoft\Templates\Charts

Windows XP:

C:\Documents and Settings\<*UserName*>\Application Data\Microsoft\Templates\Charts

If you've created SmartArt templates (*.GLOX) for your users, they live here:

Windows 7 and Windows Vista:

C:\Users\<*UserName*>\AppData\Roaming\Microsoft\Templates\SmartArt Graphics

Windows XP:

C:\Documents and Settings\<*UserName*>\Application Data\Microsoft\Templates\ SmartArt Graphics

TEMPLATES AND THEMES ON THE MAC

To make your template display in the My Templates tab of the Presentation gallery that appears when you open PowerPoint or when you choose File, New from Template, save the .POTX file here:

MacHD\Users\<*UserName*>\Library\Application Support\Microsoft\Office\User Templates\ My Templates

To have your theme display in the File, New from Template, My Themes tab, save the .THMX file here:

Mac HD\Users\<*UserName*>\Library\Application Support\Microsoft\Office\User Templates\ My Themes

COLORS, FONTS, AND EFFECTS

The Colors and Fonts XML files go here:

Mac HD\Users\<*UserName*>\Library\Application Support\Microsoft\Office\User Templates\ My Themes\Theme Colors

Mac HD\Users\<*UserName*>\Library\Application Support\Microsoft\Office User Templates\ My Themes\Theme Fonts

This enables the colors and fonts sets to show up in the colors and fonts drop-downs in the Presentation gallery in PowerPoint and in the Colors and Fonts galleries on the Themes tab of the Ribbon in PowerPoint, Word, and Excel.

Custom effects (.EFTX) files are not supported on the Mac. As noted earlier, they are rarely needed as a separate entry, so you shouldn't expect this limitation to pose problems.

CREATING A DEFAULT THEME FOR MACINTOSH USERS

Mac PowerPoint does not use a default .POTX file. Instead it uses a default theme file, Default Theme.THMX, to achieve the same effect. Put that file in this location:

MacHD\Users\<*UserName*>\Library\Application Support\Microsoft\Office\User Templates\ My Themes

CREATING THEMES AND TEMPLATES ON A MAC

Microsoft tries really hard to make Mac and PC files compatible across systems, and templates are no exception to this. Even if you're working on a Mac, you can still create templates for PC users. The information we've covered throughout this book is still completely relevant—you just have to be aware of some differences in the options and interface. This chapter covers those differences.

WHICH VERSION OF POWERPOINT SHOULD I USE?

The most important thing to consider is which version of PowerPoint the end users of the template have. PowerPoint 2008 and 2011 on the Mac share the same file format and underlying structure with PowerPoint 2007 and 2010 on the PC. You can use either 2008 or 2011 to build templates for PowerPoint 2007 or 2010 users (and vice versa).

Similarly, PowerPoint 2004 on the Mac and PowerPoint 2002 (XP) and 2003 on the PC share the same file format. You should use PowerPoint 2004 to build templates for 2002/2003 users.

Do not attempt to use newer versions of PowerPoint (2007, 2008, 2010, or 2011) to create templates for use with older versions (2002, 2003, or 2004). Conversely, do not use older versions of PowerPoint (2002, 2003, or 2004) to create templates for newer versions (2007, 2008, 2010, or 2011). You will only succeed in making users' lives difficult.

FONTS

The fonts installed onto Mac and PC systems can vary greatly. Review the section, "Theme Fonts" in Chapter 3, "Getting Started: Set Up a Theme," to ensure that you choose theme fonts that most PC users have access to. Remember also that you cannot embed fonts on Mac PowerPoint, nor does PowerPoint on the Mac recognize fonts that were embedded in PowerPoint on a PC.

Also note that you cannot create your own theme font sets in PowerPoint on the Mac. If you need a font set that doesn't exist in PowerPoint 2008 or 2011, you can create it on the PC and copy the XML file to the Mac. Alternatively, you can copy the XML file from one of the existing font sets and edit it to suit your needs. See the nearby sidebar for instructions.

If you do create a new font XML file, put it in this folder on the Mac so it displays in the Fonts drop-down menu on the Themes tab (as shown in Figure 15.1): /Users/<*UserName*>/Library/Application Support/Microsoft/Office/User Templates/My Themes/Theme Fonts. You can also choose this set from the Fonts list in the Presentation Gallery that appears when you first open PowerPoint.

FIGURE 15.1

No way exists to create custom theme font sets from within the Mac PowerPoint interface, although if you create them elsewhere, they display on the Fonts drop-down menu on the Themes tab.

CREATING A CUSTOM THEME FONT SET BY EDITING XML

To create a theme font set that's based on an existing font set, first identify a font set that already uses one of the fonts you plan to use. If there isn't a set with that specific font then choose one with a similar font.

The theme fonts XML files installed with PowerPoint are located in /Applications/Microsoft Office 2011/Office/Media/Office Themes/Theme Fonts (or /Applications/Microsoft Office 2008/Office/Media/Office Themes/Theme Fonts). To create a new theme font set, fire up the Text Edit application and open the Adjacency.XML font set located in that folder. Adjacency uses Cambria for its heading font. Open the Module. XML font set, which uses Corbel for its body font.

In Module.XML, select and copy everything from `<a:minorFont>` to `<a:/minorFont>`. (See Figure 15.2.) In Adjacency.XML, select everything from `<a:minorFont>` to `<a:/minorFont>` and paste to replace the Calibri font and its alternative non-English typeface substitutions with Corbel and its substitutions. Save the file with a new name, making sure to add the .XML extension. Locate the file here so you can select it in PowerPoint: /Users/<*UserName*>/Library/Application Support/Microsoft/Office/User Templates/My Themes/Theme Fonts.

We've also provided some Font.XML files for your convenience. You can download them from http://www.quepublishing.com/title/0789749556.

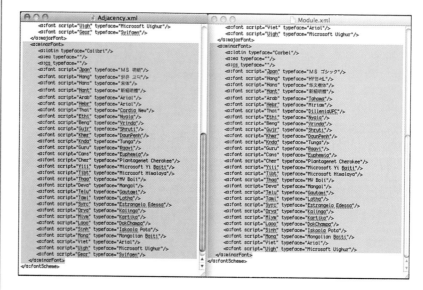

FIGURE 15.2

You can use existing font XML files to create your own custom font sets.

Be careful when specifying bullets. The Macintosh application Font Book, available in the Applications folder (Cmd-Shift-A), offers a collection titled Windows Office Compatible. Although the bulletpoint characters in these fonts might be compatible with Office on Windows, that doesn't mean those fonts are *installed* on your users' systems. If it's not installed, the font is substituted and the bullet might be replaced with a different character or symbol. Again, refer to Chapter 3 for thorough information on selecting fonts safest for use in PowerPoint. You can also stick with bullets available in the bullets galleries (see Figure 15.3), because they should be available for all users.

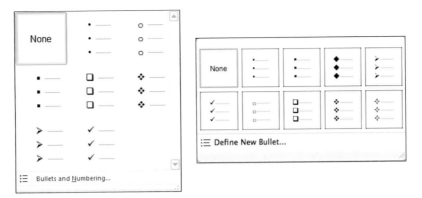

FIGURE 15.3
Default bullet gallery for the PC (left) and Mac (right).

THEME EFFECTS ON THE MAC

On both PC and Mac platforms, you cannot create theme effects sets from within PowerPoint. Additionally, PowerPoint for Mac doesn't allow you to choose a theme effects set at all. If you want to use different theme effects in your Mac-created template, you must do one of the following:

- Start with a theme or template that uses the effects set you want. You can then edit the color theme set and the slide masters and layouts to suit your purposes.

- Open the PowerPoint file on a PC and select the desired theme effects set.

- Use the Theme Builder utility (on a PC) to create a theme that uses the effects styles you want. Apply the theme on the Mac and proceed with creating your template. (See Chapter 12, "Using the Theme Builder Utility to Customize Your Theme," for instructions on using the Theme Builder.)

- Edit the XML manually. (See Chapter 13, "Editing PowerPoint and Theme File XML," for tips on editing XML.)

WHERE IS THE BLANK TEMPLATE?

Throughout this book, we tell you to begin with a new, blank template. On the Mac that is the same as choosing White from the Presentation Gallery that appears when you first open PowerPoint or when you select New Presentation from the File menu. (By the way, choosing Black is the same as a choosing a new, blank template with a dark background.) On the right of the Presentation Gallery, shown in Figure 15.4, you can select a different set of theme colors or fonts to apply before you begin.

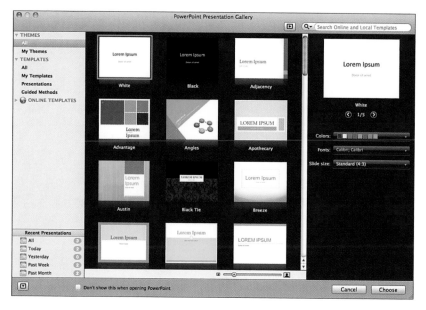

FIGURE 15.4

The Mac "White" template is the equivalent of a new, blank template on the PC.

After you've started the presentation to base your theme or template on, head to the Themes tab of the Ribbon to access the Colors, Fonts, and Background galleries. (See Figure 15.5.)

As mentioned earlier, you cannot create custom theme fonts sets from this interface, but you *can* create custom theme color sets just as you would on the PC. Click the Colors button and select Create Theme Colors at the bottom of the gallery. Custom theme color set XML files are saved in /Users/*<UserName>*/Library/Application Support/Microsoft/Office/User Templates/My Themes/Theme Colors.

Background styles are accessible on the Mac and you can apply a different style to your entire file. Unlike PC versions, though, you cannot right-click a background style and apply it to an individual slide or slide layout. To do this, you need to open the file on a PC or edit the XML manually.

FIGURE 15.5

The Themes tab on the Mac is the equivalent of the Design tab on the PC.

Finally, you can use the Save Theme button on the Themes tab of the Ribbon to save a .THMX file. To save a template file select File, Save As and choose PowerPoint Template (.potx) from the Format list in the Save As dialog. (See Figure 15.6.)

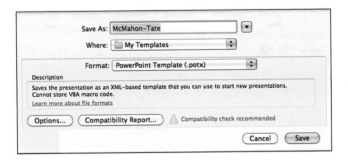

FIGURE 15.6

Although you can save a theme easily from the Themes tab of the Ribbon, to save a template, you need to open the Save As dialog.

Mac does funny things with the .POTX file extension. If you type the extension when you save the file, the filename displays with the extension. If you don't type in the .POTX extension, the filename displays without it. Both files show the .POTX icon.

TEST, TEST, TEST

If we know that our clients have a lot of Mac users, we open the PC-created template in the appropriate Mac version (2008 or 2011) and thoroughly test it out. We strongly suggest that you do the same with Mac-created templates that will be used on the PC. The more systems you can test your templates on, the better! The biggest issues are usually related to fonts, so at the very least you should ensure that no odd issues crop up with fonts, bullets, or line spacing.

Appendix

KEY STEPS TO BUILDING A TEMPLATE

For your convenience, this appendix includes a list of abbreviated steps from Chapters 3–9. After you have read the chapters and followed along with the tutorials, you can refer to this list to build your own templates.

Steps noted with an * are optional or not always necessary; whether you use them depends on your unique template design parameters.

APPLY SETTINGS TO A NEW, BLANK FILE

Create a new, blank presentation

Define the page setup

Apply theme colors, fonts, and effects

Choose from built-in theme colors or define custom theme colors

Choose from built-in theme fonts or define custom theme fonts

Choose from built-in theme effects

FORMAT THE SLIDE MASTER

Apply a background style

Customize background gradient or apply a picture fill

Set up guides

Insert and format shapes, logos, or pictures*

Format the title placeholder

Check that font is assigned to (Headings) font

Change font color, font style (Bold), font size, line spacing, paragraph alignment, vertical alignment, placeholder size and position*

Format the body placeholder

Check that font is assigned to (Body) font

Change font size for all text levels

Define bullet characters for all text levels

Adjust paragraph settings for each text level

Modify indentation settings, line spacing, and spacing before or after paragraph

Format the footer placeholders

Change font color, font size, paragraph alignment, vertical alignment, placeholder sizes and positions, as needed

Rename and preserve the slide master

Save your work in progress as a .PPTX file (save often!)

FORMAT THE DEFAULT SLIDE LAYOUTS

FORMAT THE TITLE SLIDE LAYOUT

Apply a new background style or change the background fill*

Hide background graphics*

Insert and format shapes, logos, or pictures*

Format the title placeholder

Check that font is assigned to (Headings) font

Change font color, font style (Bold), font size, line spacing, paragraph alignment, vertical alignment, placeholder size and position*

Format the subtitle placeholder

Check that font is assigned to (Body) font

Change font color, font style (Bold), font size, line spacing, paragraph alignment, vertical alignment, placeholder size and position*

Turn off footers*

FORMAT THE TITLE AND CONTENT LAYOUT

Confirm that layout matches slide master formatting

Turn off footers*

FORMAT THE SECTION HEADER LAYOUT

Apply a new background style or change the background fill*

Hide background graphics*

Insert and format shapes, logos, or pictures*

Format the title placeholder

Check that font is assigned to (Headings) font

Change font color, font style or effects, font size, line spacing, paragraph alignment, vertical alignment, placeholder size and position*

Format the subtitle placeholder

Check that font is assigned to (Body) font

Change font color, font style or effects, font size, line spacing, paragraph alignment, vertical alignment, placeholder size and position*

Turn off footers*

FORMAT THE TWO CONTENT LAYOUT

Confirm that title placeholder matches formatting and position on slide master

Format the body placeholders

Change font size for all text levels*

Adjust placeholder sizes and positions*

Turn off footers*

FORMAT THE COMPARISON LAYOUT

Confirm that title placeholder matches formatting and position on slide master

Format the heading placeholders

Change font color, font style or effects, font size, line spacing, vertical alignment, placeholder sizes and positions*

Format the body placeholders

Change font size for all text levels*

Adjust placeholder sizes and positions*

Turn off footers*

FORMAT THE TITLE ONLY LAYOUT

Confirm that title placeholder matches formatting and position on slide master

Turn off footers*

FORMAT THE BLANK LAYOUT

Apply a new background style or change the background fill*

Hide background graphics*

Turn off footers*

FORMAT THE CONTENT WITH CAPTION LAYOUT

Apply a new background style or change the background fill*

Hide background graphics*

Format title placeholder, caption placeholder, and content placeholder

Change font color, font style or effects, font size, line spacing, vertical alignment, placeholder sizes and positions*

Turn off footers*

FORMAT THE PICTURE WITH CAPTION LAYOUT

Apply a new background style or change the background fill*

Hide background graphics*

Format title placeholder and caption placeholder

Change font color, font style or effects, font size, line spacing, vertical alignment, placeholder sizes and positions*

Format picture placeholder

Adjust placeholder size and position*

Add shape outline or shape effects*

Change placeholder shape*

Turn off footers*

FORMAT THE TITLE AND VERTICAL TEXT LAYOUT

Confirm that placeholder formatting matches slide master

Turn off footers*

FORMAT THE VERTICAL TITLE AND TEXT LAYOUT

Confirm that placeholder formatting matches slide master

Adjust placeholder sizes and positions*

Turn off footers*

CREATE AND FORMAT CUSTOM SLIDE LAYOUTS*

Insert a new layout or duplicate a similar, existing layout

Adjust placeholders

Insert new placeholders as needed

Apply a new background style or change the background fill*

Hide background graphics*

Insert and format shapes, logos, or pictures*

Turn off footers*

Rename custom slide layout

FORMAT NOTES AND HANDOUT MASTERS

Apply theme colors, fonts, and effects to Notes Master and Handout Master

Format and adjust placeholders*

Insert shapes, logos*

TEST EVERY SLIDE LAYOUT

Create sample slides to test placeholder functionality

At a minimum, create one slide for each slide layout

Create slides with different types of content (charts, tables, pictures)

Delete extraneous test slides before finalizing

CREATE EXAMPLE SLIDES

Insert examples slides to be included in the final template

At minimum, create samples for Title slide layout, Title and Content layout

Create sample chart slide(s)*

Create sample table slide(s)*

Create samples for custom slide layouts*

Include instructional text*

Set default shape, line, text box, table style

FINALIZE THE TEMPLATE

Review slide master and slide layout names

Confirm theme colors, fonts, and effects are assigned correctly

Check shape, line, text box, and table style defaults

View in Slide Show mode

  Check transitions

  Confirm no animations applied

  Check legibility and visibility (for text, logos, and image quality)

Optimize file size

  Fix oversized images

  Get rid of extra fonts

Test print

  Adjust black and white or grayscale settings*

  Create PDFs to test

Set up template workspace

  Make sure you are in Normal view

  Open/close slides pane and notes pane

  Fit Slide to Current Window

  Turn Snap to Grid on or off

  Check guide positions, remove extraneous guides

Verify administrivia

  Spell-check and proofread slide master, slide layouts, and all example slides

  Run Inspect Document tool

  Check accessibility

    Add Alt Text descriptions*

SAVE FINAL TEMPLATE

Save as Template (.POTX)

Save as Theme (.THMX)*

Share with a group of users to test thoroughly and provide feedback

Implement any changes before deploying the final template

INDEX

Numerics

3D properties, modifying in Theme Builder, 209-210

7-Zip, editing XML, 234

16:9 widescreen templates, page setup, 58

A

absolute formatting, 178

accent colors, 27-30
for themes, 14
selecting, 164

accessibility, checking, 152

activating themes in Custom section of Themes galleries, 238

adding
custom colors in XML file, 224-229
data series to chart templates, 183
graphics to notes master, 128
logos to slide master, 71-72
shapes to slide master, 70

adjusting
handout master, 129
orientation of notes and handouts, 130-131

Altova XML Spy, editing XML, 235

animations, checking in Slide Show mode, 147

application templates, 238

applying
background style to slide master, 61-62
gradient fill, 63-66
picture fill, 64
built-in theme colors, 33-34
effects
to handout masters, 126
to notes, 126
fonts, 126
theme colors, 126

assembling digital assets, 162
colors, defining, 163-164
graphics, 162-163

availability of template fonts, 39

axis scale, chart templates, 179

B

backgrounds
colors, 24-27
editing in Theme Builder, 211-213
fill style, changing in XML, 229-231
formatting, 130
in Tutorial template, formatting, 66
style, importance of, 26, 61-62
gradient fill, 63-66
picture fill, 64

Black and White settings, specifying, 149-151

Blank layout, 101

body placeholder, formatting in slide master, 76-84

S

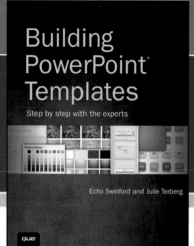

Building
PowerPoint
Templates

Step by step with the experts

Echo Swinford and Julie Terberg

Safari
Books Online

FREE
Online Edition

Your purchase of **Building PowerPoint Templates Step by Step with the Experts** includes access to a free online edition for 45 days through the **Safari Books Online** subscription service. Nearly every Que book is available online through **Safari Books Online**, along with thousands of books and videos from publishers such as Addison-Wesley Professional, Cisco Press, Exam Cram, IBM Press, O'Reilly Media, Prentice Hall, Sams, and VMware Press.

Safari Books Online is a digital library providing searchable, on-demand access to thousands of technology, digital media, and professional development books and videos from leading publishers. With one monthly or yearly subscription price, you get unlimited access to learning tools and information on topics including mobile app and software development, tips and tricks on using your favorite gadgets, networking, project management, graphic design, and much more.

Activate your FREE Online Edition at
informit.com/safarifree

STEP 1:   Enter the coupon code: TCHIDDB.

STEP 2:   New Safari users, complete the brief registration form.
          Safari subscribers, just log in.

If you have difficulty registering on Safari or accessing the online edition,
please e-mail customer-service@safaribooksonline.com

 Addison Wesley AdobePress  ALPHA   Cisco Press FT Press IBM Press Microsoft Press New Riders   O'REILLY

 Peachpit Press PRENTICE HALL QUE Redbooks SAMS SAS Publishing  vmware PRESS WILEY wrox